The Complete
ABOUT ACTING

The Complete
ABOUT ACTING

Peter Barkworth

Methuen Drama

Much of this material was originally published
by Secker & Warburg in two volumes:
About Acting published in 1980
More About Acting published in 1984

The Complete About Acting combines the two
with revision and new material by the author
and was first published in 1991 by Methuen Drama
an imprint of Reed Consumer Books Ltd
Michelin House, 81 Fulham Road, London SW3 6RB
and Auckland, Melbourne, Singapore and Toronto

Reprinted in 1992 (twice), 1993

Distributed in the United States of America
by Heinemann, a division of Reed Publishing (USA) Inc.,
361 Hanover Street, Portsmouth, New Hampshire,
NH 03801 3959.

A CIP catalogue record for this book
is available from the British Library

ISBN 0 413 66110 5

Printed and bound in Great Britain
by Cox & Wyman Ltd, Reading, Berkshire

To Tom

Contents

Foreword 1991

I am really pleased that Methuen have decided to republish my two books, *About Acting* and *More About Acting*, as a single volume. I have decided not to try to amalgamate them, but to keep them more or less as they were. A few references to things which no longer apply have been cut, and I've added one more interview, with Samuel West, to the chapter called How Do You Work On A Part? In a few places where I have changed my mind since I first wrote the books (*About Acting* in 1980, *More About Acting* in 1984) or where things needed bringing up to date, I have added a 'PS 1991'.

The books were originally published by Secker & Warburg at the instigation of the then Chairman, Tom Rosenthal. He had written to me after seeing a piece in the *Radio Times*, heralding the television series, *Telford's Change*. 'I see from that article,' he wrote, 'that we have the same taste in pictures and that you keep a diary. Do you think there's a book in your diaries?'

I went to see him in his office in Poland Street, filled with glorious things by Ivon Hitchens and others. I told him I'd already started a book, tentatively entitled *Tricks of the Trade*, and that I intended it to contain helpful hints for actors. 'It sounds a good idea,' he said, 'but I don't like the title. We'll think of something better. And your diaries?'

'Well, I'm not sure. I've brought in a few for you to dip into, as you asked me to. I'd rather it were your decision. If you think there's a book there, I'll try and make one.'

The book eventually became *First Houses*, which was autobiographical up to 1960. *Tricks of the Trade* became *About Acting*.

Tom handed out enthusiasm, help, wisdom and mirth in equal proportions, and I can never be grateful enough to him.

PART ONE

About Acting

Introduction

I started teaching at RADA in 1955. I had never intended to be a teacher and it seemed a bit pretentious to take classes there when I was a novice of twenty-six and some of the students were considerably older than I was. But I had become depressed: I was playing small supporting roles in successful plays like *The Dark Is Light Enough* at the Aldwych Theatre, and *My Three Angels* and *South Sea Bubble* at the Lyric Theatre, and was getting little satisfaction from all that repetition, night after night, and felt that my talent, for what it was, was deteriorating and my confidence was in danger of disappearing altogether.

For a while I thought seriously, but rather romantically I suppose, of giving up the whole business and going off to some far-away place, like central Africa, to do good in the world.

But then I thought, no, the thing is to do something else during the day which will take my mind off those grisly two-and-a-half hours in the theatre every evening and give me something new to be enthusiastic about. It wasn't just boredom that was bothering me, but an acute form of self-consciousness (the greatest hurdle of all for some actors) which made it harder and harder for me to perform well. I found it increasingly difficult, as a run went on, to look and feel natural and spontaneous: everything seemed too set, too patterned, and therefore lifeless. I had a great deal to learn, so, I thought, rather contrarily and boldly, why not teach? School hours would fit in well with theatre hours, except on the mid-week matinée day; and I remembered I had enjoyed my only previous experience of teaching when I was in the Army after the war, doing my compulsory National Service, and I had had to give some lectures on Pay. I thought this time I might be able to take classes in Speech and Voice Production, so I asked a friend of mine who taught at the

Webber-Douglas Academy if she thought it would be a good idea for me to approach the Principal there and ask to take a class or two.

'No,' she replied, rather too quickly. 'You see, we don't do things like that at the Webber-D. We have our own bunch of students, you see, and take them for everything . . . we direct their plays and do the voice-production and movement classes ourselves.' (I believe things have changed since then, and I'm relieved to hear it.)

'Oh,' I said, nonplussed, knowing that I would be incapable of such an awe-inspiring and responsible task, 'that's that, then.'

'Why don't you try RADA?' she said, making it sound like a huge step-down, 'I believe they do things like that there.'

Don't be ridiculous, I thought, as I put the telephone down. But emboldened by a friend who said, 'Well, they can always say no,' I wrote a brief letter to John Fernald, who was then Principal, saying that I thought I would like to teach 'perhaps something to do with speech', and if he was not interested would he please not bother to reply, but if he was I would be happy to come in and talk to him about it.

To my surprise he replied by return and suggested an immediate appointment. I was very nervous as I was ushered into his office, which, in spite of the rattling traffic in Gower Street outside, was strangely hushed, and grander than I had remembered (I had been a student at RADA in the late forties), with soft lighting from large table-lamps, and a bigger desk than I had ever seen. He seemed yards away from me as I looked at him across it from my low chair and I found it very difficult to concentrate, but certain sentences pierced my hazy brain: 'We could do with some young actors on the staff . . . I think the students would like it . . . but I don't want you to teach diction.'

'Oh,' I said, disappointed, for there was nothing else I thought myself capable of teaching.

'We've already got Clifford Turner and Barry Smith, and they're very good. And Denys Blakelock does audition speeches and things. No, I know what I want you to do: Hugh Miller is leaving, and I would like you to take over from him. He teaches "technique", you know.'

'Yes, I know,' I said. 'He taught me, actually . . .'

'Well, he is quite enthusiastic about your taking over from him, and so am I.'

So! He has already mentioned it to Hugh Miller! It's all buttoned up, I thought.

'Wow!' I said.

'I like your work,' he said, and my nervousness completely disappeared, 'and I'd like you to start next term.' He beamed at me, no doubt seeing how pleased I was, and how surprised. I think he even chuckled. He had a delightful way of chuckling, heaving his shoulders about. He sat back, waiting for me to speak, peering at me over his glasses. I stared at his bow-tie.

'Er . . . what shall I do? I mean is there anything . . . I mean . . . what shall I include?'

'Go away and think about it,' he said, 'and work out a course of eleven lessons: a term's work. Two hours a week per class; two classes. We'll start at four hours a week. Nineteen shillings an hour.'

'Is there anything you'd like me to include?' I repeated, as I got up from my chair and made for the door.

'I leave it to you,' he said . . . and then, 'Well, yes, one thing: I've noticed the students tend to be awfully clumsy with props – cigarettes, drinks, fans, books, that sort of thing . . . you could include something to do with that . . . and comedy, that's important.'

'Right!' I said, and whooped my way along Chenies Street as far as Goodge Street station. I thought of little else for the next three months and worked out a course of lectures and exercises. Occasionally actor friends would be less than encouraging: 'Those who can, do; those who can't, teach,' they would chant, reminding me that there was still a stigma against actors who taught. This had always puzzled me; why was it all right for musicians to teach at the leading Academies, for painters and sculptors to teach at the Royal College of Art and the Slade, but not for actors to teach at RADA or Central or LAMDA? I was determined to fight the stigma: now, I think, it has disappeared, and many more actors have found their way into the major drama schools, their careers not suffering because of it.

John Fernald approved of my course when I outlined it to him, and I started to take the classes which had been assigned

to me: 'I think it should be fourth-termers,' he said. Occasionally he would come in for a while to see what I was up to, but
on the whole he left me alone, and I was completely free to
get on with what I wanted to do.

He was a remarkable man and a great Principal. He trusted
his staff and loved his students, and his concern for and
knowledge of every single one of them always astonished me.
He was an innovator, too: he reduced the numbers in each
class from a staggering and hopelessly unmanageable thirty,
and sometimes even more, down to about a dozen. He
introduced a much more personal relationship between staff
and students, and inaugurated repeat performances of plays
by students in their final year: for them the Academy became
more like a repertory theatre than a school; John Fernald
always wanted students to get the feel of a professional theatre
while they were still there under his guidance.

After my first term as a teacher he asked me if I would take
third-termers as well. This meant I had to enlarge my course,
which I was only too happy to do, for it allowed me to
experiment with new methods and exercises. Later I took the
second term as well, and occasional classes for Finals students;
and by 1958 I was working there more or less full-time, which
was fine, for I was then in the middle of a three-year run of
Roar Like a Dove at the Phoenix Theatre. In that play I had a
nice, funny part, but I was on the stage for only fifteen
minutes in the second act, so the combination of the two jobs
was not too exhausting, especially as I lived nearby, in an
attic flat in Bloomsbury.

The idea of a book came from John Fernald. 'Can you write
about your classes?' he said, out of the blue one day. 'I know
you use the lecture-exercise method – don't you think you
could make a book of your lectures?'

'I'll try,' I said.

And I did, and failed. I realised that a great proportion of
my lectures was based on demonstration and needed a
perpetual comeback from the students. When I tried to write
it all down it seemed very academic and long-winded and
boring, so I gave up.

'Well, couldn't you make a book of the exercises?' he
persisted. I tried that too, but failed again, because if the
exercise is a good one the teacher has merely to set it without

anticipating the result (if he says what the result should be, he spoils the adventure of the exercise). That's all right in the classroom, for the result can be analysed and discussed afterwards, but it's no good in a book. Too much would be left in the air.

For example, one of my favourite exercises was called 'Going Round in Circles'. Here is how I used to set it: 'Next week I shall want you to perform a speech you already know – don't bother to learn a new one – and your task is to say it to someone who is standing outside a circle you keep going round. The idea of the exercise is of course to motivate properly the continuous movement, to motivate the moves towards and away from the other person, to find ways of going on an arc around him, to experiment with walking backwards and sideways, and if possible to disguise from us the fact that it is just an exercise and even, if possible, to enhance the speech because of the variety of attitudes the moves will dictate.'

This, believe it or not, is a wonderful exercise, and can teach an enormous amount about the intricacies of movement, about fluidity and about making points, about footwork and head-turns. It was often wonderfully well performed by the students and interestingly discussed by them afterwards. There seemed no way of conveying in a book the sort of excitement of discovery such an exercise can induce.

So I dropped the idea, and in time I left RADA. I wanted a break from teaching, and anyway was starting to work more on television than in the theatre, which meant that I no longer had my day-times free. I took my last class there in 1963.

Years later I was in Michael Frayn's play *Donkeys' Years* at the Globe Theatre. At every performance I gave an eight-minute party in my dressing-room. All the actors, except Penelope Keith and Andrew Robertson, who had an eight-minute scene in the middle of Act 2, used to come in, in their dinner-jackets, and drink Perrier Water (occasionally mildly laced) and talk actor-talk: we would discuss how the play was going at that performance, and what the audience was like; we would give each other occasional notes (this was allowed only within the confines of the party!) and generally chew the fat about plays, actors, directors, critics, authors and impresarios. Occasionally, too, we would play round-robin games: one rather malicious one, which had to be answered truthfully, was: 'What is the compliment you most like to receive (a) as an actor, and (b) as a person?' The answers were very revealing.

Another was: 'What advice given by other people has most helped you and affected your acting?' And it was with that question that the idea for this book dawned.

I ought to write, I thought, a book of short pieces: Helpful Hints, Golden Rules, some of which I have learnt from other people and others I have thought out for myself. Some of them may be clichés, but a good cliché has usually earned its reputation from the sheer repetition of its truth and usefulness. And rules are good, for when you know them it can be so rewarding to break them. At least you know what you are doing.

Two very dissimilar books influenced me greatly when I was considering the form of this one: J. B. Priestley's *Delight*, a compilation of 114 short pieces about things which have delighted him, and a recipe book called *The Flavour of France* by the Chamberlains: in it there is one recipe per page, accompanied by a photograph of the town or village from where it came.

So here are my few recipes. You won't like them all, for acting is a very personal business, as personal as eating. But I hope you will like some of them, for they were born out of swapping ideas with my fellow actors at my Perrier party. I was quite touched when I heard the other day that Paul Eddington and John Quentin, who played the same part after me, kept up the tradition. I wonder what they talked about!

Before Rehearsals Start

Get The Facts Right

'... remember, for all time, that when you begin to study each role you should first gather all the materials that have any bearing on it, and supplement them with more and more imagination, until you have achieved such a similarity to life that it is easy to believe in what you are doing. In the beginning, forget about your feelings. When the inner conditions are prepared, and right, feelings will come to the surface of their own accord.'

Constantin Stanislavski, *An Actor Prepares*.

This is my favourite quotation. If you are one of those people who underline memorable passages in books, here there is not a phrase you could leave out. I used to like starting a class with it at RADA, occasionally putting huge stresses on certain key words, like 'easy' and 'right'. It sums up exactly what an actor's first task should be: to go for the facts, to get them right, to dig for the details of past life and present attitudes, and, where there are gaps in the author's information, to fill them 'with more and more imagination' until the jigsaw is complete.

It is necessary to know the past life of a character because the past determines the present and the future. I was introduced to the theory of Determinism when I was a student at RADA. T. S. Eliot was all the rage then and, along with Auden, he was the poet most frequently chosen by us for diction and voice exercises. How often we listened to each other booming out:

'Time present and time past
Are both perhaps present in time future,
And time future contained in time past.'

But we never got tired of *Four Quartets*, partly because they were so fascinating to speak, but also because they were the encapsulation of the theory we were all so keen on. 'You are the result,' said one of our teachers, explaining it, 'of everything you have been and thought and done and inherited. The present is not self-contained, nor is it in a vacuum. So every character you play should be the result of what that character has been and thought and done and inherited.'

There is no substitute for detail. A vague, generalised picture is no substitute for specific facts and figures. I remember reading a review in *The Times* which included the following damning sentence: 'The actors acted with that kind of breathless intensity which actors always employ when they do not know what it is they are being intense about.'

In the beginning forget about your feelings. Get the facts right.

Springboards

Starting work on a part always feels to me like preparing to dive into a swimming pool. However many times you've dived before, there's always an element of danger. You stand there, transfixed for a moment, nervous, knowing you've got to plunge, but wondering if you dare to. The pause seems endless. Then, suddenly, as though by surprise, you're in.

I always like it, when I'm at my desk reading silently through a play, when I come to a speech which forces me to read it aloud. Often that speech becomes a model for the eventual performance; it can constitute the plunge, and is all the better for being unconsidered.

I go for the tone of voice first. That is my springboard. Precise or slack? Breathy or full-toned? Standard English or some variant? Fast or slow? Gradually a tone seems right. And by daring to read aloud a little more and a little more, the part begins to come to life: I can hear him.

Several of my friends do it this way. But not all. Wendy Hiller, for example, starts with her feet. 'Yes, I'd like to take this part,' she said, over tea at the Ritz, talking to Michael Codron, Peter Dews and Royce Ryton about her forthcoming role of Queen Mary in *Crown Matrimonial*, 'because I know what her feet will be like.' And then she demonstrated, apparently (I was not there), a delicate out-turning of her feet, and padded about on the deep carpets of the hotel. 'Yes,' she said, straightening her back, satisfied, 'those are her feet. Those feet are royal.'

Intentions And Beats

These are the two words from 'The Method' which I find the most useful. In fact they are indispensable; but so much has been written about them elsewhere that I will confine myself to the shortest possible explanation of them.

As you read and read the play and your part in it you will discover that underlying the words you are to speak there is a reason for speaking them. Why do you say that, to that person, now? Is it to convince your son, for example, that he is old enough to leave home now, and that it would be good for him to do so? Then that's your Intention. Is it to let your wife know that you know she is being unfaithful? Then that's your Intention. As soon as your son agrees with you, as soon as your wife knows that you know, those Intentions will be over and others will take their place.

A Beat is the distance from the beginning of an Intention to its end: it is the acting equivalent of a paragraph.

Write Things Down

Whatever your starting point, whatever your method, your performance will be an amalgam of the ideas which occur to you. So you might as well develop the habit of writing them down: if you don't remember your good ideas there was no point in having them in the first place, and in the hurly-burly of rehearsals it is all too easy to forget some of the valuable things you first thought of.

Remarks about the character, ideas for the subtext, and anything to do with the shaping of speeches are the things I like to scribble in my script as they occur to me.

I use a mixture of musical and other notations for the shaping of speeches:

⌒ between sentences means 'join them up'.

| between sentences or words means 'pause' or 'a beat' (a more usual meaning of the word than that given above).

⅂ between sentences or words means 'a tick pause': a very brief one.

‖ means 'a longish pause'.

∩ means 'a complete stop'.

> means 'pounce on to this new idea'.

___ under words means 'give them emphasis'.

‾‾‾ over words means 'throw them away'.

∩ is a generalised symbol for sadness.

∪ is an equally generalised one for happiness.

∪∪ means 'laughing the while'.

f means 'loudly'.

ff means 'very loudly'.

p means 'quietly'.

pp means 'very quietly'.

⋀ in the left hand margin (it can vary hugely in size: sometimes it's as big as the page) means 'enlarge the pressure or volume or whatever' and

⋁ means 'diminish it',

and a line right across the page indicates the end of one intention and the beginning of a new one.

Squiggles over words give, by their rising and falling, an indication of a preferred inflection, eg:

ɹ __ __ ɹ
'Well, I'm not sure . . .'

I wouldn't want to clutter up a whole script with these *aides-mémoire* (for that's all they are), but if an inflection has been awkward to find it's worth having a record of it.

I know a lot of actors don't like to mark up their scripts this way because they like the words to be uncluttered; but I do like to, even though I often change my mind about how things should go. My script becomes an incomprehensible mess of markings and crossings-out, but at least I can see the stages I have gone through.

PS 1991. I don't like to do this now! I'd rather see the words! Recently I've prided myself on not putting a single mark on the script except, of course, any alterations to the text. I think, now, that if the idea is a good one, you'll remember it. If it isn't, you won't.

The Voice Of The Author

The voice of the author, the voice of the character, and you: these are the three basic ingredients of any successful performance.

And of the three the hardest for an actor to realise is the voice of the author. This is especially so when the author is distinguished, for the fact that he is distinguished probably means that he is stylised, and the actor's task is to absorb that style and make it part of his characterisation.

The difficulty with performing the work of a stylised writer is that it can so easily sound as if you are quoting him rather than conceiving the words yourself. Therefore, and I'm necessarily generalising here, if he is Shakespeare, part of your *characterisation* must be that you think poetically; you are a poet, you are not merely quoting one. If he is Shaw, part of your characterisation must be that you are a good talker, high-spirited and intellectually bright. If he is Christopher Fry, you have a mind packed with images; if Tom Stoppard, your mind is even more packed with jokes, intellectual niceties and a huge vocabulary. Ibsen, Chekhov, Simon Gray, Michael Frayn, Noël Coward, John Osborne, T. S. Eliot all have their very individual voices, demanding not stylised performances but natural ones which have absorbed their style.

Go For The Life Of The Part

'Go for the life of the part,' said Edith Evans, when she was talking to some drama students in a television programme.

I was in two plays of which she was the star – Christopher Fry's *The Dark Is Light Enough* and Enid Bagnold's *The Chinese Prime Minister* – and I learned more from her than from anybody I have ever met. I wanted to include many of her Golden Rules in this book, and here is the first, for it complements what I've just been saying about an author's style. '*You* mustn't be stylised,' she said, and she started talking about how to use a fan. 'Those eighteenth-century ladies didn't use their fans for *style*, they *used* them. They would fan themselves if they were hot, or embarrassed, or poke somebody in the ribs with them if they wanted to make a point, or slap somebody on the shoulders with them if they were cross.

'You must go for the truth of a part, and know how the ladies and gentlemen of those times dealt with their clothes and wigs and make-up and accoutrements. Don't be stylised: be truthful!'

The Voice Of The Character

I have at home a book called *A Book of Make-up* by Eric Ward, originally published in 1930. Nowadays it makes very strange reading. The idea behind it is that your own face should be obliterated by Leichner No. 5 and a new face, the face of the character, should be painted on. How things have changed! Nowadays actors wear hardly any make-up, and use it only to alter something in their own face which needs altering for the part.

So it is with characterisation. There is no question of obliterating yourself and starting a characterisation from scratch. Mostly you use yourself, and change only what is necessary. 'Accept what is the same, and alter what is different,' said Fabia Drake, one of my teachers at RADA, and that's it.

Find out what the differences are (age? accent? background? speech patterns? vocabulary? period? job? intelligence? instincts?) and exaggerate them for a while, to make sure they plunge themselves into your personality. Then you can forget about them; they will take care of themselves, and you can concentrate again on being yourself.

You

Whether you intend it or not, what the audiences will be most aware of in your performance is you: your appearance, your idiosyncrasies, your persona. However accurate your characterisation, the you-ness of you will dominate it. If you don't believe me, think of, say, twenty of your favourite performers. Think how their own personalities shine through all their performances. Think of Judi Dench, Denholm Elliott, Anthony Hopkins, Imelda Staunton, Julia McKenzie, Michael Gambon.

Your private life, therefore, spills over into your acting. It is bound to. Your qualities and your attitudes will all be in evidence, your personality will be on show. What you are in everyday life will be what you are in plays.

So a lot of your early work as an actor will be on yourself, developing your strengths, eradicating your weaknesses; and this not only in the big things but in the little things as well.

If you don't speak clearly in everyday life, you won't speak clearly in plays.

If you don't speak naturally in everyday life, you won't speak naturally in plays.

If you've got a funny walk in everyday life, you will have a funny walk in plays.

Stanislavski again: 'Never lose yourself on the stage. Always act in your own person, as an artist. You can never get away from yourself . . . Always and for ever, when you are on the stage, you must play yourself. But it will be an infinite variety of combinations of objectives and given circumstances which you have prepared for the part, and which have been smelted in the furnace of your emotion memory.'

Memory

After talent (And what is that? Oh! A desire to show off? I don't know. That's where it starts, I suppose: a desire to get up and show off in front of people. Then it changes.), after that, the most important single attribute for an actor is a good memory. And I don't mean a memory for lines, but a memory for events, emotions: a storehouse of experiences. If knowing the differences between yourself and the character is the right approach to characterisation, an acute knowledge of yourself is pre-supposed, and you can get to know yourself only by remembering what you have done and what you felt like when you were doing it. You will have done a vast variety of things, and have experienced emotions from ecstasy to despair. What a pity to waste such a storehouse of experience by not using it in your acting!

Look

But your memory should be trained not only on yourself but on the people you meet and see around you. Looking, staring even, will fill you with knowledge of human behaviour, from deep revelations of loneliness, love, illness and age to the trivia of everyday existence: how people use their hands, their faces, how they walk and talk in shops, in church, in the street. Tourists are very interesting to watch, absorbed as they are in the foreign-ness of everything around them, trying to find their exact location on a yellow and green map provided by the hotel, or in their *A to Z*. Being a tourist is as near as an adult can become to being a child again, with a mind uncluttered with the paraphernalia of sophistication and getting-on-with-people; there is a simple, straightforward concentration on looking, a concentration actors could well attempt to emulate.

Models

So the world around you will fill you with ideas which, hopefully, will become deep-seated in your memory.

Sometimes, however, it is good to seek a more specific model for a part. I like to do this. I remember when I was preparing for *Professional Foul* by Tom Stoppard, in which I had the part of a Professor of Ethics at Cambridge University, I watched Professor A. J. Ayer on television deliberately to spy out some of his mannerisms and idiosyncracies. I noticed, for instance, that his words had great difficulty in keeping up with his racing intellect, so he would rush the last words of one sentence because the next one had formed in his mind. I liked, too, his habit of delaying laughter at one of his own jokes: he would crack a joke, then say another sentence, then laugh at his joke during the sentence after that. I liked his mercurial changes of mood, violent changes really, revealing themselves so quickly in his face as the thoughts flashed by. I liked the actual speed with which he spoke. All good.stuff. All grist to the mill.

Get The Job Right

Are you a soldier, a dustman, a doctor, a lawyer, a king, a Prime Minister, a housewife, a cook, a marriage guidance counsellor, a television producer, a teacher, a nurse, a company director, a mother? Get the job right, and that's half the battle. It was Clifford Evans who pointed this out to me, and I've always been grateful to him.

In the original production of Brian Clark's *Whose Life Is It Anyway?* at the Savoy Theatre, one of the glories of Michael Lindsay-Hogg's direction was that you really believed you were in the presence of doctors and nurses and psychiatrists and lawyers, and not in the presence of actors. It was the result of painstaking observation: nurses and doctors have a way of walking through wards and along corridors which is not the way you and I walk along them; doctors have a vocational caring for their patients, and carry more in their heads than they intend to reveal. They have special sorts of hands, too, sensitive, careful, instructive.

The difficulties about playing the public figures who so dominate Shakespeare's plays have always fascinated me, for the actors have the double task of finding the true public face of these characters, and the true private face as well. I have never yet seen a Claudius, for example, who has managed to achieve this duality. In his first scene he is in public, a new king, worried, obviously, by Hamlet's sulky withdrawal but nevertheless, surely, putting on as brave and impressive a public face as possible. The scene can be played with smiling, royal politeness, with its demands for compliance from Hamlet disguised as soft entreaties; but so often the actor chooses to rant and rage, making the task of the poor performers playing Gertrude, and all the courtiers, very difficult indeed! How to react? Certainly their first task will have to be to depose this madman, totally unfitted as he is to occupy Denmark's throne. And Claudius has plenty of scope, later in the play, for self-revelation: if all is revealed straight away, there are no surprises in store.

I did see one actor do the end of the play-scene magnificently. He pretended he thought the play had finished, rose and applauded. The rest of the (on-stage) audience joined in the clapping. And then, as though it were *nearly* an ordinary command, he turned to a courtier and said, 'Give me some light. Away.'

The underplaying of this superb theatrical moment, putting on the public face instead of the usual shouting and storming, doubled its impact.

PS 1991.   And Richard Easton was a magnificent Claudius
in Kenneth Branagh's *Hamlet*, directed by Derek Jacobi at the
Phoenix Theatre in 1988. His first scene contained a marvellous piece of invention – it was a small company on account
of touring so there weren't any spare actors to be just courtiers
– Claudius did not deliver his speech to his court, he merely
rehearsed it. He carried his script, and made notes and
crossings-out from time to time.

Learn The Lines

'Of course,' you say. 'What an imbecilic piece this is going to
be! Of course I shall learn the lines.'

Ah, but I think by the time you've read it you may find it
one of the hardest in the book to agree with, because the
reason I am putting it so near the beginning, when I am
concerned with the initial preparation for a part, is that I
think it best to learn the lines before rehearsals start.

Or at least to have a pretty good idea of them. When Noël
Coward directed his own plays he insisted that the cast arrive
word-perfect for the first rehearsal. And the distinguished
director Murray Macdonald often used to say to me: 'I get so
bored with actors who don't know the lines and struggle away
with them at rehearsal that I sometimes want to give up
directing altogether.'

However, my reasons for believing that it is good to know
the words before rehearsals start do not include placating
directors! Indeed the one penalty you may incur is that your
colleagues – director and cast alike – will resent your being
ahead of them. But even this can eventually become an
advantage, especially when time is short (as it always is for an
episode in a television series, or even, now, for a West End
play: four weeks always used to be allowed for rehearsals, now
it's often three), for it encourages everyone else to get a move
on. You may be accused, too, of being less receptive to other
people's ideas, less influenced by the other actors, less sensitive to the nuances they are beginning to discover in their
roles. I find the reverse to be the case. Actors who have no
knowledge of the lines, who like to start from scratch, who
bore everyone with endless arguments as to the meaning of
the lines and the attitudes underpinning them, don't even

notice what you are doing because they have their faces buried in their scripts. They don't react at all to you: they cannot. Whereas you, from the start, can look at them, speak to them, listen to them, be surprised by them (holding the script the while, of course: you won't want to throw it away right at the beginning); and this element of surprise, if you remember it, is one of the most valuable things that can happen. So often it is totally lacking, and plays become flat and bland because of the lack.

If you have learnt the lines in the leisure of pre-rehearsal days (if, as we say, you have done your homework), you will perforce have worked on their meaning and subtext. Indeed, you will have learnt them *by* working on their meaning, by reading them over and over again, until the words have gradually and unforcedly sunk into your subconscious. You will have fought over the difficult bits, and even have worked out suggestions for possible alterations. In short, you will come to rehearsals knowing what you are talking about; you will have some idea of how you want to play the part.

I have found that, if the director disagrees with elements of my homework, it is quite easy (providing the director is right, of course!) to change them. Directors are, on the whole, better at altering a positive contribution from an actor than at suggesting how a part should be played when the actor starts with nothing: I have seen disasters happen to actors who have allowed a director to tell them how to play a part.

The most important advantage, though, of having a good knowledge of the words in advance is that it enables you to assess more clearly the rightness or wrongness of the moves a director may suggest. That is usually his first task, and where you stand or sit, or when you move about, is as much as anything going to determine your eventual performance. If you know the words you can *look*. You can sense the distance between you and the other actors, you can feel when a move is a good one. You may even suggest some good ones yourself.

Edith Evans liked to do this; when a distinguished director started giving her moves she said, 'No, no, no! You mustn't tell me where to go, or when to sit! I must work that out for myself.'

'But Dame Edith,' wailed the director, 'if I'm not to give you moves, what am I here for?'

'Oh,' she said, 'we'll find something for you to do.'

I will bring this overlong piece to a sudden end with just one more observation. I think rehearsals should be fun. Work is all the better and all the quicker for a few laughs and a few jokes . . . and jokes and laughs are possible only when people do not feel the oppressive weight of work on their heads. Learning the lines in advance takes the chore out of rehearsals, lightens the load, and therefore lightens the atmosphere.

You still don't agree with me? Oh well.

PS 1991.   I still feel the same, even more fervently. Most of the cast of Simon Gray's *Hidden Laughter* had done a great deal of work before rehearsals started in April last year, and no scripts were held by anybody after the first week. They were the best rehearsals I have ever known.

Of course this learning in advance is particularly desirable for actors of advancing years! It used to take me a week, after learning lines, to guarantee that I would know them. Now it's three weeks. It is dreadful to see elderly actors struggling over lines they have only just worked on. Panic is a dreadful thing. To be avoided at all costs.

First Rehearsals

Don't Throw Away The Read-Through

Meeting the cast and director for the first time can be a nerve-racking experience. Actually it is a comfort to know that all the other actors are just as nervous as you are, and the director is probably more nervous than anyone. And if you have done your homework you will not let your nerves wreck the day for you, but will use the read-through as it ought to be used: it is, after all, your first opportunity to talk and listen to the people you are going to be with in the play.

Robert Lewis, in my favourite book about acting, *Method or Madness?*, says: 'Beginnings are extremely important . . . the things you should do in your first reading (because it is exploratory work and you are trying to find out what goes on) are *talk* and *listen*.'

Both activities will yield many surprises if you are really concentrating and, again, those surprises are worth remembering.

Talking

When you talk you are thinking of two things: what you are talking about, and the person, or persons, to whom you are talking. Sometimes what you say has most of your attention (if it's a memory, for example, or something which is difficult to think out or to find the right words for); sometimes the person you are addressing has (if you are telling him what to do, or asking for his sympathy or advice). It is one of the most interesting things to work out: where does the majority of your attention lie at any given moment?

But you talk for the benefit of other people, not for yourself. If they weren't there, you wouldn't talk. It is for them.

Obvious, and yet it is distressing to see – particularly in 'speechy' plays by, say, Shakespeare and Shaw – how many performances are ruined by actors who forget they are actually talking *to* someone.

Listening

'Listening,' said Edith Evans, 'is paying attention. It is *not* reacting. I can't bear it when I'm talking to another actor on the stage and he *reacts* to everything I say. Listening is blank-faced usually . . . if it's gracious listening a smile is allowable. But listen! Don't react!'

I love that. It's true.

As is Flora Robson's dictum, in a speech she gave to RADA students, that 'Listening is receiving. Talking is giving, listening is receiving.'

Your Attitude To The Director 1

Continuing for a moment my theme of talking and listening (and doing one of those two things is how you will spend most of your time in most plays), I would like to tell you what my first television director, Lionel Harris, said to me: 'Don't try to convince *me*, don't try to convince the *camera*: convince the people you are with. Convince them that you are really talking to them and really listening to them. Try to pretend I'm not here. When you're in the studio, try to pretend the camera is not there. You won't succeed, but the attempt is worthwhile.'

This really is a Golden Rule for acting in television; but I think it has enormous relevance to acting in the theatre as well. It is so tempting, there, to talk to the audience and to listen to them, instead of talking and listening to the other characters.

Your Attitude To The Director 2

Lionel Harris also said: 'I always say to my casts and, when I'm lecturing, to students at drama schools, that they should not take too much notice of what I say. You see, the actor is the one who has to do it, and do it night after night, and he must be comfortable. Clever actors will remember what they like about what I've told them and conveniently forget what they don't like, and I never reprimand them for it. So. Don't be too obedient!'

I had been immensely worried when I was being directed by John Gielgud in a revival of *The School for Scandal* at the Haymarket Theatre in 1962. I was Sir Benjamin Backbite, and I remember that just before the read-through he suddenly turned to me and said, 'I think it would be amusing, Peter, if you said all your R's as W's. For example, let's see, yes, here, your third speech: instead of "To say truth, ma'am, 'tis very vulgar to print", you should say, "To say twooth, ma'am, 'tis vewy vulgar to pwint."'

The rest of the cast laughed, but it threw me into consternation because, to say truth, I didn't think it was the best idea in the world; but I felt I couldn't start the rehearsals by having an argument with Sir John, whom I admired and liked so much – no one is kinder and more generous than he – so I let it go. I tried to do it straight away and of course made an utter mess of it and felt wretched and humiliated.

At later rehearsals he gave me an immense amount of business, including, I remember, trying to balance a small cane on my chin! This not while I was speaking but while Margaret Rutherford was. I could feel the rest of the cast didn't like it but, again, because it was John Gielgud, and I was in awe of him, there seemed nothing for it but to be obedient.

Eventually I confessed my worries to Meriel Forbes, who was playing Lady Sneerwell, and she said: 'Darling, you mustn't be so obedient! John would be shocked if he knew you were so worried. What he is doing, darling, is offering you pearls. But you have to supply the string yourself, and any pearls which won't fit on to your string, you must discard.'

But the W's remained, I'm afraid. By sheer repetition both good things and bad things stick; and the good things get better and the bad things get worse.

Your Attitude To The Director 3

Television has brought about a much more democratic relationship between actors and directors, for a television director is a performer too, supervising the cameras' moves and the cuts from one camera to another. He is not just an onlooker.

This new democracy has permeated through to the theatre as well, and is to be applauded. It is up to actors to maintain it, and there is one area where I think we often fail, and that is in the giving of praise.

Actors are known to thrive on praise. 'Don't criticise me,' Dame Edith implored Peter Brook, during a rehearsal of *The Dark Is Light Enough*, 'praise me! What I want is praise!'

We all do. In our hearts we all do. We can take anything from a director who starts by saying: 'It's coming along beautifully, your performance . . . it gets better every day . . . there's just one thing . . .' As John Fernald says in his book *Sense of Direction*: 'All actors incline towards insecurity some of the time, and the best of them much of the time; a director may well be judged by the rapidity with which he can dispel this inclination.'

True; but what we are not good at is giving praise. To praise the director for his good and helpful ideas, the author for his skilful writing is, if it's truthful, nothing to do with sycophancy: it is to give encouragement and confidence in exactly the same measure as we would like to receive them.

Praise should be a two-way affair.

Your Attitude To The Cast

Take care to acknowledge that they have as many insecurities as you have, will probably prefer not to be watched too closely at early rehearsals when they are finding their way, and will be much happier to think that you are not sitting there criticising them, either silently or in whispers to someone else. We are all so damn' sensitive, that's the pity of it! I remember my confidence falling through the floor at an early rehearsal for a stage play when I caught sight of a girl exchanging a kind of deprecating grimace with another, while I was struggling away with a long speech. When confidence goes, boldness goes and daring goes, and boldness and daring are too valuable to be allowed to evaporate in early rehearsals. I like it when the rest of the cast seem not to be taking too much notice of what I am doing, when they read newspapers (as long as they don't rattle the pages), or do the crossword, or knit.

We are a critical lot, and I think it is better to curb criticism of your fellow performers as much as you can. If you criticise them you can bet your bottom dollar they will criticise you.

Do as you would be done by.

Concentration

If your attitudes to the director and the cast are as kindly as I have recommended, you will more easily gain the enormous and necessary bonus of concentration; concentration is impossible in unfriendly surroundings.

To be able to concentrate easily, and ignore the many distractions in a rehearsal room, a theatre, or a film or television studio, is a knack which has to be acquired. And the place to acquire it is in everyday life.

Train yourself to listen well, to remember people's names as you are introduced, to remember, like a photographer, the look of people and places and things, and to see them in your mind's eye in colour.

Give yourself these exercises:

1. Concentrate, when alone, on a memory, without allowing distracting thoughts to invade and spoil it.
2. Work out arithmetical problems in your head, or argue, in your head, through a personal problem.
3. Read. (Have you noticed that people who read a lot, or write, are particularly good at concentrating?)
4. Learn to talk well, so that there is a clear connection between what you are thinking and the words you use to express those thoughts. 'Talking-practice' is what I call it, this exercise of talking alone over a wide range of subjects: half an hour of continuous chatter (your family will think you've gone mad) and the sentences will flow out of you, connecting your voice to your head.

Look. Listen. Read. Talk.

Moves

Sometimes called 'Blocking', 'Plotting', 'Seeing What Happens', or – Barry Davis's favourites – 'Busking', 'Bluffing', or 'Finding Your Feet'.

I like it best when everybody pretends to be very casual about it. 'OK,' said Michael Lindsay-Hogg, one of our finest television directors (we were finding our feet in *Professional Foul*), 'OK. So. There's this hotel room. I tell you what's already been decided and that's where the walls are because the scenery is now being made and so that tape on the floor indicates where the walls are and there are a couple of doors, one into the corridor, there, and one into the bathroom, there. So. There'll have to be a bed somewhere, and a chest-of-drawers like they have in Czech hotels, and a couple of chairs, I suppose. But they can be anywhere. The only thing is, of course, that when we've decided where we'd like them to be in *this* room, the other rooms – you know, for the reporters and footballers and all – will have to be sort of similar, because they are in Czech hotels. So . . . Peter . . . er . . . well, look, just come in, eh? . . . and . . . er . . . well, come in . . . see what happens . . .'

This approach, which allows everyone to chip in and feel their way through a scene, is very relaxing, and moves invented in a relaxed atmosphere need less amending at later rehearsals because they start from a premise that comfortableness is what counts. Not cosiness, comfortableness. Only when an actor is comfortable will his performance grow.

'OK then, Peter? . . . Stephen? . . . Looks good . . . feel OK? We'll come back to it tomorrow . . . but that's the groundwork . . . OK?'

I can't bear being given arbitrary moves arbitrarily preconceived by the director. Only sleepless nights and awkward arguments ensue, for such a director discards one of the most precious ingredients in the making of a play: the actors' instincts.

Anchors

This and the next eleven pieces are just a few tips about blocking and moves and positions and things.

'I must have my anchors!' said Edith Evans when we were rehearsing *The Chinese Prime Minister*. When I asked her what they were she said: 'Anchors are the people or things around you on the stage, onto which you can latch your thoughts. They are, quite simply, the people and things you look at. Where you *look* is extremely important.'

She pointed out to me how they helped her in a particular scene. 'I'm here, d'you see, and you're there. As I have the most to say, I'm sitting in the upstage chair. So you're down there. Sitting. And sitting still, I hope. Ah yes,' she said, 'you must be still when I am talking to you because I'm like a horse, d'you see: if you move about, I shy. Like a horse shies at a hurdle. Anyway. There you are down there, on my left. You are my left-hand anchor. I need something on the other side of me. I need a right-hand anchor. Now: there's nobody else on the stage, so it has to be a thing. I've made it this little table to the right of my chair. I shall drink during this scene, d'you see, and from time to time I shall put my glass down on this little table. If the table were on the same side of me as you are it would be no use to me, because the importance of having anchors on both sides of me is that it enables me to *turn* from one to the other. This means that the audience sees much more of my face, and it also enables me to make points . . . you know that rather cross little line I have to you? Well, just before, I shall have taken a drink and put my glass down on the table, so that I can *turn* to you, suddenly, and make a point of my moment of crossness.'

Anticipation

The example Dame Edith gave me of her use of anchors leads to the truism: 'What you are doing now must be right for what you are doing now, and right for what you are going to do next.'

I have forgotten which bit of the play she meant now, but her lines were something like: 'Yes, he was a splendid man, your father. A pity you don't live up to him.' Putting the glass down during the first sentence was good, for pictures of my father were in her mind and the audience could see them; and it was also good because it was right for what she did next, which was to turn to me suddenly for the second sentence, 'that rather cross little line'.

Talking Off

I learned this from a wonderful American actress called Evelyn Varden, who was in Lesley Storm's play *Roar Like a*

Dove. Unhappily she became very ill during the course of the three-year run at the Phoenix Theatre, and died shortly after her return home.

Here is an example of 'talking off': you are looking round a room and remarking on various ornaments and pieces of furniture. Once you have seen an object you can turn away from it *while talking about it*, so that your eye can alight more readily on the next object to which you are going to refer.

Evelyn's part was Muriel, an American matriarch, visiting her daughter who was married to a Scottish Earl. On her first entrance she looked around the library, inspecting it. Her speech went:

'The lamps are new . . . and those drapes . . . (*she wanders up to the yellow curtains, touches them*) Very nice . . . but in America we got over that yellow craze years ago . . . (*She glances at a small table*) Gracious – where's the snuff box that belonged to Prince Charlie?'

Now. Having looked at the lamps, she turned 'off' them and looked towards the curtains while saying, 'The lamps are new', so that she could say almost immediately, 'and those drapes'. She used the line 'but in America we got over that yellow craze years ago' to look towards the small table.

This device is very useful, for it is extremely natural, and it helps you to get a move on.

Aftersurge

'Do you play golf?' Edith Evans asked me one day, and went on, without waiting for a reply, 'because if you did you would know what I mean by the follow-through. You hit the ball, d'you see, and then afterwards you lift the club high above your head like that, and hold it there. That's the follow-through. It's the same in a play, d'you see: you say a line, but the thought behind the line does not stop the moment you've said it: there's a follow-through.'

A nice Golden Rule from this is 'Go on thinking about what you were thinking about until the next thought occurs to you.'

The aftersurge is a development of the follow-through. I learned the word from Hugh Miller. 'The aftersurge of emotion' was how he described it, and he explained it like this: 'When one of those enormous anti-aircraft guns, or those the Germans used to shoot at us from across the Channel, has been fired, it immediately recoils and then slowly resumes its firing position. Even a rifle does this. When you've fired, it jerks back at you for a moment. It can be quite a nasty surprise the first time you experience it. Well, when in a play you have powerful emotions to express, the emotions do not stop at the ends of the lines. There is an aftersurge. This aftersurge is best expressed in a move. Aftersurges can provide some of the most effective moves in a play.'

Then, without any warning, he turned on one of the students and said, really angrily: 'Don't you ever behave like that again!' – and he turned slowly away, in deep anger, walking a step or two, and then turned back and said, even more viciously: 'I've had just about as much from you as I can stand!' – and again he moved away, this time in another direction, occasionally looking at some of the rest of us, and we were all scared in case we were going to be the next recipient of this apparently unwarranted anger; a pause ensued, but his anger with the same student was inexorable, for he turned back again and shouted: 'You have no right to upset the class in this way!' The poor student was distraught, wondering what on earth he had done to incur such displeasure, but still Hugh Miller, after another move away, turned back (by now he had travelled more or less round the room): 'You don't *listen* to what I say, you criticise it, you argue with it; your stupid face gives you away!' By now the student had gone quite white, and Hugh Miller, like a stalking lion, went to the far end of the classroom. Then he pointed to the door and yelled: 'Now get out! Get out! Get out!' And the student got up and left the room.

Hugh Miller rescued him. 'Come back!' he said, all kindness and niceness, 'Sit down!' Then he turned to the rest of us. 'That's the aftersurge. It allows you to go anywhere, and it has the huge advantage of making moves away from people easier to perform; it helps you to break up your speeches: you noticed how I was able to walk away and then turn back, to walk away again and then turn back.

'Of course,' he said, beaming at his poor victim, 'the emotion doesn't have to be anger. But it's the easiest with which to demonstrate.'

Footwork

Anchors, Anticipation and the Aftersurge (the three 'A's', I used to call them at RADA) are to my mind the most helpful of all technical devices, the most useful to know about.

They all rely for their effectiveness on really controlled footwork. 'Watch my feet,' said Hugh Miller, as he demonstrated the aftersurge again – we had been so mesmerised the first time that we hadn't really noticed what he was doing – 'and you'll see how smooth, how slack, how relaxed they are, and how walking about on a stage does not always mean walking forwards: you can walk sideways, like a crab, or you can walk on an arc round a person, or even walk backwards.'

Laurence Olivier said, when he was talking to me about technique in acting, that his two favourite commands to himself were: 'Relax your feet!' and 'Always have more breath than you need!'

Years later, I was in a production for television of Royce Ryton's play *Crown Matrimonial*, and Anna Cropper, who played the Princess Royal, was rehearsing a scene where she was walking along a corridor talking to a Lady-in-Waiting. Anna was walking somewhat faster than the actress playing the Lady-in-Waiting, so in order to keep talking to her she suddenly turned and started walking backwards. Having stopped talking, she turned forwards again and walked into a room.

I was standing with the director, Alan Bridges, and he whispered to me: 'There's an actress for you! She knows how to walk backwards.'

New Move On A New Thought

A new thought can be a good springboard for a move, especially if the two things coincide, almost jerkily.

It is good to go through your part to find which of the things you say can be things which just occur to you. Comb through your part for new thoughts, and moves may well spring out of them, for new thoughts come with energy, and it is that energy which converts itself into a move.

Follow Your Thought

Put a look in the direction in which you are going before you go, and the move will look and feel more natural.

For example, you are sitting talking to someone. Over there, on the other side of you, is a table with drinks on it. Contrive while talking to look round at the drinks. Some time afterwards, go and get one.

Or, for example, you are in a bad mood, and you turn away from the person who is hurting you. Wherever you look when you turn away can establish the direction you take for your next move.

Or, look down before you sit; look up before you stand.

A bit bald, but it's not bad, and it works.

Practical Moves

Many moves can be made for emotional reasons, but it is easy for them to become clichés: how tired one becomes of the perpetual rise in anger, or sit in despair! 'I think that would be a good moment for you to rise and walk round the back of the sofa,' I can hear a director say, or, 'I think that would be a good moment for you to sit.'

One way to avoid such clichés is to give the move, if possible, a practical purpose as well: you rise not only because you are agitated but to look for an ashtray as well; you sit not only because you are feeling more relaxed but to tie up a shoe-lace as well. Etc. etc.

Suit The Action To The Word

There was an electrifying sequence in Tom Stoppard's *Night and Day* at the Phoenix Theatre. Diana Rigg, as Ruth Carson, had just been told of the death of Jake Milne (played by Peter Machin), a young reporter she had just got to know and to whom she was attracted. When his death was announced she was standing with her back to the audience at a table with drinks on it. She put her glass down and clinked another one with it. A little later she walked, apparently calmly, across the stage and suddenly banged a pillar with her fist, and hugged it for a while. Her face gave nothing away, for her husband was there.

I can imagine – I do not know, for I haven't asked her – that those brilliantly chosen actions were an immense help, night after night, to the re-creation of the feelings induced by the news of the death of the boy.

It's a bit like praying, really. Why is it easier to pray if you kneel down, close your eyes and put your hands together? I don't know, but it is. The action reminds you of praying.

Thoughts inspire actions. Actions, rightly chosen, inspire thoughts. Suit the action to the thought.

Do Things At Different Speeds

This, again, is from Laurence Olivier, who pointed out the value of walking slowly if you are talking quickly, and walking quickly if you are talking slowly. 'Much better,' he said, 'than the cliché of rushing about and talking quickly, or strolling and talking slowly.'

Try it!

Use The Visual

This is one of my favourites. It means refer, either by look or by gesture, to things which are outside the set in which you are acting. 'He's upstairs,' can be accompanied by a look or a gesture (however small) to the room upstairs. It makes 'upstairs' more vivid, and therefore more believable. 'No, he's not here, he's in Kent somewhere,' can be accompanied by an albeit vague gesture in the direction of Kent – at least it places your room geographically, and even that helps believability.

Penelope Keith, as Lady Driver in *Donkeys' Years*, used the visual for a wonderfully comic moment. We were standing in an Oxbridge courtyard, and she was telling me that her husband Harry was 'away this weekend'.

'Oh, Harry's away, is he?' I said.

'He's in Montreal,' she said, pointing vividly in the direction in which she assumed Montreal to be. The audience caught the ludicrousness of it, and hooted.

Using the visual can apply not only to looks and gestures but to moves as well. I had a line in a television play which referred to my garden outside and how proud I was of it. The director wanted me to go on sitting where I was, chatting to a visitor.

'Can't I get up and look out of the window?' I said.

'No,' he said.

'Why not?' I said.

'Because actors aren't good at looking out of windows,' he said.

What an odd thing to say, I thought. But then I thought, no, I know what he means: some actors forget that when they look out of windows they can see specific things in specific places; instead they give a generalised look in the direction of the generalised world outside.

'Why do you want to look out of the window?' he asked.

'Because it will make the garden more vivid. The audience can't see it, but if I look at it they'll believe it's there.'

'Well, you won't get a close-up,' he said, 'because I can't get a camera outside the window.'

'I don't mind,' I said.

'Show me!' he said.

I showed him.

'All right,' he said, 'I see your point . . . and . . . yes . . . that's good . . . because it means you're nearer the door, so you'll be able to lead the way into the dining-room. Yes, that's good. And I'll give you a close-up in the dining-room!'

Turn Your Back

'If you've got a long part,' said Clive Brook, when I was acting with him in a revival of *A Woman of No Importance* at the Savoy Theatre in 1953, 'spend some of the time on the stage with your back to the audience. It stops them getting bored with your face.'

Homework

Planny-Anny

Having plotted the play you will want to do another long session of homework: there are so many things to be chewed over away from rehearsal, in the relaxation and privacy of home. This is what I call my Planny-Anny stage. A silly phrase, but it's stuck with me now. Actors, unlike painters, writers and composers, have to do much of their creating in the company of colleagues, and however relaxed you try to be at early rehearsals, there is always a certain tension, and it is good to reconsider the ideas you've had and the decisions you've made in more tranquil surroundings.

Often, during these homework sessions, new and delicious ideas will occur; and you can use them, too, for more precise work on those bits which seemed awkward at rehearsal. Do you need, for example, to work out what to do with your hands? Is putting them in your pocket for the entire scene good enough? Some actors don't need to work on their hands, others do. Every actor finds some things difficult; you may be ashamed to mention your particular difficulties to your colleagues, so home is the ideal place to solve the problems they induce.

Your imagination is freer to roam, and you may well think of using props rather more than you had anticipated. 'Yes,' you might think, 'I've got to go from my office to hers – why don't I take something with me, even if it's only a file, and plonk it on her table? That'll help that move.'

The first rehearsals, and the Planny-Anny sessions which follow, are for working out what you are going to do. That, for me, is the part of acting which is the most fun.

After that it all gets a bit more serious!

Further Rehearsals

Attitudes

At this stage you will be deeply engrossed in yourself and your performance; you will be trying new ideas at rehearsals, and testing the results of your recent homework.

To counteract all this self-absorption you must now start considering what your attitudes are to the other people, not as *actors* (I have dealt with that already) but as *characters* in the play. How do they affect you? Do you like them, are you in love with them? Do they make you shy, do they bring you out of your shell? Are you at ease in their company, are you suspicious of them? Do you hate them? If you do, how much are you prepared to reveal that hatred, how much do you keep it a secret?

If you are like me, you will, in everyday life, feel very differently in the company of different people. So it should be in your acting too. And yet it rarely is, is it? I mean, when you look at plays you get some idea of the characters, but you rarely sense that a character changes when his companions are different.

Especially should you know how much, and in what way, your attitude to each character *develops* as the play progresses.

Affections – mother-and-child, friends, lovers – are very differently expressed in everyday life, and should be in plays, too. C. S. Lewis is marvellously clear about affections in his book *The Four Loves*.

Cover-Ups

I'm shy, but I'm damned if I'm going to show it.
I'm ill, but I'm damned if I'm going to show it.
I'm angry, but I'm damned if I'm going to show it.
I'm in love, but I'm damned if I'm going to show it.
I'm happy, but I'm damned if I'm going to show it.

I'm scared, but I'm damned if I'm going to show it.
I'm on the run from the police, but I'm damned if I'm going
to show it.
I'm a spy, but I'm damned if I'm going to show it.

Acting the cover-up can often be more interesting and
revealing than merely demonstrating the underlying emotion
or situation. It is amazing how far you can go with covering-
up, especially if the story-line is strong enough for the
audience to know what's going on.

The Story

Never stop telling yourself the story of the play, for this will
illumine the story of your character within it: it will tell you
what *happens* to him, and how much he is altered by the
circumstances.

Each scene will have a story. An excellent television director, David Reid, used to start the early rehearsals of every
scene by telling the actors the story-so-far, like TV announcers
do for the later episodes of a classic serial. And he used to say:
'So. That's the situation at the beginning of the scene. At the
end of it the difference will be . . .'

The scene *travels*, therefore. It has, or should have, a starting
point and a destination.

When I was rehearsing the last scene of *Professional Foul*,
the scene in which John Shrapnel (Professor McKendrick)
and I (Professor Anderson) were flying back from Prague to
London, Tom Stoppard was very dissatisfied with the way I
was doing it.

'You're too smug,' he said, 'too light. It's a more serious
scene. You should be more concerned about Chetwyn, that
he's been held by the customs officer at the airport, and isn't
allowed to travel home with you.'

'More serious?' I said.

'Yes,' he said.

So I did the scene more seriously.

'Well?' I said.

'It's still not right,' he said.

'Why?' I said.

'It's too serious,' he said.

'But you said you . . .'

'Yes, I know,' he said, 'but I can't write a play which starts a comedy and ends as a tragedy.'

'So you want me less serious,' I said, lost.

'No, not at the beginning of the scene.'

'Ah,' I said, inspired, 'you mean I should travel further?'

'Yes,' he said.

So I started seriously, concerned, found a moment for a change of mood, and ended flippantly.

'That's it,' he said, 'travel further. Good.'

Telling yourself, or having the director tell you, the story-so-far is especially valuable for filming. Shooting out of sequence always bothers me, but if the story is in everyone's mind mistakes are less frequently made. And I don't mean just physical mistakes, concerning the state of clothes or the tidiness of hair or the dirtiness of hands, but emotional ones too.

The Before And After Of Each Scene

Clifford Evans, in *The Power Game*, always wanted to know what had happened immediately before a scene started. We used to invent little scenes (one of the many uses of improvisation, this) to lead up to the scene we were about to rehearse. Oh, how doing this helped us decide what to do!

And afterwards he would say: 'Now, if this scene had gone on, what would have happened?' and just asking this made the end-line seem not like an end-line at all, and prevented that curious foreknowledge an audience has that a scene has finished.

The Before And After Of Each Speech

An audience can often tell not only when the end of a scene has arrived, but when the end of a speech has, too; you have signalled it somehow, and they know you have got nothing more to say and it's the other person's turn. Of course, in everyday life we often do signal to our family, friends and acquaintances that we have finished, but a lot of the time *we would have gone on talking if someone hadn't interrupted us.*

In your play, what would you have said if the other character hadn't interrupted you?

Similarly, what launches you into interrupting the other character?

Words In Brackets

I was working with Patience Collier on some of the parts she played for the Royal Shakespeare Company, and she found the addition of words in brackets to a speech could clarify its meaning and colour its intentions. (These words in brackets are not to be spoken, of course, they are merely aids to spontaneity.)

Here's a speech, not by Shakespeare but by me, just to illustrate the sort of work we did and the sort of phrases we invented. Here it is without words in brackets.

She to him: 'You said that to me on my birthday last year. We were in Brighton, and we'd been for a walk through the Lanes. It was just getting dark and we'd had tea in a little café. I thought I would never forgive you, but I did, and I do now. But please don't say it again. I forgive you now, but I won't again.'

There are two main ingredients of this speech: a memory and a request. A simple memory and a simple request may be all that is required, but possible, illuminating, words in brackets could be:

'(*Now I come to think of it*:) You said that to me on my birthday last year. (*Do you remember?*) We were in Brighton, and we'd been for a walk through the Lanes. (*Oh yes, I've just remembered*:) It was just getting dark and we'd had tea in a little café. (*Anyway, getting back to what I was saying*:) I thought I would never forgive you, but I did, and (*do you know?*) I do now. (*But mark my words*:) But please don't say it again. (*As I said*:) I forgive you now, but I won't again.'

Spontaneity

This and the next few pieces are attempts to help you with the most difficult but essential task for an actor: the achievement of spontaneity. And spontaneity has to be *achieved*, it has to be worked at, for the trouble with being in a play is that you know it so well. You know the words, you know the business, you know the story, you know the moves. And you know everybody else's words and moves too. And yet you have to give the illusion that you are doing it and thinking it *for the first time*.

I said earlier in this book that we actors are a critical lot: but we are always disarmed when we see a performance of supreme spontaneity. 'You are so truthful, it's hard to believe you've ever done it before' is a compliment we would all like to receive.

A starting point can be to comb through your part for the bits which are easy to say and the bits which are difficult.

Easy bits might be:

> Things your character often says, from habit.
> Things which are not new to him (you will have to decide what those are).
> Small talk.
> Things which require no switch of attention.
> Things which require no change of mood.

Difficult bits might be:

> Things your character has never thought of before.
> Approaches to other characters involving hesitancy.
> Ideas your character is trying to clarify.

You will find lots of examples in every worthwhile part, and it is worthwhile making the effort to discover them.

Preambles

The performances which sound least spontaneous are those in which every sentence sounds like a statement of intent. Nothing gets thrown away, nothing is rushed over, nothing is slack; and the performance therefore seems wooden and heavy. One way of preventing this is to underline in your script the really important statements you make, or questions you ask, and to use what you can of the preceding dialogue as a preamble.

In the following speech every sentence could be given equal weight, in which case the final question, the pivot of the speech and the reason for its existence, would go for nothing.

'It's cold today. That's why I'm so well wrapped up. But it's warm in here. Do you mind if I take my coat off? It's always so snug here. It feels comfortable. Always. How lucky you are to live here. How's Harry?'

Treat the earlier part as a preamble, distracted, knowing that eventually you have got to ask how Harry is, and it's a different kettle of fish.

Forget

Flora Robson, in *Black Chiffon* at the Westminster Theatre and *The House by the Lake* at the Duke of York's Theatre, was the first actress I ever saw who electrified the audience by appearing not to know what she was going to say next. She was apparently so distraught that her mind went blank; only gradually did she recover.

It's a risky business, drying deliberately; but it's worth it occasionally.

Feel For Words

Certainly I think it's good to hunt around in your mind for the right word, from time to time. We often have to search for words in everyday life, so why not do the same in plays?

Ers and ums can be added too, providing they are properly motivated and not merely a mannerism. And I like it when an actor back-tracks in a speech to add a word he has omitted. Say the written sentence is: 'I feel very distressed about what you've just told me.' A good 'actor's addition' could be: 'I feel dist – very distressed about what you've just told me.' 'Very' becomes a more important word thereby. All this, of course, applies to modern, realistic plays. It would be a bit dangerous in Shakespeare!

New Move On A New Thought

This has already been a title in this book, but I feel I must use it again here, for it is a splendid aid to spontaneity. A new thought, as I said, comes with energy, and that energy can be channelled into a move. The move can be big or small; it can be just a sudden look.

As a simple example, imagine a man talking to two others who are standing on either side of him. He starts a sentence by looking at one of them, and during the sentence his gaze drifts off into the space between them. At the beginning of the next sentence he suddenly looks at the other hearer, and drifts off, mid-sentence, again. At the beginning of the third sentence he looks at his first hearer again. And so on. It is too mechanical, of course, to go from one to the other alternately like that – one hearer is usually more important than the other. But it will suffice for this imaginary exercise.

To convert it into a real one, try this speech of Casca's in *Julius Caesar*. It was very well done by the actor in the BBC Television Shakespeare series: Sam Dastor was talking to Richard Pasco as Brutus and David Collings as Cassius. Brutus says:

'Tell us the manner of it, gentle Casca.'

Casca replies:

'I can as well be hang'd as tell the manner of it: it was mere foolery; I did not mark it. I saw Mark Antony offer him a crown—yet 'twas not a crown neither, 'twas one of those coronets—and, as I told you, he put it by once; but for all that, to my thinking, he would fain have had it. Then he offered it to him again; then he put it by again; but to my thinking he was very loath to lay his fingers off it. And then he offered it the third time; he put it the third time by; and still as he refus'd it, the rabblement hooted, and clapp'd their chopt hands, and threw up their sweaty night-caps, and uttered such a deal of stinking breath because Caesar refus'd the crown, that it had almost choked Caesar; for he swooned and fell down at it. And for mine own part I durst not laugh, for fear of opening my lips and receiving the bad air.'

Interrupted Actions

You are about to drink but you don't drink because something has occurred to you. You are about to smoke but you don't smoke because you've suddenly thought of something you want to say. You are about to sit but you don't sit because you've seen something out of place on the mantelpiece.

Interrupted actions: a wonderful aid to spontaneity. I learned about them from watching Humphrey Bogart. Over and over again, in his films, the glass of whisky would be raised to his lips, but he didn't drink, not just yet, not until he'd made one more laconic remark. Then he'd drink.

Look, Move, Speak

Actions happen in the order: look, move, speak; or, more deeply: idea, confirmation of idea, utterance of idea.

If you feel unspontaneous in a part, the application of this formula may provide the remedy.

A nice homework exercise for this is to pretend that you are showing a prospective buyer round your home, pointing out its features, good and bad, and its contents (you're selling the lot, lock, stock and barrel!). Be quite conscious of looking at a thing, pointing and/or moving to it, and talking about it, in that order.

Then, as a further exercise, show some people round an imaginary place: you could be talking about a beautiful view from the top of a hill, say, or showing them round a garden. See the objects, indicate them with a move, and speak about them.

'Look, move, speak,' I used to say at RADA, 'and you can't go wrong.'

Well, you can. But every little helps.

Get Your First Scene Set

As soon as you can, get your first scene set. It's often quite a task, this, because your first scene is rarely the easiest (in fact I often find it the hardest of the lot), but your mood at later rehearsals, and during the recording, if it's television, or the performance, if it's the theatre, will be determined by how well you think you have done it. It's worth making quite sure it's as secure as iron.

Later scenes you can leave a little more to chance. But do not risk it with the first one.

Act Sideways

Have you ever thought that the essential difference between acting in the theatre and acting in front of cameras is that in the theatre you need to *widen* your performance so the whole audience can see you, whereas for the cameras you need to narrow it down?

In the theatre, the actor is the apex of a triangle and the audience is the base-line:

ACTOR

AUDIENCE

In television and films, the actor is the base-line, and the audience is the apex:

ACTOR

AUDIENCE

Acting sideways, then, is for the theatre. It is necessary for you to open out your performance, to use 'anchors', to 'talk off' people, and to use the fourth wall properly, keeping your eyes up as you turn from one side to the other.

The Fourth Wall

If the set-designer had designed the fourth wall, what would he have put there? What is there to look at? You will have to agree with the other actors about this, but it's worth discussing.

Technically the fourth wall is there to receive the thoughts for which you do not need to look directly at the other players. And technically the easiest level for your eyes is the darkest part of the auditorium, just below the Dress Circle; in most theatres that will be your own eye-level.

PS 1991. It's a bit harder to keep your eyes up in those steeply raked modern auditoria, for fear of looking someone in the audience straight in the eye. It is worth working out, when the theatre is empty, where your eyes can safely land, like the aisles or an exit door or something.

Play The Opposite

A: How are you today?

B: Oh, marvellous, thank you. Yes, I feel really good today.

A (*turning to C*): And how are you?

C: Oh, dreadful. I've got a terrible headache. I couldn't sleep last night. No, I feel dreadful.

B *could* be solemn-faced, quite serious. Because he is *saying* how he feels, he has no need to demonstrate it.

Likewise C could smile, or even laugh. Because he's saying how he feels, he has no need to demonstrate it.

Play the opposite! Notice how often you do this in everyday life . . .

A: What do you think of it so far?

B (*solemnly, frowning*): Wonderful!

A: And you?

C (*laughing*): Terrible!

PS 1991.   Similarly, I think it is not a good idea to colour already colourful words.

For example, if a mother says of her teenage daughter, 'I'm worried about her obsession with boys,' it's a mistake to say, 'I'm worried about her – oh, her OBSESSION with boys.' The meaning is diminished thereby. Obsession is such a rich word it doesn't need working on. And if she continues by admitting she has been a neglectful mother because of other ambitions and says, 'I'd do it all again: harden my heart, if necessary, all over again,' it's a mistake to colour the words 'harden my heart' with hardness. It diminishes the meaning. Colour them with a tinge of regret, maybe, or a tinge of amusement. But not with the colour which the words themselves indicate.

Be Monotonous

'For God's sake be monotonous!' said Alan Bridges, when he was rehearsing Greer Garson and me in a scene from *Crown Matrimonial* (we were doing the television version). 'You actors, you're all the same: you're all so good at *explaining* the text . . . you've got the right inflections, the right emphases, you know exactly what you mean, and you're determined to let us know. Come on, you two,' – I looked across at Greer to see how she was taking all this, and was relieved to see that she was still smiling – 'come on, you two, for God's sake Stop Acting! Mumble! Mutter! Anything . . . but don't explain it all!'

So we did. And it was wonderful.

I never do a play without remembering his golden advice. Mind you: care, care, care! It's a corrective to be used against being over-emphatic. If your speech is already monotonous, ignore this!

Telephone Conversations

If it's a two-way conversation (as it often is in television plays or films) it is easy enough. The hard thing is when you are on your own.

It certainly is worthwhile (of course it is) to invent and write down what the other person says; and I think the main trick about doing telephone conversations is to give the other person time to say what he has to say, but only just. If you don't give him enough time, well, the conversation will have no truth in it and the audience will dismiss you; if you give him too much time, you will be boring and the audience will get restless.

It's a curious thing, being just one end of a telephone conversation: you have to bring the other person to life for the audience; you are doing the acting for two, as it were, for the price of one. So let the other person interrupt you, if you can; and interrupt him; and talk at the same time. This makes him very vivid.

If you interrupt him, you have to stop him talking, so go a little louder. If he interrupts you, let him do so on a consonant. It is much easier to stop at a consonant than it is on a vowel. If your sentence is:

'I'm not sure I could manage that,' and he interrupts you, it is easier to say

'I'm not sure I could m . . .' than

'I'm not sure I could ma . . .'

I don't know why, but I think it's because 'I'm not sure I

could ma . . .' will result in a glottal stop, and will not sound (or feel) nearly as convincing.

Try laughing, if it is apt, at something the unseen person says. It's quite hard to do, this, and needs practice. I have no tips at all for laughing, but it is, of course, something you must be able to do; but oh, when you bring it off, how it convinces the audience there is somebody there at the other end of the line!

Dialling is always a problem because it takes so long. Again, you cannot cheat – if it's a London number, and you're in London, you must dial at least seven digits, and if it's a long distance call you must dial even more, and you must start with o! What you *can* do, though, to speed up the whole dreary business, is choose the lower numbers for as many of the digits as possible. So a Birmingham number could be, 021-422-1311.

And, usually, hold the mouthpiece low enough for the audience to see your mouth. It looks better.

PS 1991.   Of course now you can get a number by pressing digits. But you have to wait longer afterwards to hear the ringing tone. Or not, with the newest technology.

I have yet to meet anyone in stage management who knows how to do a British telephone ring properly. It should go: 'Brrr Brrr 1 2 3 Brrr Brrr 1 2 3 Brrr Brrr.' But it never does. The correct pause seems too long and panic sets in. So it's usually 'Brrr Brrr beat Brrr Brrr beat Brrr Brrr.' Or even 'Brrr Brrrrrr, Brrr Brrrrrr.' Hopeless.

Do Not Cheat

There are many other activities which, like listening on the telephone, should not be cheated.

Writing, for example. Those hurried squiggles we have all seen, usually in period plays, really will not do. A period character sits at a period desk with period parchment and a period quill pen, and he says aloud what he is writing and says it so quickly in an effort not to be boring that you *know* he can't possibly be writing the actual words he is speaking. And sometimes he writes without even bothering to form letters and you *know* that what's on the parchment is:

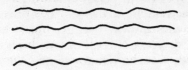

Reading must not be cheated either. If you've got to read a letter silently, well, you've got to read it. Quickly; but you've got to do it. If you have to look at a list of figures and come to a conclusion about, say, a customer's account, you have got to look at it and have time for the assessment. I remember the producer of *Telford's Change*, Mark Shivas, saying to me at a rehearsal: 'I don't believe you could have read all those figures in Maddox's account. I mean, in the story you've never seen them before, have you? They are news to you.'

'But Mark,' I said, 'it'll take so long.'

'Never mind,' he said, 'you've got to do it!'

If you are going to gossip about somebody who is leaving the room, you must wait until they have gone out and closed the door, or are out of earshot, before you start. 'Oh, I can't wait that long,' you may complain.

'But you must,' the director should say.

Exits And Entrances

When you exit you are going somewhere else.

When you enter you have come from somewhere else.

Where?

Someone once told me, I think it was Nigel Patrick, that it can be a good idea sometimes to be in the middle of doing something as you enter, like putting a handkerchief back in your pocket; it means no more than that you have blown your nose in the place from which you have come, but at least it means you did *something* there. If you're coming from upstairs, I suppose you could just be finishing putting on your jacket or cardigan or whatever. It makes 'upstairs' a bit more vivid.

But it is to be used sparingly, this.

Drinking

A lot of drinking goes on in plays. If it's a nice middle-class room, there's bound to be a drinks table somewhere. The director will want one anyway because it will help him with the moves. But have you noticed how, with all that drinking going on, the actors seem to remain stone-cold sober? Actors are either sober or drunk (in 'Drunk scenes'). There are lots of states in between which are worth exploring.

Incidentally, if you breathe in before you drink you cannot choke.

Eating

Quite a lot of eating goes on in plays, too. Especially in television plays. And commercials. How do the actors do it, I often wonder, when they have to do retake after retake of eating a chocolate bar? In plays, well, you have got to eat; but the trick is to eat the easiest foods – the mashed potato, for example, rather than the meat, which can be so very, very chewy and embarrassing – and to have smaller quantities on your fork or in your spoon than you would in everyday life. For some unfathomable reason it takes longer to eat in plays than it does in everyday life, and it is harder to swallow. 'Will it never go down?' one so often thinks to oneself.

Smoking

A lot of smoking goes on, too, though it is nice to note that writers and directors are now far more loath to insist that you smoke if you are a non-smoker, because they know that you can't smoke in plays unless you smoke in everyday life: it will look all wrong and it will make you dizzy. Of course, if you are in *Who's Afraid of Virginia Woolf?* you will just have to smoke, and there are herbal cigarettes on the market now which make it more bearable for a non-smoker.

An odd thing about smoking in plays is that it's harder to *taste* the smoke. So to confirm that your cigarette is alight, puff out the first intake of smoke straight away. You (and the audience) can then *see* that it is alight, and you (and the audience) can relax.

James Mason said to me, when we were doing a scene in a film called *Tiara Tahiti*, 'Never smoke in films.' This was after he had witnessed my appalling discomfort in the scene. For each take of each angle, I had to light up again; my mouth was so dry at the end of the day I could hardly speak and wanted to vomit. Continuity problems are acute, too. 'Sorry, sorry, sorry,' I would have to say, stopping a take for an agonising moment: 'my cigarette's not the right length. I'd smoked about half of it by now, hadn't I?' So a cigarette would be broken in two, and the frayed end would flare up in flames as I lit it.

James Mason was right. 'I never do,' he said.

Switching Things On And Off

Usually lights, lamps, radio sets and other gadgets are operated by someone else. The lighting people will be doing the lights, the sound people will be doing the radio sets.

Well, if they switch things on or off *before* you have actually got there, there's nothing you can do except look a Charlie. You'll look a Charlie, too, if there is a long delay after your hand has gone to the switch. But here you can save yourself by not giving all your attention to the switch. You can go up to the switch and, having touched it, look away from it (talking or listening the while, or just looking at something else); that half-mind left on the switch accounts for the delay.

Bad Dialogue

A few tips now about how to deal with poor dialogue. It is not only in films or television where an actor has to face this problem, but these are the two media where it is most prevalent.

Most importantly, I think, I would advise that if you can bring yourself to say the lines, do, rather than try to alter them. Time and again I have seen a scene get worse instead of better as actors nit-pick over the words. And it's terribly time-consuming, too. My least favourite rehearsals are those which develop into script conferences between the director and the actors.

Of course, sometimes you have got to change the lines, particularly in a television series where a new author has been brought in and gets facts wrong about the story and about the characters and their idiosyncracies.

But a lot of dialogue is much more speakable than many actors allow. A bad line can be made to sound almost like a good one, provided an actor has a very clear attitude towards it: an attitude which prevents it from being a mere statement of fact. How often a line can be saved by the attitude:

(This is not really how I want to put this, but . . .)

We're back to Words In Brackets, and other helpful ones are:

(I know it's a cliché but . . .)

(You'll probably think this is funny but . . .)

(I'm talking nonsense, I know, but . . .)

(Look, I'm trying not to be intense; let me put it to you lightly and quickly:)

Actors' Additions

True and original attitudes towards the words you speak and the people you are addressing are fundamental to dealing with poor dialogue, but even after days of struggling you may feel inadequate and defeated. What to do? Well, a number of things you might be able to add could just yield the silk purse you are looking for.

Drunkenness, for example. Could you be drunk in this scene you are faced with? Among other things, drunkenness allows you to switch more violently from one emotion to another, releases your anger and your tears, excuses you from making coherent sense, and it is interesting in itself! I was once driven to using drunkenness to get away with appalling dialogue (In an episode of a televison series.) and it seemed to work: the rubbish I had to say was apparently caused by drink. Drink talks, as they say.

Tiredness is another useful addition (rarely used). Tiredness, or illness even, can mean that only half your mind is on what you are saying and hearing: there will be an abstracted air about you; and, like drunkenness, tiredness is interesting in itself.

Jollity, too, can cover many a cliché, and has one advantage over drunkenness and tiredness: it will make you act quickly. Speed can be a life-saver in awkward passages.

Laughter can sometimes help. I often think we laugh more in everyday life than we do in plays; why not even it up a bit?

Temperature is a nice addition, too. How hot are you? How cold? When the door opens is there a draught? Being cold can yield more for you than the clichéd rubbing of hands and warming them at the fire, and being hot more than the clichéd mopping of the brow and neck with a handkerchief.

You don't need to wait for poor dialogue, of course, to employ some of these additions. They are good for good stuff as well.

Secondary Tasks

'I'm going to make it hard for you,' said Alan Bridges, when we were rehearsing *Crown Matrimonial*. 'You actors, you always have it so easy in plays. I'm going to make it hard. Now, let's see. You're talking to Queen Mary and the Princess Royal, and there's a fire in the grate. You know that bit where you're just about to say you love Mrs Simpson, well, what if a piece of coal fell out of the fire and rolled dangerously near to the carpet?'

'Oh no, Alan, not *then*! It's my best bit.'

'Yes, why not? Could happen. I mean, if a piece of coal rolls away from a fire someone's got to get the tongs and put it back. Haven't they? Otherwise the carpet will catch fire.'

'Oh, Alan . . .'

'Try it!'

I did, and, at the second attempt, we all agreed it was really rather good. It didn't interrupt the scene, it took the expectedness out of the moment, and converted it into one of surprise.

I like secondary tasks. Well chosen, they can give surprising new colours to a scene:

Two people are talking, but reading at the same time.

Two people are talking, but washing up at the same time, or laying the table, or dressing, or undressing, or cooking, or eating, or looking at a view, or walking along, or being overheard, or having a rest, or doing exercises, or dancing, or dusting, or playing games, or working at something.

Overlaps

Alan Bridges also likes overlaps. 'If you can answer before Queen Mary finishes her speech, do; talk while she's still talking.'

'Do you mind, Greer?' I said, 'because I don't want it to throw you.'

'No, of course not,' she said, 'I think it's good.'

'There you are, you see,' said Alan, triumphant, 'you've both just done it. Greer answered, "No, of course not" to your question, "Do you mind, Greer?" The fact that you went on speaking did not stop Greer from interrupting you, nor did it stop you from finishing what you wanted to say. You've just done it. So do it in the play.'

Used sparingly, I like overlaps too.

PS 1991. I like them even more since I saw that great production of Eugene O'Neill's *Long Day's Journey into Night* by Jonathan Miller in 1986 which, because of extreme use of overlaps, shortened the play by a reputed 40 minutes.

Criticism

Everyone has faults, and it is good to have them pointed out occasionally by the director or by friends. If the fault is one which applies to your acting in general, as opposed to just your performance in the play, do take special heed and work as hard as you can to eradicate it.

People may tell you that you fade out at the ends of sentences, that your speech is not clear enough, that you blink too much, that you fidget, that you smile too much, that you don't smile enough, that you don't listen properly, that you gesture too much, that you don't gesture enough, that you're content with too little, that you complicate things unnecessarily, that your hair-style doesn't suit you, that you've got a funny walk.

Listen, and work!

But don't listen to everybody. Rely on the director and close friends. If you listen to everybody you will get awfully confused, for you will hear so many different things. If you are very, very good everybody will say so and have similar reasons for thinking so. If you are very, very bad everybody will say so, behind your back, and have similar reasons for thinking so. But if you are somewhere in between very, very good and very, very bad, which is where most of us are most of the time, everybody will know that all is not perfect, but will have differing reasons for thinking so.

It's as well to remember, always, that you can't please everybody.

Bad Rehearsals

There will always be those days when, in spite of all the work you have put in, in spite of all the ideas you have thrown into the melting pot with the director and the company, nothing seems to come of it: self-consciousness takes over, concentration becomes impossible, your face freezes, your arms and legs are as heavy as lead, and you feel that your very talent is in danger of disappearing, as *you* would like to, through the rehearsal room floor. I have seen actors and actresses of great distinction weep from the sheer panic and embarrassment caused by such feelings. And you never really know what sets them off; it can be anything: you might be tired, off-colour, worried about something at home; or it may be that somebody new has come into the rehearsal room and is watching you before you feel ready to be watched. It can, as I said, be anything.

These days are dangerous, and hard to recover from. But they do have one advantage: they make you go home and WORK.

Further Homework

The Mirror

Should you use it?

It is good for correcting pointed-out faults, for the sight of them in the mirror will confirm that they exist.

Certainly I do not agree with those who say you should never use it. It provides a very useful check, particularly on bits you have found awkward. 'Oh, of course,' you say to your reflection, 'I'm standing in the wrong way for this bit: I should face you squarely, feet and all, shoulders and all, not just turn my head sideways to you and look at you over my shoulder.' Pictures of yourself looking wrong will help you to start looking right. And then you will start feeling right.

Fluffing

If, in rehearsal, you have fluffed a line several times, or if you fear you might fluff it, or if it's just hard to say, it's worth taking it out of context and practising it over and over again like a tongue-twister.

The most noticeable mistake an actor can make is a fluff. An audience might not know you have dried, they *might* not know you have giggled, but they will always know you have fluffed.

And while I'm on the subject of tongue-twisters, I think it's worth being able to do a few really well; you can always use them as warm-ups before a performance. All RADA students who were taught by the late Clifford Turner will remember what emphasis he put on 'quick diction exercises', and will be able to do his favourite:

> lah lay lee lay lah law loo law
> lah lay lee lay lah law loo law

and on and on, over and over, at breakneck speed. It gets the tongue moving, just as 'Peter Piper' gets the lips.

Reality Tests 1

With the constant pressure of rehearsals, when you have to go over and over each scene, thinking of so many details, making alterations, cuts and additions, coming to conclusions, it is very easy to lose your instinct. You had it when you first started, but now you've lost it, and cannot see the wood for the trees. You've got to get it back.

Doing 'reality tests' at home is one way. It's curious how well they work and, thankfully, they are quite amusing to do, too.

Go through the words of your part, aloud, but change the circumstances. For example, whatever the scene, do it this time with a duster in your hand, and clean the room. Place the other character or characters in chairs, so you know where they are, and do the scene while you are dusting.

It will tell you many things, this exercise: it will tell you when your concentration can be mostly on the dusting and you needn't look at the other characters; it will also tell you when you *have* to look at them and stop dusting. So, for the play, it will tell you when you must look at the other characters and when you needn't. It will freshen up the dialogue too.

You will think of many variations on this exercise: a good one is to be working in one room – washing up, or making a bed, or just sitting reading – and saying all your lines to someone who is in another one; you are talking through the walls, as it were, to someone you cannot see. If your instinct is really returning to you, you may find that at some moment you have to leave what you are doing and go into the other room to say something to them directly. But leave them as soon as you can, for your secondary task is very important, and you want to get back to it.

Reality Tests 2

The idea behind these reality tests is to keep some things the same but alter others in order to bring back your instinct.

This time, try changing the people you are talking to. Try saying the whole part as though to your oldest friend.

No, try it! You'll be surprised!

Reality Tests 3

This is John Hurt's idea, and it is very good. Instead of acting your part, tell the story of the scenes, including your lines and what you can remember of the other characters', to an imaginary person (or a real one, if you want) sitting in a chair. Your story will sound something like this:

'So he comes up to me and says, where were you last night at eight thirty, and I say to him, oh, well, I was having dinner out with some friends, and he looks very suspicious and says, would I mind telling him their names, and for a moment I want to refuse but I realise that if I do it will make me look guilty, and of course I'm not, so I tell him their names, and the name of the restaurant . . .' and so on.

This exercise will tell you where you have been overacting, and remind you of the true content of each scene.

Reality Tests 4

If a line or speech just won't come right, change the words. Put it in your own words. Improvise.

It would be very tedious to do this for your whole part, but for those sticky bits you may find, when you go back to the author's words, they feel a bit fresher.

Never Bring A Sick Mind To A Part

Richard Gatehouse, who was with me at Sheffield Rep. in the early fifties, said: 'If you're not feeling well, or just not in the mood, don't work. It could do more harm than good. Never bring a sick mind to a part.'

And often it's amazing what a good rest and an early night will do!

Final Rehearsals

Pace

This will be the word on everyone's lips now. The play will probably need to be speeded up.

Lionel Harris used to say, at one of the final run-throughs, 'Everybody, when we go through the play this time, I would like you to go too fast . . . I don't mean gabble, but just a little too fast for comfort.' And when the run-through was over he would invariably say: 'Good. That was about the right speed for the play.'

A play should always be acted as quickly as possible, though 'as possible' is very much the controller of that dictum. Some bits are bound to be slow; but cues can often be more sharply taken, changes of tone more surprisingly used, and the four varieties of speech more vividly brought into play.

The Four Varieties

Speed, pitch, volume and tone.

And the one most frequently under-used is 'speed'.

It is all too easy to get a uniform speed for a part – fast, leisurely, slow – and stick to it. And although in everyday life people are slow- or fast-speakers, nevertheless, within that generality, the speed at which we speak is changing all the time; and whenever this variety can be used in a play, it should be. Along with the other three, of course.

They do help to stop an audience being bored.

And they help an overall sense of pace, because coming-in-on-cue, which everyone knows is desirable, is quite all right if you don't take the other person's speed, pitch, volume or tone.

Don't Pause

'Don't pause!' said Edith Evans when she was giving a lecture to RADA students in the Vanbrugh Theatre, and she looked sternly about. 'Never pause!' And she paused, giving our disbelief ample time to register. 'Young actors nowadays are always pausing,' she said, 'and I don't like it. You see, if you pause you are saying to the audience: Ladies and Gentlemen, this pause is more interesting than the author's next line. Now, if you *can* say that and *mean* it, *then* you can pause.'

A change of tone is a good substitute for a pause. Suppose the dialogue to be:

A: Did you enjoy today's rehearsal?
B: Yes. No.

Between 'Yes' and 'No' there is, for whatever reason, a complete change of heart. It could be easy enough to have a really long think between the words. And in certain circumstances that may be what is required. But if the two words sound completely different, if, for example, 'Yes' is firm and loud and 'No' is doubting and quiet, you will be able to cut the pause to a minimum.

Just one more thought about pausing. Never forget that if you pause, either before or during a speech, everyone else is pausing with you. They cannot speak because the author has not given them anything to say. How often one has heard an actor plead with another:

'Look, boy, if you pause there, I'd come in, I'd say something . . . I mean, I've got egg on my face during that pause . . . do you need it?'

The answer has to be 'No'.

Give The Scene To The Other Actor

This is another of John Hurt's ideas, and it's very relaxing. Concentrate on the other people rather than on yourself. After all, this is what you do in everyday life; you might as well do it in plays.

'Chuck it to them,' he said, 'and say to yourself: it's their scene, not mine.'

'But if it really *is* your scene, grab it!'

Comedy

This is the subject I dreaded teaching at RADA. A joke is only really funny the first time, and after five people have tried it there's no laughter left. The classes in comedy were the glummest of the lot.

And it's such an idiosyncratic subject, too, so much to do with personality and flair, that it's very hard to talk about. Athene Seyler's book *The Craft of Comedy* is as good as you'll get.

I can only say, 'Watch comedians! Learn from those who appeal to you!' I learned a lot from acting with Penelope Keith in *Donkeys' Years*. She is a fine comedienne and a remarkably truthful actress. She never strains for comic effect. Truth comes first.

But there are one or two things all good comedians do which are perhaps worth listing here:

Speak clearly and brightly.

Don't fade out at the ends of sentences.

Keep the rhythm of the lines. Keep the flow of the feed-lines and the laugh-lines right through to the very last word. Remember that when you have a laugh-line you are not only inviting the audience to laugh but you are inviting them to laugh at a particular moment . . . that moment, usually the last word of your line, could do with an extra little punch.

Don't be slow.

Don't try to be funny but know what it is that's funny about the funny bits.

Be as relaxed as possible, and know the value of slack turns of the head during a laugh-line. I don't know why they work but they seem to, as do small involuntary movements like crossing your legs, rubbing your eyes, putting your hand to your forehead, wiping ash off your jacket, putting a glass down, taking a drink, taking a puff of a cigar – remember George Burns and Groucho Marx? – taking your glasses off, putting them on, anything except stroking the lobe of your ear: that's the only one which has become such a cliché it's unforgivable.

Sense the house: laughter is largely a matter of audience-temperature, hence the phrase 'warming them up'. Use as much energy as the part can stand.

'Timing' is a difficult thing to write about: it is so much a matter of sensing. What most people mean by 'timing' is using a beat-pause between the feed-line and the laugh-line, but of course it depends very much on the meaning of the lines; it can often be just as funny to come in on cue.

But let me give an example.

One of my favourite comedy sequences was near the beginning of *Donkeys' Years*, when Christopher Headingley (a politician) and David Buckle (a doctor) meet, after twenty years, at a reunion party at their old university. They don't know what to say to each other. Here is the dialogue, as written by Michael Frayn:

HEADINGLEY: Well. How *are* you, and so on?
BUCKLE: Well, all right, Christopher. Not too bad. In quite good working order. And you?
HEADINGLEY: Oh, fine. Fine, fine, fine, fine fine, fine.
BUCKLE: Oh, good.
HEADINGLEY: Yes, fine.
BUCKLE: Oh, good. Good, good, good, good, good, good.
HEADINGLEY: Fine
BUCKLE: Good.
HEADINGLEY: And you're . . . sawing people up?
BUCKLE: That's right! Whhht! Out with their waterworks!
HEADINGLEY: My word.
BUCKLE: And you're . . . Parliamentary Under-Secretary, is that what they call it, at the Ministry of, isn't it in fact Education?
HEADINGLEY: Whhht! Off with their heads.
BUCKLE: Goodness me.
HEADINGLEY: Tell the Vice-Chancellor where he gets off.
BUCKLE: Well, well, well.
                        Pause.

Here it is again, with notes on the timing which Peter Jeffrey and I eventually found secured the most laughs.

HEADINGLEY: Well. How *are* you, and so on?
BUCKLE: (*brightly*) Well, all right, Christopher. (*tick pause*) Not too bad. (*pause, then equally bright*) In quite good working order. (*longer pause, lost*) And you?

HEADINGLEY: (*immediately*) Oh fine. (*pause, lost; while thinking of something to say, absently*) Fine, fine, fine, fine, fine, fine.

BUCKLE: (*immediately*) Oh, good.

HEADINGLEY: (*pause, louder, reassuringly*) Yes, fine.

BUCKLE: (*immediately, reassured*) Oh, good. (*pause, lost; while thinking of something to say, absently*) Good, good, good, good, good, good.

HEADINGLEY: (*slight pause, while getting the next question sorted out*) Fine.

BUCKLE: (*immediately*) Good.

HEADINGLEY: (*more or less immediately, depending on the audience's laughter*) And you're . . . sawing people up?

BUCKLE: (*immediately*) That's right! Whhht! Out with their waterworks!

HEADINGLEY: (*immediately, impressed*) My word.

BUCKLE: (*pause; slowly, not at all sure he's right*) And you're . . . Parliamentary Under-Secretary, is that what they call it, at the Ministry of, isn't it in fact Education?

HEADINGLEY: (*immediately, wittily*) Whhht! Off with their heads!

BUCKLE: (*immediately, impressed*) Goodness me.

HEADINGLEY: (*laughing, loudly*) Tell the Vice-Chancellor where he gets off.

BUCKLE: (*laughing*) Well, well, well.

      Pause. Both lost.

Walking away after a laugh-line (the laugh-line's 'after-surge'!) can help: Morecambe and Wise often do this; and I suppose ideally a feed-line should be slightly louder than a laugh-line, but the reverse can often work, and really, it's impossible to lay down laws, but what I *do* know is that it is necessary to be good at comedy in your own way because all the skills you develop from it will be useful for your acting in general, and when you come to think of it all our very best actors are very good at comedy.

Having got a laugh, incidentally, remember that while the audience is laughing you are pausing – the laughter does not *belong* to the stage – and the pause must be filled.

And come in with the next line as the laughter is dying. Do not wait for it to finish.

Relax

Now you are getting near to the performance, and are concentrating on polish and pace and comedy and attack and team-work, you should balance all this with a conscious attempt to be as relaxed as possible, especially in those bits you have struggled over. A tension may have crept in and you may be able to do with a gesture or two fewer, a delivery less emphatic. Your first scene in particular may well benefit from a dose of relaxation. I always like it when an audience is led gently into the world of the play, and if a first scene is too 'acted', too loud, unnecessarily quick, the audience will be put off, and it will take them a long time to recover.

Do A Rehearsal For Something

Lionel Harris again.

'Now everybody,' he would say, clapping his hands for attention – he always called the cast 'everybody' – 'I want you to do this run-through for listening. Don't think of anything else except listening. Remember: by now you already know what everybody else says to you. It's so easy to anticipate your reply. Really listen, right up to their last syllable.

'Everybody: this time I want you to pretend you've never said any of it before. Do this rehearsal for spontaneity.

'Everybody: do this rehearsal for a sense of place. Where are you? What are you looking at? What is the room like? Do you know it well, or is it new to you? When you go up and down those stairs, are they stairs you know well so you don't have to look at the treads, or are they stairs you don't know at all so you have to look at the treads?'

And speed, of course. We'd do a run-through for speed.

I always derived great pleasure and amusement from his later rehearsals, although he could sometimes send one up most horribly.

'Lionel,' I said, after many run-throughs of a television play we were about to take into the studio, 'Lionel, I feel I'm getting stale. Give me something new to think.'

'Oh, I can't think of anything,' he said, crossly, 'make up something for yourself.' A moment's pause, while he made sure the cast was listening. 'No, *I* know,' he said softly, a smile just beginning to show on his face, 'do it,' and he paused again, looking furtively around at everyone else, 'do it as though you are wearing an enormous picture-hat.'

I don't think we got through that rehearsal.

Emotion

There will be other rehearsals, run-throughs, when the play seems to take off. Suddenly new things happen. Suddenly there is a flow, a continuity. Your instinct is taking over, and, with it, your emotion.

It is like making a cake: you got together all the ingredients and mixed them and refined them according to the recipe. Now all you have to do is put the mixture into the oven and let it bake. The work is done and the heat takes over. If the work has been right the cake will rise.

As Stanislavski said: 'When the inner conditions are pre-pared, and right, feelings will come to the surface of their own accord.' Emotions have nothing to do with will. You do not will yourself to laugh, to cry, to be angry, to be ecstatic . . . these things happen in spite of yourself: you laugh because you cannot help it, you cry because you cannot help it, you are angry, you are ecstatic, because you cannot help it.

Let these emotions have free rein now. They will bind your performance, give it a shape. For soon it will be performance-time, and it is nice to go into the studio for the recording, or into the theatre for the First Night, knowing that the cake is still rising, still in the ascendant, and the heat is doing its work.

Your memory will be at work too, allowing you to recollect the changes which are now taking place; and your taste will also hopefully be at work, telling you when your emotions are getting out of hand, and when it would be more moving to control them. Nothing is more affecting than bravery; you can will yourself to *stop* laughing, to *stop* crying, and this attempt to control yourself, this conflict between the natural expression of an emotion and a desire to control it can become the most moving part of your performance.

'All right, I'm ready now,' you will say, with that mixture of longing and dread which we all have, 'I'm ready for the First Night, or the television or film or radio studio, or the recording booth, or wherever. I'm ready.'

And the cake comes out of the oven.

The Performance

Relax And Enjoy It

Your performance is determined by what you have rehearsed. If you have rehearsed well your performance will take care of itself. Just do what you have practised.

If you feel your performance take wing, let it fly – it can be the most exhilarating feeling in all the world. If it doesn't, if it remains stubbornly earth-bound, don't worry. If it's accurate it will be all right.

Try not to judge yourself: you will so often be wrong. When I watch myself on television I am always surprised. The bits I thought I did well at the recording are often my least favourite when I see them, and the bits I thought were terrible are not so bad after all.

If you judge yourself while you are performing, you are judging your present form, not the validity of the decisions you have taken during rehearsals, and it is those decisions which more than anything determine the quality of your performance.

So. Just do it. Relax and enjoy it. The *Telegraph Sunday Magazine* (25 February 1979) quotes Dorothy Tutin as saying: 'Michael Bryant . . . told me he looks on acting as a hobby. I thought: yes, I'll do that too. It makes such a difference. Now, instead of thinking, right, I've done all the chores, now I've got to go to work, I think, good, now I can go and do my hobby.'

Retakes

In the film or television studio, when several takes of a scene may be recorded, it's very hard not to start comparing one with another.

I remember when Stephen Rea and I had done several takes of a long scene in a hotel corridor in *Professional Foul* he

said to me, reverting from his Czech accent to his native
Northern Irish one, 'Oh, it's terrible, it's terrible! You do a
scene once, and you just do it. You do a scene twice, and you
just do it. But after that! You start judging yourself! I just
couldn't do it that last time.'

He could, and was brilliant; so even judging yourself is not
too harmful. But what can help, in the pause between one
take and another, instead of merely regretting you've got to
do it again, is to think of just one bit you could do better. Aim
for that. And you'll be glad to do the retake.

Rehearse/Record

With the advent of discontinuous recording and shooting a
play out of sequence, acting for television has become a very
different thing. The 'performance' days can be very long,
sometimes over twelve hours, and I often think on those days:
you know, even an uncut version of *Hamlet* is only four-and-a-
half hours!

What to do, just to keep going and keep at performance
pitch?

Three things:

Don't waste your energy on anything but the play. It's
amazing how tiring an hour's clatter-chatter in the canteen
can be at meal-breaks. If you've got a lot to do, have food in
your dressing-room and rest your body and your voice.

If it's a rehearsal, don't try to do it well. It's better to do it
badly. If you do it well you'll think, damn, I'll never be as
good when we record it, and you'll probably be right. Just
'mark it', as Ralph Richardson used to say: just go through
the motions.

If it's a recording, try and think not so much about what
you are going to do but about what you have just done. Where
have you come from? What did you see there? Was it a view
over the Yorkshire moors, or a street in Islington? If you were
walking – over the moors or in the street – has that left you
slightly out of breath? (It's a nice last addition, this.) And if
what you are about to record is the continuation of a scene
you have already embarked on, go through the last few
speeches you had before this bit. You will know where you
are then.

Television Cameras

Should you know when the camera is on you and when it's not?

Up to a point you can't help but know because when the camera is on you its little red light will go on, and when it is not it will go out, and you will see it out of the corner of your eye.

But I prefer not to notice it, if I can, and to trust the director to have noticed my moments of change in the rehearsal room and to include them in his camera-script. Well, if he doesn't, he doesn't. He obviously thought that what somebody else was doing was more interesting, or more relevant to the story, and chose that.

I used to like to know what every camera cut was, but this can lead, as Gordon Jackson put it, to 'clunk-click' acting: every time the camera cuts to you you feel you must do something, so you nod, or open your eyes a little wider, or do some sort of reaction. 'Cut!' says the director. 'React!' says your mind.

No. On the whole I prefer to forget the cameras as much as possible, and to get back to what Lionel Harris told me so many years ago: 'Don't try to convince the camera: try to convince the people you are with.'

Filming

Although television is becoming more and more like filming there is one big difference, and that is that for a television play you will have spent days or weeks rehearsing for it, whereas for filming you will be lucky if you have rehearsed in advance at all.

So the main thing, I think, is to know the lines backwards, forwards and inside out, so that the small amount of time you spend rehearsing before you shoot will not throw you into consternation. You will be able to give all your attention to the circumstances of the scene and the contributions of the other people; and you will more easily find time for working out the details of your movements, so that continuity is not just the prerogative of the Continuity Girl. 'Was this parcel in my left hand or right hand?' She will be able to answer you, but it's quite nice not to have to ask.

The director Guy Hamilton told me: 'For filming, speak as quickly as you can and act as slowly as you can.'

I have never really known what that means. But I know it's good. 'Speak as quickly as you can' is the one bit he did explain. 'I never know until I'm editing,' he said, 'how fast a scene should go. If you've spoken quickly I can slow it down, if I want to, with reaction shots and pauses. If you've spoken slowly, I can't speed it up.'

I *think*, by 'act as slowly as you can' he meant, don't jerk, don't move about too much. But I'm not sure!

He also said, 'Save up your reactions until just before you speak. I shall probably cut to you, when I'm editing, for your speeches. Probably. Not always, of course. But as often as not. So save up any acting you want to do until just before you speak. It would be a waste if it ended up on the cutting-room floor.'

Radio

'"You must see with your ears": that is the note I give most often to actors,' said David Spenser, one of the best directors of radio drama. 'And I say, "try to convince the microphone that you are looking at the other people, or *not* looking at them; or that you are calling after them, or talking to them on the telephone, or talking to them while you are doing something else, like looking through a microscope or reading a book; and you should be able to do all these things without looking up from the script. You must see, you must look, with your ears."'

'Quite hard,' I said.

'Yes, it is,' he said.

'Demands a lot of observation, a sort of aural observation, I suppose?'

'Yes,' he said. We were talking on the telephone. 'But you see, what I'm using now is a telephone voice. I know that to talk on the telephone is different from talking outside, or in a car, or to the cast of a radio play. Yes. A good radio actor will know all these differences. And he will also know how to ignore punctuation, so that the thought-line matters more than the sentences.'

'Oh yes,' I said, 'good. Of course, when you've learnt the lines for the theatre or television you forget about punctuation altogether, but there it is, staring the radio actor in the face.'

'That's right,' he said.

'Anything else?' I said, for my own benefit really, for I'm not an experienced radio actor.

'Oh, just, oh, play the microphone. The microphone is your audience, and it's an audience of one. You don't have to project. As long as your thoughts are accurate, the microphone will accept them.'

Commentaries And Voice-Overs

Commentaries for films and voice-overs for commercials: delightful jobs, both, delightful perks, both. And they both rely on your having a sort of microphone-presence – a good forward voice, a voice with an edge to it – and on your diligence in acquiring certain knacks.

As far as I understand it, the knacks are these:

1. Keep as steady a level of volume as you can, even trying to make the ends of words no quieter than the beginnings. This is harder than it sounds. You know when you hear a tape played backwards and it sounds like Russian? That is because in Russian words get louder as they progress, whereas in English they tend to get quieter. Say 'Quieter'. 'Qui' is louder than 'er'. The more you can level it up the more the microphone likes it.

2. Keep a steady tone. Don't change gear.

3. Don't breathe audibly. The microphone doesn't like those sudden, rushed intakes of breath. Hard to avoid sometimes, when one long sentence is immediately followed by another, but a huge breath just before you start will help.

4. Develop an acute sense of timing, coming in immediately the cue-line has whizzed across the screen or immediately 'the

pack-shot' (the final close-up of the product being advertised) comes up at the end.

'Brutal soap. The soap you can trust.'

It's nice if the B of Brutal coincides with the cut to the pack-shot.

5. Be obedient. They have worked for months on their film, and you are the last arrival. They have fought and argued over every shot and every word. They know more or less exactly how they would like you to sound. If they tell you, be obedient. But . . .

6. . . . be sincere. It is important to believe, for the moment of doing it, that Brutal soap really is the soap you can trust.

7. Be quick. For a usual fifteen-, thirty- or sixty-second commercial you will not normally have had a previous sight of the script, and the recording-studio will have been booked for only half-an-hour or an hour. It is important to be quick at grasping what is required, and to use the utmost concentration. You can help yourself achieve this, and make fluffing less likely, by reading something aloud, at sight, for fifteen minutes at home before you go. It will put you into a good reading mood.

Voice And Concentration

It is worth doing similar exercises at home before you go to the theatre for your performance, for you will enjoy yourself much more and feel much better if you are 'in voice' (in the singer's sense) and in a good concentrating mood.

One's bad nights – regrettably more numerous than one would like – are often due to being out of voice (husky, throaty, quiet) and being unable to concentrate.

Bad Nights

Wendy Hiller calls these bad nights No Man's Land. 'Darling, I'm in No Man's Land,' she would wail. 'I don't know who I am, where I am, or what I'm doing.'

There are always nights like this in a long run. And you

just have to say to yourself, well ... it'll be better tomorrow ...

If it's not, then a little homework might help, especially if it yields a new idea, something you have never put into the part before. It's like having a new picture or ornament at home. It makes you look at the pictures and ornaments you already have all over again, and makes you realise how long it is since you looked at them properly.

A good wheeze is to pretend that the next performance after a bad night is not a performance at all but a rehearsal. 'Pretend the tabs are down,' said Murray Macdonald, 'and there's no audience there.'

Wendy Hiller and I used to say to each other, when one of us had been in No Man's Land the previous evening: 'Let's do it for each other. Not for the audience. You talk to me and listen to me, and I'll talk to you and listen to you.' We both found this an enormously helpful corrective, for it pointed out to us just how much we had been forgetting each other, and merely addressing the audience and listening to their coughs and sneezes.

But don't forget that whereas you are comparing your performance with your previous ones, the audience is not. It won't be nearly as bad, or as different, as you think.

You And The Audience

Nevertheless, there will be those nights when you feel the audience is decidedly hostile towards you. Towards you personally. 'They hate me tonight': I think I must have heard every actor I have acted with say that at some time or other. I have certainly said it often enough myself. 'They cough in my quiet bits and I just cannot get the laughs I am used to. It's all right for the rest of you, it's me they hate.'

It can be very demoralising; confidence can sink to a surprisingly low level and self-consciousness set in. Of course the changes to the performance are minimal, but they hurt. What I have noticed is that, when confidence goes, attack goes too. And speed. So a good way to get the audience back on your side is to go a little louder and a little faster. 'Dow ' nights are quiet, and slow, nights.

Laughs In The Wrong Place

One of the most unpleasant things that can happen to an actor is to get titters in the wrong place. You are being derided in public and it is terribly dispiriting. It can happen in modern plays when the dialogue is of questionable quality, but it can more easily happen in plays of a few decades ago: those by Wilde, Shaw, Ibsen, Galsworthy and others. The serious bits in *A Woman of No Importance*, for example, can present an unconvinced audience with a field-day, so mawkish are the sentiments the poor actors have to deliver.

Besides bringing the utmost sincerity and clarity of intention and attitude to such awkward passages, there are a number of remedies you can try, and they are all, really, the opposite of some of the ideas for comedy which I outlined earlier.

So: *Do* fade out at the ends of sentences.
Don't keep the rhythm of the lines: split them up and *don't* do slack turns of the head.

In particular, fading out at the ends of sentences is a good antidote: it makes that possibly funny line sound much more serious; a melancholy fills the air, and the audience will probably be stilled.

Good Nights

On your good nights everything (as that other soap commercial says) feels 'fresh and alive', and you feel especially pleased with yourself when this happens after the play has been running for a long time. 'I'm still capable of spontaneity, even after all these months,' you think.

You can help yourself to these good nights, and give your performance a wash-and-brush-up, by telling yourself little stories before you go on, like:

1. Pretend the play is by somebody else. If it's by Alan Ayckbourn pretend it's by Chekhov.
2. Pretend, if it's comedy, it's a serious play.
3. Pretend, if it's a serious play, it's a comedy.
4. Pretend you are another actor playing your part.

5. Pretend it has never been written down, and that you are improvising it.

These secret games are amusing to play and, don't worry, they won't alter your performance much: they will just freshen it up.

Giggling

I used to be a dreadful giggler, and am still capable of it, as the cast of *Donkeys' Years* knew only too well. I'm not as bad as I used to be because I'm more nervous now, but it is a terrible affliction, and of course it can ruin a play for the audience.

I remember two dreadful nights in *Crown Matrimonial* at the Haymarket Theatre.

Half-way through a very tense scene, Wendy Hiller, Amanda Reiss and I noticed that Andrew Ray's stiff white collar had come away from his shirt, for the stud had broken and flown off with a ping. We managed to keep going but saw to our horror that his collar started rising up his neck until it covered his chin. He then had to say: 'All this passion is very fine. But what is happening now?'

I was supposed to be the next to speak, but couldn't because all I could think of as a reply was, 'Your collar's come undone.'

And in the last scene of the play, a duologue between Queen Mary and David, the Duke of Windsor, there was this exchange:

QUEEN: As to the question of a job, what job? You refused Bermuda.

DAVID: Whose macabre idea was that? I cannot agree to be shunted from remote island to remote island. It's a wonder I wasn't offered St Helena.

QUEEN: Bermuda would have accepted you. Nowhere else will . . .

One night I just couldn't remember St Helena. The only island I could think of quickly was the Isle of Wight. So I said it. Wendy Hiller paused for what seemed like an eternity, then decided to say: 'The Isle of Wight would have accepted you. Nowhere else will.'

I don't know how we finished the scene.

The best remedy I know is to say to yourself: 'All right, go ahead and laugh, you fool . . . go on . . . show the audience you are laughing.' It's the most relaxing antidote there is – giving yourself permission to laugh if you want to – and it sometimes works.

Mistakes

I like the old actors' adage: If you make a mistake, acknowledge it. It is no use pretending it hasn't happened.

If you trip over a rug, acknowledge it. Look at the rug. Straighten it.

If ash drops on a carpet, acknowledge it, and do something about it.

If you drop a glass and it breaks, pick up the pieces. If your cigarette goes out, re-light it.

Of course, if you are recording a television play, you'll get a retake!

A Happy Company

A happy company is essential, and anything you can do to prevent unhappiness and induce happiness will be worth it. As I have said before in this book, it is impossible to concentrate in an unfriendly atmosphere. Nip any kind of crossness in the bud, and keep a sense of humour to the fore.

A happy company is based in generosity. And generosity on the stage consists of not upstaging your colleagues any more than you have to, of downstaging yourself whenever you possibly can, of not distracting when the focus of attention should be on someone else, and of really listening. I suppose the general rule is that you can move about as much as you want to when it's your turn, but you should remain as still as you can (without freezing) when it's someone else's. If you move about the audience will look at you. So if you move about, say, in the pause between a feed-line and someone else's laugh-line, you can bet your bottom dollar their laugh will be diminished, and they will not thank you for it. Actors become very sensitive to laughs in a long run, and one of the main causes of argument and, possibly, friction, is the loss of a laugh on account of what someone else is doing.

'Acting is like tennis,' said Edith Evans. 'We hit the ball to each other and the audience follows the ball. Now it's your turn, now it's mine. And when it's my turn you must not distract. You must just listen to me. And try to listen to me as though for the first time. Never forget, you do not know what I am going to say, right up to my last syllable. You must not anticipate what I am going to say.'

Tennis. Yes. Now it's your turn, now it's mine. That helps keep a company happy. And it helps keep the audience happy, too, for they know where to look.

Do Your Best

This was one of the last things my dear old friend Edith Evans said to me. *The Chinese Prime Minister* was coming to an end and I had no job to go to. 'Don't worry,' she said. 'Just do your best. That's all you can do. If you do your best, good things will come.'

She meant, of course, do your best at every rehearsal, at every performance (including the matinées), and in everyday life as well: at dinner-parties, at meetings, whenever you are with people.

Speak The Speech

I said right at the beginning of this book that I liked to start classes at RADA with that quotation from Stanislavski.

I always used to end the last lesson with every class by reciting a speech which the students knew only too well, Hamlet's advice to the players, for I had used it for many an exercise during their course; but it is full of gold, and so I'll end this part of the book with it too.

'Speak the speech, I pray you, as I pronounc'd it to you, trippingly on the tongue; but if you mouth it, as many of your players do, I had as lief the town-crier spoke my lines. Nor do not saw the air too much with your hand, thus, but use all gently; for in the very torrent, tempest, and, as I may say, whirlwind of your passion, you must acquire and beget a temperance that may give it smoothness. O, it offends me to the soul to hear a robustious periwig-pated fellow tear a passion to tatters, to very rags, to split the ears of the groundlings, who, for the most part, are capable of nothing but inexplicable dumb shows and noise. I would have such a fellow whipp'd for o'erdoing Termagant; it out-herods Herod. Pray you avoid it.

'Be not too tame neither, but let your own discretion be your tutor. Suit the action to the word, the word to the action; with this special observance, that you o'erstep not the modesty of nature; for anything so o'erdone is from the purpose of playing, whose end, both at the first and now, was and is to hold, as 'twere, the mirror up to nature; to show virtue her own feature, scorn her own image, and the very age and body of the time his form and pressure. Now, this overdone or come tardy off, though it makes the unskilful laugh, cannot but make the judicious grieve, the censure of the which one must, in your allowance, o'erweigh a whole theatre of others. O, there be players that I have seen play – and heard others praise, and that highly – not to speak it profanely, that, neither having th' accent of Christians, nor the gait of Christian, pagan, nor man, have so strutted and bellowed that I have thought some of Nature's journeymen had made men, and not made them well, they imitated humanity so abominably.

'O, reform it altogether. And let those that play your clowns speak no more than is set down for them; for there be of them that will themselves laugh, to set on some quantity of barren spectators to laugh too, though in the meantime some necessary question of the play be then to be considered. That's villainous, and shows a most pitiful ambition in the fool that uses it. Go, make you ready.'

PART TWO
More About Acting

Out Of Work

I had arrived at the last room of the *Picasso's Picassos* exhibition at the Hayward Gallery. No one else was there except an attendant who was sitting in a far corner, reading a book. My shoes squeaked on the tiled floor as I wandered round the pictures and sculptures, trying to concentrate. It was a brighter room than the others, with skylights and a view over the river. But I'd had enough and wanted to go. The idea of walking briskly across Waterloo Bridge in the hazy winter sunshine and having lunch somewhere in Covent Garden seemed infinitely preferable to staying there any longer.

The attendant turned a page and looked up. Some more people came into the room. Right, I'm off, I thought. But the attendant was standing now with a vague look of recognition on his face. I don't know him, do I? I wondered. He made straight for me, right across the room. Damn, I thought. I really did want to go.

'Hello,' he said, hushed, not wanting to distract the new arrivals.

'Hello,' I said, equally hushed but more impatiently than I had intended.

'Don't you remember me?'

'Erm . . .'

'We met in that pub opposite the Cambridge Theatre during the interval of *One Mo' Time*. I was with Marianne Bates.'

'Oh, of course,' I said, only barely remembering. Marianne was a mutual friend and had done most of the talking. 'What are you doing here?'

'Well,' he said slowly, 'trying to make ends meet, actually.'

Oh that's right, he's an actor. I remembered he'd said so. He was about twenty-five, I guessed, and was tall, and had straight fair hair.

'Is work bad at the moment?' I asked.

'Terrible,' he said, and smiled, and looked around.

'When did you last have a job?'

'Well . . . I did a couple of plays at Northampton about six months ago.'

God, what a profession, I thought. 'A long time,' I said.

'Yes,' he said. 'Feels endless. It's just getting started again . . .'

'In London, you mean?'

'Yes. Well anywhere really . . .'

'Yes.'

'. . . because I think I'm all right: I mean I got good notices and people said nice things.' He looked quite bewildered for a moment. 'Never mind,' he said, 'I've got an interview for a beer commercial the day after tomorrow, so that's something. But I don't suppose I'll get it: there are always hordes of people there. And I'm up for a small part in *Juliet Bravo* in about three weeks. My agent says it sounds an ideal part for me, so I'm afraid I'm pinning a lot of hopes on it. Mustn't, though.'

'You can't help it, though, can you?' I said. 'Would it be your first telly?'

'First for the BBC. I had a tiny part for Granada about two years ago.'

'I hope you get it.'

'Thank you,' he said. And then: 'I must tell you. I meant to tell you the other evening but I was too shy. I've read *About Acting*. A friend of mine lent me his copy. It's very good.'

'Thank you,' I said.

'The only thing is . . . I don't know if I should say this . . .'

'What?'

'He said, this friend of mine, that your book was all very well if you've got work, but it doesn't tell you anything about how to get it, does it?'

'No,' I conceded, 'he's right, it doesn't. It wasn't meant to. It was just meant to be about what it says it's about. And I'm not sure if you can tell people about how to get jobs. There's no golden formula.'

'I know,' he said. 'But although being out of work has nothing to do with acting, it has a great deal to do with the average actor's life. Don't you think?'

'Yes,' I said. 'Yes, it has. Unfortunately.'

'Anyway, that's what my friend said.'

'Yes,' I said. 'Thank you. And good luck with the interviews.'

'Fingers crossed,' he said, and went back to his corner.

And I walked back over Waterloo Bridge more slowly than I had thought I would.

Several months after that I went to Equity's offices in Harley Street to ask Peter Plouviez, then General Secretary, for a few facts and figures.

'Well,' he said, picking up a lightweight office chair and bringing it round his desk so that we could talk more easily above the clatter of his assistant's typewriter, 'let's get the numbers in perspective first. There are about 30,000 members of Equity. But of these 6,000 are Variety performers and over 4,000 of the rest are not actors: they are stage managers, opera singers, ballet dancers, television presenters, broadcasters, directors, designers, extras and so on.'

'So there are fewer than 20,000 actors on your books?'

'Yes.'

'And on any given day about how many of those actors would you say are not working?'

'Between sixty and seventy per cent. But figures for this can be misleading on account of the sporadic nature of an actor's work. For example, someone may be working for a film on a daily rate. The fact that he is used, say, on only one day in a week, and in some weeks not at all, hardly puts him in the same category as someone who is completely out of work. The same applies to people who do commercials, or commentaries or broadcasts.'

'But unemployment is still a major problem? There are still too many actors chasing too few jobs?'

'Oh yes. Yes,' he said, 'it's an ever-present problem. So we have to try and keep the numbers down to a reasonable level. That's why we introduced the Control of Entry scheme. It seemed the fairest way. We have to protect, as far as we can, the job prospects of our existing members. I think it's worked out quite well, really. It isn't that we prevent talented young people from joining the Union: we've just made it that little bit harder.'

'You mean by restricting the allocation of Equity cards and

by imposing the forty weeks of provisional membership to start with?'

'Yes.'

'There are some absurd anomalies in all this, though, aren't there?' I said. 'A new member has to have forty weeks of employment under his belt before he is allowed to have a part in the West End or a Number One tour, but can appear in a leading role on television straight away.'

'Yes. It's silly. Silly. It's the result of different negotiations with different bodies at different times. We have to get what we can when we can. There's a long way to go . . .' He relit his pipe and asked if I would like a cup of trade union coffee.

'Thank you,' I said. It was a hot day and I'd taken off my jacket and loosened my tie. He was wearing a dark pinstripe suit and kept his jacket on.

'Let's have two coffees, Anita, please,' he said, and got up and looked out of the window at the view of all the other windows, walls and chimneys which he knew so well. 'We can just see the top of the Langham,' he said, pointing it out to me. It was quiet now in the merciful lull from the incessant typing. 'When I came here over a hundred years ago there were only 8,000 members. But it wasn't all plain sailing, even then. Not by any means.' He puffed his pipe. 'Employers are more responsible now, you see: they respect Control of Entry and the Closed Shop. The problem used to be that when they wanted people for small parts in provincial theatres or television they'd just take them off the streets. They don't do that any more. And drama schools are better on the whole now, and more responsible, with smaller classes and higher standards. There's a long way to go there too, though I'd like to see a more professional approach to drama schools, with employers showing more interest in the training of actors. By interest I mean of course that they should help pay for that training. The BBC pays a fortune on the training of its technicians, but not a penny towards that of the people who are the life-blood of so many of its programmes. I'd like to see drama students being invited to be associate members of Equity, with a subscription of, say, a pound a year, so that they would be more inclined to take an interest in their Union and find out how it works. I would like standards to be more controlled by professionals, and grants from local authorities to students who are accepted by accredited drama schools to be mandatory. It's absurd that grants are still at the whim of different local authorities.' He stared moodily at the roof-tops and the sunny weather going on outside.

His face was brown ('My Muswell Hill tan') with a lot of laughter-wrinkles round his eyes: a good public face, photogenic and recognisable for when he has to appear on television. Affable, you would call him, but with plenty of steel inside. A born Trade Union leader, you would say, who has remained loyal to Equity through all its turbulent years and with all its shades of Councils. He has a politician's (or Trade Union leader's) way of speaking, with its careful, syllabic progress through instantly edited sentences, biting away at the consonants, so that 'politician' can sound like Polly Titian, the daughter of that well-known painter. 'We're lucky to have him,' said Hugh Manning, the on-and-off President of Equity. 'We don't know how lucky we are.'

Anita Saunders came back with our coffee and resumed her hectic, electronic typing.

'When actors are on the dole, does Equity have any official attitude as to whether or not they should apply for Social Security?' I asked, having to concentrate harder all over again.

'Not officially,' he replied, sitting down again and picking up his brown cup and saucer, 'but if asked I would always advise that should it be needed it should be applied for. Why not? It is their right. They've paid towards it in taxes and National Insurance. Why not?'

'Someone said to me the other day he would never stoop to accepting Social Security.'

'An older actor?'

'Yes.'

'Yes. A lot of them do find it difficult. They still think of it as a stigma. Younger ones don't any more, partly because so many of them have to apply for it. And it's not just actors: it's white-collar workers and all.'

'And what about temporary jobs – Alfred Marks type – does Equity have any connection or liaison with those employers who welcome actors who are out of work?'

'Again, not officially, though we know who they are and they occasionally contact us. The good ones are very good and allow time off for interviews and auditions and things. There are quite a lot who really like actors: many of the big stores, for example, and I don't just mean for their Father Christmases. They think that actors, with their outgoing personalities, make good salesmen. Pubs too, for the same reason, welcome actors as barmen, and restaurants as waiters. Agencies for domestic work do too: people like to employ actors to clean their flats and houses, because they feel it gives them a certain cachet and they talk about it afterwards to their friends. Companies who need telephone operators for surveys of public opinion and sales promotions are particularly keen to employ actors because of their persuasive and pleasant voices, so much so that they often put advertisements in *The Stage*.'

While Peter Plouviez was methodically going through this list of temp jobs, I was thinking of some of the actors I knew who had had, at some time, to take them. Drab jobs, compared to what they'd had in mind for themselves during their passionate and heady days at drama school. But they're a godsend, really, providing an easy but soul-less way of keeping body and soul together. And it's something to do. There's less time to brood. You can get quite drawn into this strange, new world with its little intrigues and funny things that happen, and as often as not there will be other actors around, so at least you can have the comfort of confirming that there are a lot of others in the same boat; though sometimes you can look round and think, God, and these are only a few of the masses of actors who are out of work! What hope is there! How futile it all is! How demeaning!

But after work you can go off for a drink somewhere and feel low and cynical, and moan to each other, until eventually you get on to the subject of theatre and actors and performances and productions and reminiscences, and somehow manage to chatter about them as though the temp work never existed.

Unfortunately, in addition to the depression a temp job can induce, there is a deeper snare lurking. Most actors, I believe, have an uncomfortable attitude towards their real work: they love it, otherwise they wouldn't be doing it; but there are dreads as well. There's the dread of not being able to do a part adequately when it comes, and the particularly nasty dread that after the interview or after the audition, when the part is offered, it will prove to be rubbish: you've got to take it, your agent would be furious if you didn't, and beggars can't be choosers. A friend was recently landed with such a part (mercifully quite short) in a dreadful television play. 'Oh dear,' he said, 'I ought to feel elated: I've got a job, I'll earn some money. But I don't. I dread it. It's hopeless. And I'll be hopeless in it. Oh dear.' And he panicked.

There's the dread of making a fool of yourself in front of everybody, the dread of being off form when it's important to be on it, the dread of being found out. A most distinguished actress said to her most distinguished director during rehearsals for *Much Ado About Nothing* at Stratford many years ago, 'This part is the one in which I am going to be found out to be such a fraud.' The actress was Peggy Ashcroft, who proceeded to enjoy great acclaim for her performance as Beatrice.

Most of us have a love-dread attitude to our work. For myself, I love it and dread it in about equal proportions, I think. Sometimes love gets the upper hand and I think, oh good, things are on the up, I'm going to be rather good in this, and then, unaccountably, with the next job, dread does, and I can't fathom out where my talent has sunk to. And the snag about temp work is that, compared to acting, it can be insidiously attractive. It's dull, yes; it's not what you were put on this earth to do; but it's easy. It doesn't involve your emotions and you're not on show all the time. And all this can take the edge off your enthusiasm to leave no stone unturned to get an acting job. Gradually you can allow yourself to drift out of the main stream and settle for this little eddying backwater, where there is a bit of peace and quiet, and where the turbulence passes you by. I have known several people who dreaded acting more than they loved it, and who opted therefore for the quieter life of the temp job they found themselves doing. Well, maybe they would have given up anyway: maybe the temp job merely hastened the change.

Nevertheless, for many dedicated actors who would never dream of abandoning their chosen profession, who live with a vast ambition tucked securely under their skin and an undying hope that one day their turn will come, a temp job is a necessary part of their working lives, especially if they have a family to keep, or any expensive outgoings, like a mortgage or a car. I suppose the actors who are in the happiest position are those who have, either by their own endeavours or those of their agent, managed to find a niche in sidelines which are connected with acting: radio commercials, and voice-overs for television commercials, commentaries for films, broadcasts (I don't mean to call broadcasting a sideline: it's an important part of the world of drama; but actors who were once members of the BBC rep., and who therefore know and are known by all the directors, often continue with the odd broadcast from time to time), teaching at drama schools, or being the presenter of audio-visuals for internal commercial use. Mostly these jobs require expert use of the voice and mostly they are well paid. Of course, they are so desirable that they are also hard to get, but it's worth persevering. Again, it's just a question of getting started. One thing leads to another.

'I wouldn't have your job for all the tea in China,' said Peter Plouviez, waking me out of my reverie. He was standing now. It was time for me to go.

'Why not?' I said, getting up and putting on my jacket.

'Because there's no logic in it,' he said. 'I want a job which befits my merit. If I do that job well I expect promotion; and if I continue to do well I expect further promotion. And so on and so on. With actors it doesn't happen like that at all. People rise and fall with alarming rapidity, often for no discernible reason. And when I see the figures of some people's earnings I am continually amazed: Joe Bloggs, who's had a good year with a few commercials, can earn more than the Prime Minister, while a highly esteemed actor can be below the poverty line.'

'Nevertheless, there are reputations which, once made, seem to stick and to carry longevity with them,' I persisted, 'and up to a point one thing leads to another. But I know what you mean. An agent was telling me yesterday about two of his clients. One, a young actor, had the leading role in a television series and was remarkably good in it. But nothing came of it. The other, a young actress, had a bit part in an episode of a half-hour sitcom. The following day the telephone never stopped.'

'Typical. Typical,' said Peter Plouviez, as we moved out of his office on to the landing. 'Of course the trouble is that too many of you are just too bloody good. When standards are high we – by "we" I mean the public and employers alike – *expect* you to be good. And you make it look so easy. People get used to it. If you were a member of the National Theatre of Uzbekistan, where the standards are indescribable, people would sit up and take a bit of notice. They would see that good acting is really rather difficult.'

'The National Theatre of where?' I said, not cottoning on.

'Uzbekistan.'

'Where's that?'

'Oh, somewhere in outer Bengal.' He started to laugh.

'How do you spell it?'

'Look. I've told you where it is. You don't expect me to spell it for you as well, do you?' He laughed some more and went back into his office. And I went out into the street, glad of the hour I had spent with this committed, generous and guarded man.

And as I walked up Harley Street and across Marylebone Road into Regents Park, on my way home, I thought about what he had told me and remembered how I had felt during a long period of worklessness: ill with depression, brooding endlessly and losing every particle of confidence in myself, not only as an actor. An actor without confidence is nothing. Good acting takes courage and daring.

So the sensible thing is always to be ready; life can change in an instant, at the ring of a telephone: an interview, an audition, or the offer of a part. Out of the blue. It's important to keep up with things – to look good, to sound good, to feel good – and to try to be positive and not bitter, to add constantly to a store of audition speeches, and to keep in trim by doing all sorts of exercises (if possible by attending occasional classes, which have a therapeutic value as well) and by watching and considering other people's acting and your own.

Easier said than done, but . . .

PS 1991. Peter Plouviez writes:

'There have been some significant changes in the way in

which entry into the acting profession is regulated. This has resulted both from a desire among Equity members to relax restrictions, particularly on those who have got through accredited courses at drama schools, and from the effects of successive Acts of Parliament during the Thatcher years which have made any form of Union closed shop legally unenforceable.

'It now needs only thirty weeks of work as a provisional member to qualify for full membership.

'More importantly, there is now a scheme whereby all those who graduate from courses which are accredited by the National Council for Drama Training (that is most of those who leave the leading drama schools each year) can be employed straight away in Repertory, the Equity Fringe and the Commercial Provincial Theatre provided always that they can find someone willing to give them a job. There is still, in addition, a quota of other newcomers without previous professional experience who can be offered work.

'The effect of these changes can be seen in the Equity membership figures. Although under the new Laws no-one can any longer be compelled to be an Equity member, there has been virtually no change in the position wherein all performers in the major areas of work remain in the Union. The total membership at the end of 1990 had grown to about 46,000. Equity has been one of the tiny number of Unions which has shown an increase during a period when, overall, Trade Union membership has rapidly declined.

'Alas, there has been no appreciable increase in opportunities for work. When we conducted a survey of earnings and employment a few years ago, more than half our members earned less than £5,000 a year from the business. We are still only marginally better off than our American colleagues who throw parties when they get an audition!

'The Casting Agreements remain intact and by and large are still appreciated by the employers, as well as ourselves, no doubt because they do not relish the prospect of opening their auditions to the thousands who still would like the chance to join the profession, but who have shown no willingness to equip themselves for such a demanding and unrewarding occupation.

'Despite this, if I had to make a prediction today, on the eve of my retirement, I would say that in a decade or so actors may well find that the only way they will be able to be protected and respected will be by turning acting into something which might properly be described as "a profession". Not, as now, meaning simply that they will be paid for what they do, but, like the older professions, indicating that the members of it are qualified and subject to codes of professional conduct laid down by their peers.

'There will always be opposition to this, particularly from older actors who remember when drama schools were often indistinguishable from finishing schools. However, I expect some of the older barbers, while applying their leeches, felt much the same about the establishment of a separate medical profession.'

Exercises

Here are some exercises you might like to choose from. You won't want them all, but you'll know which ones to ignore. Some you can do on your own, while for others you'll need a friend or two.

Stretch Your Voice

Two actors, Colin Blakcly and Robert Stephens, were talking to two members of the Moscow Art Theatre, in London for a season, who had studied under Stanislavski. Naturally they asked them what the great master was like and how intricately he followed the methods described in such detail in his books.

'Oh, he was very practical and encouraged us to be as true and as natural as possible,' said one of the Russians, hoping that would be enough; they got asked it a lot.

'What he was really writing in all his books, you see,' said the other Russian, taking over, 'was an antidote to the heavy, Germanic, melodramatic style of acting prevalent in those days. He wanted a style more suited to the new, gentler, realistic plays of Chekhov and others.'

'But of all the things he must have said to you,' said Colin Blakely, anxious to know as much as possible, but without wanting to turn the conversation into an interview, 'were there any which stand out particularly in your memory?'

'No, no,' said the first Russian, disappointingly, 'none particularly. He didn't preach much. He assumed we'd read his books, I think. He was good, but no special remark, no.'

'Oh, come on,' said Robert Stephens, 'there must have been something . . .'

There was a long pause while they both thought about it. Then from the second Russian came the surprising answer: 'Actually, I do remember something he often said, "The three most important things for an actor are voice, voice and yet again voice."'

Far be it from me to pontificate on what you should do to improve your voice: there are many experts who have taught and written books on the subject. I have indeed had my share of problems with my own voice; so I thought I would try to remember here what some of them were, and what I did, or was advised to do, to overcome them.

First of all, I think an actor should be able to speak loudly. Easily loudly. Without strain.

'Louder! You should be louder!' said the director Michael Rudman to me, during rehearsals and after early performances of *Donkeys' Years*.

I had spent the previous three years working mostly in television. 'But it feels as if I'm shouting,' I remonstrated.

'Well you're not,' he said, 'and you should practise till it doesn't.'

And he was right. That's it. An actor with a naturally loud voice can easily quieten it and will still be heard; whereas an actor with a naturally quiet voice will always be full of strain, because it feels wrong when he has to go loud.

I have often been envious of the superb voices of stallholders who cry their wares in market-places, or the vendors of evening papers who shout at street corners. Hour after hour they do it, sonorously and tirelessly. And I've noticed that when I've been acting in a large theatre for some time, or more especially when I've been on tour, trying to adjust to the varying acoustics of large and not-so-large houses, something happens to my voice, giving it a deeper resonance, a wider capacity. It can go on for longer, at full theatre-pitch, just as those toy cars powered by a certain battery can outlast those using the inferior sort. When I go loud, or shout with full force, it doesn't hurt any more.

And I've regretted that, when I haven't been working in the theatre, I haven't compensated by doing regular exercises, at home, for speaking loudly. I remember being humiliated once in a broadcasting studio when I had to shout in a scene. We did several takes, and afterwards my reddened and unpractised throat hurt unbearably, and I was hoarse, and therefore inadequate, for the rest of the play.

Stretch your voice. Half an hour a day, say. A little but often.

Breathe in deeply. Start with a prolonged 'h' and gradually, without any hint of a glottal stop, build in some sound, 'ah', in your middle register. Increase the volume gently, without any strain, and keep it going for as long as you can. If you get a frog in your throat, cough as gently as you can to release the phlegm and spit it out. Cough only to get rid of the phlegm. Frogs in the throat tend to happen at the beginnings of practice, or at the beginnings of plays. I've often had one in the first scene, never, as far as I can remember, in the last.

Now let your 'hah' go up and down the scale: mouth nicely open, plenty of breath, so that you can feel that the tone comes from the chest and passes, without any interruption from the throat, into the room (or remote place in the open countryside!). When a certain volume feels easy, try going a little louder. Then, a week or so later, louder still. What you will hope for is to combine a new capacity for loudness with a tone which is as pure and uncluttered and musical as possible. If you feel there is something really wrong or something you don't like about the tone of your voice it would be worth consulting an expert. Actors with dry, rasping voices, with no liquid notes in them, suffer a disadvantage, I think. We can't all be like Derek Jacobi, Patrick Stewart or Greg Hicks, Susan Fleetwood, Eileen Atkins or Frances de la Tour (and some may say, well, we don't want to be: we are ourselves, and we want to do things our way); but there they are, they and others, possessors of true theatre-sized, musical, expressive voices. Object-lessons.

You'll soon get tired of 'hahing' so you can 'mah' for a while. Let the 'm' be prolonged until the lips are tingling and then open them gradually into the same 'ah' sound.

There are lots of variations of this exercise, using different consonants – L, B, D and K are good ones – and all the vowel sounds. Try to keep the mouth as open for 'ay' and 'ee' as it is for 'ah'. Well, the great teacher Clifford Turner used to say that, but it's a bit hard and feels silly, so nearly as open will do. A nice alternative to going up and down a scale is to do off-beat alterations of the note so that it sounds like modern plainsong or a Moslem call to prayer.

Strengthen your voice, and sing. When Mary Martin was appearing on Broadway in *South Pacific* she used to make a point of doing an hour's vocal warm-up in her dressing-room before every performance. She did all the exercises she could think of, and was apparently mortified to learn that her partner Ezio Pinza, the bass-baritone, with his highly developed, magnificent voice, merely said, loudly and slowly, 'Carolina' four times before he went on the stage and sang his heart out.

Diction Practice

This is the actor's equivalent to a musician's scales and arpeggios and an athlete's daily slog. There's something of a musician, and of an athlete too, in every actor.

You'll already have your favourites, but here are some more which, if you don't know them already, you might like to add:

Go through the consonants from B to Z, including the double ones like Br, Dr, Tr, Thr, Pr, Cl, Shl, Gl, Pl, St, using the vowels:

ah ay ee ay ah aw oo aw

So the first one would be:

bah bay bee bay bah baw boo baw

Etc. Faster and faster.

Do tongue-twisters, especially for those consonants you find difficult. An actress who has had trouble with her 's' (it whistles easily) gave me these:

Six thick thistle-sticks.
The shrewd shrew sold Sarah seven silver fish slices.

The same actress had to say, in a recent part, 'Spanish specials', which was none too easy for her, though it was child's play compared to these four cruel lines:

Amidst the mist of smoking frosts,
With stoutest wrists and loudest boasts,
He thrusts his fists against the posts
And still insists he sees the ghosts

Or, an extension of her first one:

Theophilus Thistler, the thistle-sifter, in sifting a sieve of unsifted thistles, thrust three thousand thistles through the thick of his thumb.

Some more consonants, to be practised until they sound easy and uncluttered:

Betty bought a bit of butter, but she found the butter bitter, so Betty bought a bit of better butter to make the bitter butter better.

'Do daring deeds! Do damage!' demanded Dr Doolittle.

Five flippant Frenchmen fly from France for fashions.

How has Harry hastened so hurriedly from the hunt?

James just jostled Jean gently.

Keencut cutlery cuts keenest and cleanest of all. Keencut cutlery.

(That was the wording for a television commercial. The actor who did it, years ago, had four seconds in which to get it out. 'It was the nastiest session I ever had,' he said.)

Lucy lingered, looking longingly for her lost lap-dog.

Quickly, quickly, quickly, quickly, quickly, quickly, quickly, quickly.

(To be done quickly; and can you manage it without a whistle, ever, before the 'i'?).

Two toads, totally tired, trying to trot to Tewkesbury.

Vera valued the valley violets.

To strengthen the tongue:

Red leather, yellow leather

and

Red lorry, yellow lorry

over and over again, faster and faster, can hardly be bettered. And what about the 'r' sound? To roll or not to roll? It doesn't matter much but it's nice to be able to do both easily. Try:

Round the rugged rocks the ragged rascal ran

and

Reading and writing are richly rewarding.

For the lips there's obviously, and probably best of all:

> Peter Piper picked a peck of pickled peppers.
> If Peter Piper picked a peck of pickled peppers
> Where's the peck of pickled peppers that Peter Piper
> picked?

But if you want a change, here's

> Pearls, please, pretty Penelope,
> Pretty Penelope, pretty Penelope,
> Pearls, please, pretty Penelope,
> Pretty Penelope Pring.
> I would like to buy pearls for Penelope,
> Pearls for Penelope, pretty Penelope,
> I would like to buy pearls for Penelope,
> Pretty Penelope Pring.

or, alternating 't's with 'p's:

> Tippetty-Tippetty was an elfin,
> Tippetty-Tippetty, Tippetty-Tee.
> Tippetty-Tippetty tripped so neatly,
> Tippetty-Tippetty, Tippetty-Tee,
> Tippetty-Tee, Tippetty-Tee,
> Tippetty-Tippetty, Tippetty-Tee.

It is the leaping from the guttural consonants to those formed by the lips which can sometimes be so appallingly difficult. What about

> Peggy Babcock,

for example?

But you'll know what you find difficult, and practice will make perfect. Or should. Some obstinacies will cling. After doing a play for months and months I still found 'seriously neglected' hard to say. Time and time again it would come out as 'serious 'n' glected'. And 'traditional' can easily become 'trujjnal'.

A microphone can point out many things that go silly, like additional mouth-noises that creep in unawares. When you open your lips to speak, especially if they are a bit dry, you can make an involuntary 'p' sound. There can be a tongue-crack, a clatter sound, between the 'fierce' and 'ly' of 'fiercely', for example, or in any other word ending in 'ly'. Did it happen to you when you were saying, 'Reading and writing are richly rewarding'? And your throat can click in the pause after an 'ing' sound, too, so you could be recorded as saying: 'Are you comingk? No, I'm goingk.' Just to make this absurd, you might have a slow go at: 'Readingk and writingk are richkly rewardingk,' but if it sound like that, somethingk is really wrongk!

Nevertheless, the beauty of becoming very practised at tongue-twisters and quick diction exercises is that they will give your speech such precision that when you come to act you will not have to bother about precision. You can forget it, be slovenly, even, if you want to be, if the part calls for it. When a rule or an exactness is mastered, it can be thrown away.

There was a time when, led by Laurence Olivier, actors caught the habit of separating similar consonants which ended one word and began the next. 'That day,' would never be allowed to sound like 'tha' day' (I mean with a silent 't', felt, but not pronounced), or 'Yes, Sarah' like 'Yessarah'. It often presents a problem, this. For example, should our favourite afternoon beverage be described as 'Best drink of the day' or 'Bes' drink of the day'? I think the unpedantic solution is the better.

Finally here's an exercise, very well known, which combines a number of difficulties, and which you could never do too often, because it's such a help. It's from *The Pirates of Penzance*:

'I am the very pattern of a modern Major-General;
I've information vegetable, animal, and mineral;
I know the Kings of England, and I quote the fights historical,
From Marathon to Waterloo, in order categorical;
I'm very well acquainted too with matters mathematical,
I understand equations, both the simple and quadratical,
About binomial theorem I'm teeming with a lot o' news,
With many cheerful facts about the square of the hypotenuse.

I'm very good at integral and differential calculus,
I know the scientific names of beings animalculous.
In short, in matters vegetable, animal, and mineral,
I am the very model of a modern Major-General.'

(I was surprised by the word 'pattern' in the opening line.
I had learnt it, when I was a student at RADA, as 'model',
and that's how I have said it and heard it from that day to
this. But there it is, in an original edition by W. S. Gilbert:
'pattern'.)

I have proved to myself all over again recently, during a
tour of a play, that half an hour spent doing some of these
manipulative exercises, either before leaving for the theatre,
or in your dressing-room when you arrive, will make all the
difference to your performance. When your lips and tongue
and voice are ready, your batteries are charged.

Check Your Vowels

It is interesting to hear, when you watch British films made
during the war or in the early 'fifties, how pronunciation of
so-called Standard English has changed. Some of the sounds
they made then have become curiously affected to our ears:
their 'o's, as in 'coat', were thinner, and their 'a's were much
less flat than ours, so that 'flat' could sound like 'flairt' or
even 'flet'. I was struck by this all over again when I was
watching, for the umpteenth time, Celia Johnson and Trevor
Howard in *Brief Encounter*.

It's worth checking through your vowels to make sure they
are the vowels you really *want* to make. I stress 'want' because
if you have a regional accent there's no reason why you
shouldn't keep what you want of it. It's up to you. After all, it
would be dreadful if we all spoke in precisely the same way
without any idiosyncracies, though I suppose you could say
that 'good speech', whatever its flavour, is required of actors
who, along with writers, public speakers and television people,
have a responsibility to maintain and maybe, even, occasionally to enhance our language. (So it's good to refer to your
dictionary whenever you are in doubt about pronunciation.
Controversial words like 'controversy', 'applicable', 'explica-
ble', 'transport', 'often', 'either', are worth getting right.)

Again, it's easy to find or make up your own vowel checks. But here are a couple, for 'aw' and the dastardly 'oh':

I ought to call at Dawley Hall
Where my friend Paul, who is not tall,
Has had a fall from off a wall.
His sister Maud has bought a shawl:
I can't afford a shawl at all.

Golden in the garden, golden in the glen,
Golden, golden, golden September's here again.
Golden in the tree-tops, golden in the sky,
Golden, golden, golden September's going by.

Get Your Sight-Reading Good

Yes, do! It's worth it. We often have to do it. And it comes only with practice. Do it whenever you feel like it, and go on with it until you make no mistakes of either diction or meaning. Go on with it until you feel you are actually *elucidating* the meaning. Go on with it until it feels like talking, not reading: personal and natural.

A rather more boring exercise (because, after all, when you are reading at sight you can read anything that interests you, from a novel to a newspaper, though technical books are a challenge, with their sudden shocks of the names of flowers or diseases) is to prepare a reading, a longish one, as though for *A Book at Bedtime*, say. Scribble around the words whatever markings you feel you need to help you with the meaning and the phrasing. Among those markings I like to put a little squiggle over bits I know I might fluff on account of having already fluffed them more than once. The squiggle means, watch out, here's a difficult bit, take care over it.

When you've got your reading prepared, go through it three or four times each session, trying never to lose either the meaning or whatever freshness it had when you first read it, but at the same time allowing new nuances to creep in when they occur to you. Try to make it better each time. Go for the words. Go for their meaning. Go for their feeling.

I've put this bit in, about preparing a long reading, because I find it so difficult myself. My least favourite job is reading a book for cassette or radio. A lot of actors love it but I hate it. The recording sessions seem endless: I can manage the first hour or two, but when they extend for a whole day, as they often can, my concentration withers and I don't know what I'm talking about any more. Shame sets in as the tape is rewound after yet another mistake, and I leave the studio humiliated. If the job lasts for more than one day, as it often can, I arrive the following morning with dread.

I'm still trying to get better at it. But this is more about sustained concentration than reading, and I'll come on to some exercises for that later (having had yet another go through them myself).

What Do You Mean?

For my entire eight years' teaching at RADA I shirked this whole question of *meaning*, and how it was an actor's duty to extract the true meaning from any prose or verse he has to deliver in a way that makes people want to sit up and listen because they know he is being so clear. Harold Innocent once told me he thought the first duty of an actor is to be clear; and that's no bad thing to aim at. When I say I shirked the subject I didn't shirk pronouncing such generalities as those I've just pronounced: I shirked finding examples and setting exercises. I nearly shirked it here because it's such a difficult subject to be clear about.

But last Christmas I had to read the ninth lesson at an annual carol service at St. George's, Hanover Square; and the ninth lesson, for which the whole congregation stands, is always that bit from the beginning of St. John: 'In the beginning was the Word.'

'Oh no, not that!' said one of my friends when I told him about it. 'That's the impossible one. Nobody ever understands it.'

'Consult a priest!' said another. 'Try and get him to explain it to you.'

Well, I didn't: I decided to try and work it out for myself. But there are problems, as you'll see:

In the beginning was the Word, and the Word was with God, and the Word was God. The same was in the beginning with God. All things were made by him; and without him was not any thing made that was made. In him was life; and the life was the light of men. And the light shineth in darkness; and the darkness comprehended it not.

There was a man sent from God, whose name was John. The same came for a witness, to bear witness of the Light, that all men through him might believe. He was not that Light, but was sent to bear witness of that Light. That was the true Light, which lighteth every man that cometh into the world. He was in the world, and the world was made by him, and the world knew him not. He came unto his own, and his own received him not. But as many as received him, to them gave he power to become the sons of God, even to them that believe on his name: Which were born, not of the blood, nor of the will of the flesh, nor of the will of man, but of God. And the Word was made flesh, and dwelt among us, and we beheld his glory, the glory as of the only begotten of the Father, full of grace and truth.

'Christ,' I thought, blasphemously, 'what have I let myself in for! I've always thought this bit good but boring; how can I make it good but not boring?' So here it is again with notes about what I attempted. The meanings I ascribe may be thoroughly questionable theologically, but I was concerned primarily with performing it:

In the <u>beginning</u> was the <u>Word</u> (*I tried to find a substitute for the word 'Word'; something more mystical, like 'Idea', 'Life Force', or 'Space', to make 'Word' sound larger*), and the Word was with <u>God</u> (*uniting, in my mind, the two mysteries*), and the Word <u>was</u> God (*they were one and the same*).

(*The next sentence was the hardest of the lot. Is it just an emphatic reiteration of the first? It seems weak and rather boring. Well, I thought, I'll do it emphatically.*)

The same (*i.e. the Word*) was in the <u>beginning</u> with God.

All things were made by him (*big statement*); and <u>without</u> him was not <u>any thing</u> made that was <u>made</u> (*throwing the last three words away slightly, to rid them of any possible absurdity and to make the meaning sweeter. Usually readers choose to emphasise the penultimate word, 'was', but eventually I decided that was silly*).

In him was <u>life</u> (*new word, 'life'; big word, 'life'; felt word*);

and the life was the light of men (*their inspiration; another theme introduced*).

And the light shineth in darkness; and the darkness comprehended it not. (*And that was the end of that for now: all the foregoing was ignored, for now.*)

(*New paragraph, new brightness*:) There was a man sent from God, whose name was John. The same came for a witness (*go for the word 'witness', and throw the rest away, so it sounds conversational; and wherever 'witness' occurs again, emphasise it each time, and do this whole passage about John slightly more quickly than the previous paragraphs, so that the word 'witness' ties it all up*), to bear witness of the Light, that all men through him might believe. He was not that Light, but was sent to bear witness of that Light. (*Awkward change to follow: it needs to sound different because suddenly you're talking about Jesus, and that needs to be clear; so let the first three words lead up to the fourth quickly, and then slow down and be as simple as possible*:)

That was the true Light, which lighteth every man that cometh into the world. He was in the world, and the world was made by him (*still very simple, straightforward and true*), and the world knew him not.

(*Putting it another way, but linking it surely with the previous sentence, as though to underline it*:) He came unto his own, and his own received him not (*and throw all the words away except those underlined*).

(*Another awkward transition to follow: so try to make 'But as many as received him' sound as near as possible to 'However, there were some who did receive him'*:) But as many as received him, to them gave he power (*make quite a lot of that word*) to become the sons of God, even (*odd word, 'even': it must mean something like 'I mean'*) to them that believe on his name: Which were born (*make a nice list here of the 'nots' and 'nors'*), not of the blood, nor of the will of the flesh, nor of the will of man, but of God.

And the Word (*hark back in your mind to the beginning of the piece – remember the Word?*) was made flesh, and dwelt among us, and we beheld his glory (*make much of that word, and do so again straight away: make a feature of this repetition, just as you did of 'witness'*), the glory as of the only begotten of the Father, full of grace and truth. (*I think those last words 'grace' and 'truth' are so felicitous and deep that they could be separated.*

'Grace' gets a bit lost if you just say 'grace and truth'. It could go: 'full of grace. And truth.' But I don't know. That's what I did, but it's not as simple as 'grace and truth' and maybe stands out a bit too much. On the other hand it's a good curtain-line.)

I found that what I had to do after analysing it like that was try to throw the analysis away, and not exaggerate anything, so that the whole piece would flow in as relaxed and spontaneous a way as possible. The analysis remained, but only just.

It will already be clear that the clear way through to the meaning of a piece is not at all by trying to make the most of every word.

There's a spoof of a voice-over session for television commercials. It's called *Blooper's Soap*, was made in America and is very famous in advertising circles. I have a pirated copy of it at home, recorded from a recording which was recorded from a recording *ad infinitum*, I should think, judging by the appalling quality of my little cassette.

The actor arrives, and is given his one end-line, 'Blooper's soap is real good', with the instruction from the director, 'It's just a statement of fact, you know: we want sort of a simple, straight, sincere, throwaway kind of reading.' The actor does it perfectly and the director says, 'Perfect. I mean what the hell can you do with a simple sincere line? Just say it.' The actor enters the recording booth and does a test for level. Then it goes:

RECORDING ENGINEER:	Take one.
ACTOR:	Blooper's soap is real good.
DIRECTOR:	Sounds fine. Nice easy reading. We'd better take another for our protection, and as long as we're doing it again I was thinking, the Account Executive is a real stickler for client-name identification, so maybe you could goose Blooper a little. OK?
ENGINEER:	Take two.
ACTOR:	BLOOPER'S soap is real good.

DIRECTOR: I think we got it. Fine, fine . . . er . . .
                 wait a minute. The only thing is our
                 Copy Chief is pretty adamant about
                 product-mention.

ACTOR: You mean soap? I mentioned it.

DIRECTOR: Yes, but not with pride. Mention it
                 with great pride.

ENGINEER: Take three.

ACTOR: BLOOPER'S PRIDE is real good.

DIRECTOR: Perfect. That was it . . . er . . . but you
                 said 'Blooper's pride' . . . no, no, it's
                 'Blooper's soap'. Have you got a script
                 in there?

ENGINEER: Take four.

ACTOR: BLOOPER'S SOAP is real good.

DIRECTOR: Getting there. Don't lose that nice easy
                 sell . . . could I make one suggestion?
                 The Agency Head is very particular
                 about qualifications. You should hit
                 'real' a bit more, don't you think?

ENGINEER: Take five.

ACTOR: BLOOPER'S SOAP is REAL good.

DIRECTOR: That just about wraps it up. I'm
                 satisfied . . . er . . . wait a minute. The
                 Client loved the word 'good'. He's used
                 it in his copy for years. He's tried to
                 copyright it several times. He spent a
                 fortune, but no soap, you know. Make
                 more out of 'good', will you?

ENGINEER: Take six.

ACTOR: BLOOPER'S SOAP'S REAL GOOD.

DIRECTOR: Terrific. But it sounds like 'Blooper's
                 soap's real good.' You're making a
                 contraction out of 'is'. Will you give
                 that 'is' great conviction?

ENGINEER: Take seven.

ACTOR (*yelling now*):   BLOOPER'S SOAP IS REAL GOOD.

DIRECTOR: That's it. We got it. That's just the
                 amount of undersell I wanted.

No. The way through to the meaning of a piece is to know what to emphasise and what to throw away. I think the secret is (and I swear I wrote all this before interviewing Prunella Scales) to go for as few words as you can and throw as many as you can away. Then there will be a rhythm to it, a vitality and a life. Let's look at a bit of King Magnus's great speech to his Cabinet in *The Apple Cart*, and see how few words need emphasis:

MAGNUS (*very grave*): The Prime Minister has been good enough to pursue the discussion with me in <u>private</u> to a point at which the issue is now <u>clear</u>. If I do not accept the ultimatum I shall receive <u>your</u> resignations and <u>his</u>; and the country will learn from his explanatory speech in the House of Commons that it is to choose between <u>Cabinet</u> government and <u>monarchical</u> government: an issue on which I frankly say that I should be very sorry to <u>win</u>, as I cannot carry on without the support of a body of ministers whose <u>existence</u> gives the English people a sensation of self-government. Naturally I want to <u>avert</u> a conflict in which <u>success</u> would <u>damage</u> me and <u>failure disable</u> me.

I won't go on; but if the idea appeals to you try the whole speech for yourself. It's a great piece of dramatic prose.

Oscar Wilde's plays can be awkward and hard to follow, and unless the acting is splendid the wit can sound stale and the sentiments mawkish. One of the best readings of an awkward line I ever heard (and I heard it a lot because I was in the same production) was by Nora Swinburne in the 1953 revival of *A Woman of No Importance* at the Savoy Theatre. We were coming up to the curtain of Act Two. I was Gerald Arbuthnot and I had just found out that Lord Illingworth (Clive Brook), whom I had hitherto greatly admired, had made advances to my girlfriend, Hester Worsley (Frances Hyland); according to the stage directions I had to be quite beside myself with rage and indignation, uttering the lines:

GERALD: Lord Illingworth, you have insulted the purest thing on God's earth, a thing as pure as my own

mother. You have insulted the woman I love
most in the world with my own mother. As
there is a God in Heaven, I will kill you!

MRS
ARBUTHNOT (*rushing across and catching hold of him*):   No! No!

GERALD   (*thrusting her back*):   Don't hold me, mother.
Don't hold me – I'll kill him.

MRS
ARBUTHNOT: Gerald.

GERALD: Let me go, I say!

MRS
ARBUTHNOT: Stop, Gerald, stop! He is your own father!
(*Gerald clutches his mother's hands and looks into her
face. She sinks slowly to the ground in shame. Hester
steals towards the door. Lord Illingworth frowns and
bites his lip. After a time Gerald raises his mother up,
puts his arms round her, and leads her from the room.*)

One can imagine how imperiously Mrs Arbuthnot's last
line will have been delivered by the actress in Wilde's own
day. Nora Swinburne said it very quickly and urgently, all in
one, in spite of herself: she hadn't meant to spill the beans.
Then in the pause afterwards, she realised what she had said.
And we all looked at her and didn't do any of the other actions
suggested in the stage directions. The curtain managed to
come down during a rapt silence from the audience, which
then broke into considerable applause.

No actors are more skilled than John Gielgud and Derek
Jacobi at keeping the meaning of a speech rippling clearly
along through mazes of clauses and parentheses in very long
sentences.

You will see the difficulties involved if you try these three
excerpts, which I won't mark up at all: I include them as they
are, as fine examples of complicated prose and verse, the like
of which you could well be faced with next time you are in a
broadcasting studio.

1. The opening paragraph of *The Life and Opinions of Tristram
Shandy* by Laurence Sterne:

I wish either my father or my mother, or indeed both of them, as they were in duty both equally bound to it, had minded what they were about when they begot me; had they duly considered how much depended upon what they were doing; – that not only the production of a rational being was concerned in it, but that possibly the happy formation and temperature of his body, perhaps his genius and the very cast of his mind; and, for aught they knew to the contrary, even the fortunes of his whole house might take their turn from the humours and dispositions which were then uppermost: – Had they duly weighed and considered all this, and proceeded accordingly, – I am verily persuaded I should have made a quite different figure in the world from that in which the reader is likely to see me – Believe me, good folks, this is not so inconsiderable a thing as many of you may think it; – you have all, I dare say, heard of the animal spirits, as how they are transfused from father to son etc, etc – and a great deal to that purpose: Well, you may take my word that nine parts in ten of a man's sense or his nonsense, his successes and miscarriages in this world depend upon their motions and activity, and the different tracks and trains you put them into, so that when they are once set a-going, whether right or wrong, 'tis not a halfpenny matter; – away they go cluttering like hey-go-mad; and by treading the same steps over and over again, they presently make a road of it, as plain and as smooth as a garden walk, which, when they are once used to, the devil himself shall not be able to drive them off it.

2. From *Eccentric Travellers* by John Keay, the subject here being William Gifford Palgrave, who travelled in the Middle East in 1862, on camel-back:

We were now traversing an immense ocean of loose reddish sand, unlimited to the eye and heaped up in enormous ridges running parallel to each other from north to south, undulation after undulation, each swell two or three hundred feet in height, with slant sides and rounded crests furrowed in every direction by the capricious gales of the desert. In the depths between the traveller finds himself, as it were, imprisoned in a suffocating sand-pit, hemmed in by burning walls on every side; while at other times, labouring up the slope, he overlooks what seems a vast sea of fire, swelling under a heavy monsoon wind, and ruffled by a cross blast into little red-hot waves. Neither shelter nor rest for eye or limb amidst torrents of light and heat poured from above on an answering glare from below.

3. A long, single sentence, spoken by Perpetua in Christopher Fry's play *Venus Observed*.

> There isn't any reason
> Why a sentence, I suppose, once it begins,
> Once it has risen to the lips at all
> And finds itself happily wandering
> Through shady vowels and over consonants
> Where ink's been spilt like rivers or like blood
> Flowing for the cause of some half-truth
> Or a dogma now outmoded, shouldn't go
> Endlessly moving in grave periphrasis
> And phrase in linking phrase, with commas falling
> As airily as lime flowers, intermittently,
> Uninterrupting, scarcely troubling
> The mild and fragile progress of the sense
> Which trills trebling like a pebbled stream
> Or lowers towards an oath-intoning ocean
> Or with a careless and forgetful music
> Looping and threading, turning and entwining,
> Flings a babel of bells, a carolling
> Of such various vowels the ears can almost feel
> The soul of sound when it lay in chaos yearning
> For the tongue to be created: such a hymn
> If not as lovely, then as interminable,
> As restless, and as heartless, as the hymn
> Which in the tower of heaven the muted spheres
> With every rippling harp and windy horn
> Played for incidental harmony
> Over the mouldering rafters of the world,
> Rafters which seldom care to ring, preferring
> The functional death-watch beetle, stark, staccato,
> Economical as a knuckle bone,
> Strict, correct, but undelighting
> Like a cleric jigging in the saturnalia,
> The saturnalia we all must keep,

Green-growing and rash with life,
Our milchy, mortal, auroral, jovial,
Harsh, unedifying world,
Where every circle of grass can show a dragon,
And every pool's as populous as Penge,
Where birds, with taffeta flying, scarf the air
On autumn evenings, and a sentence once
Begun goes on and on, there being no reason
To draw any conclusion so long as breath
Shall last, except that breath
Can't last much longer.

And now to balance these initial exercises for voice and speech, here are a few for your body.

Keep In Trim

Again, I wouldn't dream of pontificating on how you should keep in trim, except to say that any time you spend exercising your body to help keep it fit and strong will not be time wasted. An actor requires stamina. An actor needs to be well. He is, after all, someone who is looked at: stared at, even; so you will want to do everything you can to keep your appearance as you would like it to be. Exercise will help. The right food, and not too much of it, and not too many cigarettes will help, too. Of course there are parts for fat actors and if that's what you want, so be it. But it's easy to let yourself go unwittingly, and it's such a waste. And when you're not in trim it can be quite hard to get back, especially as you grow older.

Start From Scratch

All these initial exercises accompany my belief that acting, or rather good acting, is difficult enough without having to bother about a heap of extraneous things which can get in the way of whole-hearted concentration on a part. As I've said, if your speech is right, you don't have to bother about it. Similarly, if your body is right, you don't have to bother about it. Get your everyday self right, and your acting tasks will be halved: I'm such a believer in this that I'm going to dwell on it for some time. Whether you are indeed starting from scratch, or would like a quick overhaul, here are some of the things you can do. Use the mirror if you want to, but when you've got something really right in the mirror, go away from it and do the exercise again without it, so you *feel* the rightness of it rather than merely observe it.

1. Stand. Just stand. Look at yourself standing. Be conscious of relaxing your shoulders, arms and hands. The hands by your sides hang slightly forward, don't they? Stand with your feet slightly apart. Check your stance. Not too wide, not too turned out, just a little. Feet which are too turned out are hard to act on: circular moves become cumbersome, and corners too awkward to turn. Look at your head and neck. Relax them. And make sure your head is level. Neither up nor down. It is very desirable for an actor to have a level head. Turn your head, from side to side, and keep it level.

2. Walk. Go out for a walk. Don't hold anything in your hands and don't put them in your pockets. Let your arm-swing be as natural and as relaxed as possible and keep your head level.

Of course it is nice to hold things in plays, and to put your hands in your pockets, and it is nice to let your head go up and down when you want it to; but it is good to be able to do these simplified stances and walks until you feel comfortable doing them, because they will give you an ease.

If you feel easy in everyday life you will feel easier in plays.

3. Now go back to standing, and investigate, without holding anything, as many different positions of rest as you can think of. There are a lot, and it's worthwhile having as large a vocabulary of them as you can, because they will all come in useful some day. Investigate, particularly, positions for hands which are not identical: not both hands on hips, both hands behind your back, both in pockets, etc. This doesn't mean *never* have identical positions for your hands, but there's a tendency (you will have noticed it in plays) for identical positions to be over-used.

Once you've done this exercise thoroughly, and feel you have plenty of resources, forget it, and even more will occur to you involuntarily. But it's worth doing at some time or other: I recently met an actor who had hardly any resources at all, and it hampered him.

4. Look at your hands. I think a good actor's hand is one which is relaxed and in which all the fingers are visible, equally slightly curved, and slightly separated from each other. This doesn't mean (of course it doesn't) you can't point or clench your fists or strain your hands into peculiar shapes for certain gestures. But it is the hand to fall back on – the basic hand. And the basic gesture is one in which the power travels down the arm towards the hand *getting slightly less as it goes*, so that the hand does not easily become distorted by tension.

Do Everything Separately

You know that one where you pat the top of your head with one hand while doing circular movements round your tummy with the other? Or you pretend to be conducting an orchestra and strictly use the right hand for beating time and the left for expression or bringing in the instruments and not at all for beating time? Well, what follows is an extension of that.

Stand again. As in the previous exercise. And say a known speech. Anything. A nursery rhyme, a speech from a play you've done before, a poem or any of the speeches included here and there in this chapter and which you might like to learn for the specific exercises to which they apply. Stand and speak and do not move about. Do not fidget. Do not *accompany* your speech with anything. 'I felt quite proud of myself tonight,' said Hannah Gordon, after a performance of *Can You Hear Me at the Back?*, 'I managed that whole speech without a single gesture or twitch and with my hands by my sides.' And that she felt so triumphant about it, after several months in the play, shows just how difficult it can be. 'It felt good,' she said.

'It looked good,' I said.

Now add one thing. Allow yourself, say, the freedom to gesture with one arm and hand. Be sure that there is no accompaniment from the other. Find helpful gestures for 'Jack and Jill', 'Little Jack Horner', 'Little Miss Muffet' and others.

Nursery rhymes are useful for cultivating what I call 'echo' gestures, by which I mean gestures which are not a full-force indication of what happens, but a mere echo of it. We use echo gestures a great deal in everyday life, but they can easily get left out of plays. For example:

> Little Jack Horner
> Sat in a corner
> (*Well, if you're going to have any gestures at all you might as well indicate where the corner is. It could be with a full-arm point. But it needn't be. It could be only just indicated. Slackly. And is it a good idea to indicate the corner to your left if you're using your right hand, or to your right if using your left?*)
> Eating his Christmas pie.
> He put in his thumb
> (*See in your mind's eye what he does, then do half of it.*)
> And pulled out a plum
> (*This time a quarter.*)
> And said, 'What a good boy am I!'
> (*Anything at all?*)

Similarly, Jill can tumble downhill with an echo gesture, and Miss Muffet's tuffet is only just small, with a gesture similar to that which might accompany a line like, 'Of course I was only so high then.'

One more thing to notice, before you go on to the other hand: there is a tendency (especially in beginners) for the majority of gestures to be made with the palm of the hand turned outwards; a whole new range of possibilities can emerge from the hand which is turned the other way: I mean the hand which smooths a table-cloth.

Now try other gestures, expressive and nicely slack, with the other arm and hand, unaccompanied.

At last use both hands; but for the purposes of this exercise, avoid making identical movements with them. (You don't have to gesture all the time, incidentally! Only when you feel like it and you've got a good one.) What you could experiment with here is putting the main force of a gesture into one of your hands, while letting the other do a similar thing but with half the force, so that it accompanies the first, or is an echo of it. Very useful, this, and very natural.

Now add walking about, and stopping when you want to.

Finally, as the aim of this sequence of exercises has been to get your everyday speech and movement on the right lines and to give you a feeling of easy control, be just a bit aware of what you are doing as you stand and walk about at home and in the street, and talk to people. And watch how other people do it too.

NB: Since I wrote these last two exercises I have begun to study the Alexander technique. This has not made me want to alter what I have written here, except to add that the technique explores similar themes with a more fundamental penetration and depth.

Consider Your Qualities

'Oh, I don't know why some people get work while others don't,' said Patience Collier to me – years ago, but I've always remembered it. 'I suppose it's a mixture of talent, rightness for the part, and niceness. Probably in that order,' she added, cautiously.

Niceness. 'Oh I do like him', 'Oh I always like her': typical remarks from the public. This likeability is an important ingredient in a long career. What is it that makes people like an actor, that gives them that undefined feeling that if they met him they would take to him, no matter how bad-tempered or even evil he may be in a particular performance. Kindliness, or charm, will be at the base of him. If he is charming he will never have to 'act' it. He can go far away from it when he needs to. Only those who are not charming have to act it, and usually it doesn't seem to work, quite. It's like a posh voice: when people put it on, there's always something wrong.

Sincerity, warmth and humour are other desirable attributes. If you've got them you won't have to act them. So the greater your stock of qualities, including temperament, softness, sensitivity, ruthlessness, unpredictability and a capacity for rages, the less you have to pretend. Danger has long been regarded as very desirable, the sort of quality which makes stars. 'Richard Burton is fascinating,' said the director Brian G. Hutton one day while we were working on *Where Eagles Dare*, 'because he's so dangerous. You never quite know where you are with him. You're always on your guard. However charming he's being, affable and funny, you know there's something there, dormant now, but waiting to explode.'

Brightness is also very desirable. I don't mean just smiling, but a true, inner, energetic feeling, the sort of extrovert brightness all good comedians have. Though to have a nice smile is desirable too. I remember watching, at an award ceremony, Lee Remick weaving her endless way among the tables to collect hers for Best Actress. Her smile was bright, true and unflinching for the whole of that horrendous journey, and my neighbour Peter Jay, who also won an award, whispered to me, 'Americans are very good at that, you know. They work at it more than we do.'

I've put all this here, among the Exercises, hoping that you might like to make it one. Remember times past, times when you will have experienced all these feelings. Dredge around for them, search for as many details as you can. Check your moods and notice yourself.

For Concentration

The places we act in are full of distractions. In the theatre there are people in the wings, walking about and whispering, and in the auditorium there are latecomers and coughs in the wrong place. In film or television studios, or out on location, there are people herded behind the camera, or standing in your eyeline, shifting about restlessly and looking around, clicking stopwatches and checking the lighting. Even in a radio studio the clock ticks loudly; you can hear the Bakerloo Line if you're in the basement of Broadcasting House in London, and you watch, fascinated, as an actor turns the page of his script, oh so very slowly so as not to make a noise, and then at the last moment the paper cracks like a piece of sheet metal and everybody in the control room looks up, startled, wondering if it will mean a retake. An unheard discussion then takes place and, yes, sure enough, the scene is interrupted: 'Go back to speech three on page 46 and, Donald, it's all a bit slow, you know, that's why I'm going back so far, it's *frightfully* slow, so it wasn't just your script noise, Joan, I'd have gone back anyway, but do be careful everybody. All right. Green coming.' And you wait for the engineer to restart the tape and flick the green cue-light.

So an actor has to do everything he can to acquire the knack of being able to concentrate easily in order not to be deflected by all these distractions. Anyway it's much nicer to act when you're concentrating, and really 'in it', rather than merely observing what you are doing from somewhere outside yourself. And that, truly, is the difference that concentration makes.

Here are some exercises:

1. Try to think of anything you would like to think about for five consecutive minutes, undeflected, unhindered. Think through an argument, organise your reasons for your belief in something, go through details of a memory or of jobs to be done: something like that.

Make it easy for yourself, to start with, by doing this at home, alone, and with your eyes closed. Later, make it more difficult. Try it when you are in a bus or a train, or when you are walking down a street.

2. The important thing is to be able to concentrate *at will*. We can all concentrate when the mood takes us. For example, after you have been to see a really gripping film and you come out into the street afterwards, you know you have the mood of concentration. You know that the people you pass in the street (those who ignore you and those whose eyes you catch), the lighted shop windows, the traffic lights, the cars and buses and taxis swishing by, all have a heightened dramatic significance and you are part of the drama. It is tempting, no, it is delicious, when you get back home, to open your wardrobe door and look at yourself in a full-length mirror, and act out some tremendous scene. You are very dramatic, and full of meaning and intent. You are very talented. Was there, really, ever any doubt? If only people could see you now!

There is some conjunction, then, between concentration and talent. What you were doing was concentrating. What you felt was talent.

Notice and examine this mood when next you have it. It won't spoil it. It will teach you a lot.

3. Can you generate this after-cinema mood at will? It's hard. But try this:

Think: 'Let my thoughts go back from my eyes. Instead of projecting them forwards, out of me, let me keep them inside my head. Let them go back. Back to the back of my skull. My head contains my thoughts. They go back, back, back to the back of my head . . .'

Try it, easily, hypnotically, for a few minutes at a time.

4. At your party, play Kim's game. A tray is put in front of everyone for about three minutes with thirty to forty small articles (a pin, a penny, a nail file, etc.) on it. After it has been taken away, lists must be written of what was on it. He who remembers most wins. But subtract a mark for anything listed which was not on the tray.

5. Another game to make your party swing! You all sit round and the first player says, 'I went to market and I bought a bar of toilet soap.' The second player says, 'I went to market and I bought a bar of toilet soap and a second-hand vacuum-cleaner.' The third: 'I went to market and I bought a bar of toilet soap, a second-hand vacuum-cleaner and a pound of cooking apples.' And so on, round and round.

Notice the desperate devices you use to cling to your memory: the association of one article with another, consecutive articles which begin with the same consonant, or, more importantly, the association of the article with the person who thought of it. In the game I've just started here, you might think, ah yes, Joan always wants to be clean, ah, so does John, but round the house and, ah, in the house Marilyn likes to cook pork.

I once played this game with a class of twenty students, at the excellent City Lit. in Stukeley Street, as a rather frivolous end to a three-day seminar, and we managed to go round six times before everybody started to collapse. Not bad though: 120 articles, remembered in the right order!

6. And if your friends will still stay with you for another, more serious, exercise, you might like to try this one. I first saw it done in a television programme a long time ago, in which the late Harold Lang, a talented and volatile teacher, was taking a class of Central School students. They sat round in a semi-circle and, to a student at one end of it, Harold

Lang handed a piece of screwed-up paper. The paper had to be passed from one student to the next until it reached the end of the line; each time it represented some specific object: a mouse with a broken leg, a valuable small painting, a sparrow, a piece of very fragile glass. The purpose of the exercise was to point out the sort of concentration that objects command; and I remember Harold Lang being particularly emphatic about the difference between true, straight, unaffected concentration on the *object* and a self-indulgent concentration on their personal *reaction* to it. One student, in advance of receiving the paper the first time round, had obviously thought, I know, I'll act being squeamish about mice, and when it came to his turn his face was a model of distaste and displeasure. He was concentrating so hard on his face that he gave no thought to how he was actually handling the mouse, which, from his ridiculous grasp, would have escaped, or been dropped. The *task*, after all, was to receive a mouse and hand it on. The *mouse* had to be concentrated on, not the emotional reaction to it.

7. To follow from that, observe how you use objects in everyday life. Notice in particular the difference between the attention you pay to objects you know well and to those you don't know at all, like staircases, paintings, streets, ovens and kitchen utensils.

   Oh yes, there's a lot you can do in everyday life. But when it's done, it's done. Habits will be formed, and it won't be such an effort any more.

For Listening

Two simple exercises: one for practising listening, the other for observing it. Both are best done with a group of people.

1. Get someone to tell you a long tale: a personal reminiscence, or an event they witnessed, or the story of a film they have recently seen. After the tale is ended, you must relate as much as you can remember. Re-arrange the facts if you like. It's good to do this. Clarify them. But include them all. Add any observations you made about the story-teller's

attitudes to the subject. The story-teller and the others will mark you out of ten.

Good listening, like everything else, is habit-forming. 'I don't like her very much because she never listens,' said one actress about another. She was talking about her behaviour offstage, not on: but she didn't listen on, either. It was the word 'never', unstressed though it was, which was so indicting.

2. Recently I met two people who listened perfectly. One was a detective, the other a solicitor. Of course it is their job to listen; but what an object-lesson they both were! I met the detective in the company of other actors (he was giving advice about an investigation scene) and after he'd left us we exclaimed, severally, 'Did you notice how he answered Tony's long list of questions in the right order? Point one, he said, point two, and so on. He'd just stored them up.' 'Did you notice how still he was?' 'Yes, he didn't move his legs at all when he was sitting over there in the corner watching the scene. He didn't cross or uncross them or anything.' 'Yes, and his face was still, too, and gave nothing away. Only his eyes moved. He just . . . well . . . he just listened.' 'And watched.' Unforgettable, that afternoon's rehearsal.

And I thought again, when I was talking to the solicitor, privately this time, and watching him listening to me, that because there was so much energy going on in his head, there was none left for any fidgets or reactions. You can see the same thing on television when a politician receives complicated questions from an acute interviewer. You can see him storing them up, icily assessing them and sifting them and working out his necessarily edited replies.

The following exercise for observing listening adds one more ingredient: that of transferring attention from one person to another. So place two people, who will be the talkers, in chairs on either side of the room, and add the third, who will be the listener, between them, the arrangement to be something like this:

⊓

the listener's chair

⊏ the talkers' chairs ⊐

Ask the talkers to discuss any topic they mutually agree to. Ask the listener to listen and not to participate at all, but warn him that you will be asking him questions about the content of the discussion afterwards.

Watch the listener. How relaxed is his posture? How absorbed is he? If he is absorbed, how do you know? How does he transfer his attention from one to the other? Does he always look at each, full in the eye? Does he turn on cue? Or is there a delay? Does he know, instinctively, which of the two speakers is the protagonist at any given moment? If he does, does he ignore, at any rate physically, questions thrown in from the other? But if a question is an elaborate one, does he turn to the other in advance, waiting for the reply?

Of course, the listener here is in an extreme position: upstage centre. But if the listening has been good, you might have found he helped you, in the audience, to follow the discussion, instead of distracting from it, by guiding your attention to the most important place.

For Talking

This is my favourite exercise with which to start a class, or seminar, or workshop or whatever it's called, at the Actors Centre or wherever, because everyone learns a lot from it and it's such a good ice-breaker. It has the advantage of being as exciting for the onlookers as it is for the participants: it is like looking at life through a microscope.

I ask someone to volunteer to tell as personal a story as they will to one other member of the group, both sitting, the listener downstage of the talker. Particularly vivid in my memory are the story one girl told of what it was like giving birth, and details from another of the day she moved house and all the awkwardnesses involved. One boy told of an exhausting journey on a Greek ferry from Kos to Patmos and another described how, when he was a boy, he and a friend tired of throwing darts at a dartboard, so decided to throw them at each other, until one lodged itself firmly in the middle of his forehead.

There is no time limit. But after it is over I will ask the class if they think that, had it been learnt and acted instead of improvised, they would have judged it good. Or not.

'Oh yes, good,' chorused the class, after the girl's story of the birth of her baby.

'Why?' I asked.

'Well, because you could *see* it all. It was so vivid.'

'Why was it so vivid?'

'Well, because she was seeing it all herself. You knew it was true.'

'She was backing everything with pictures in her mind, was she?'

'She must have been. It was as if the words just floated out, because of what she saw and everything she'd gone through.'

'So you felt, did you, there was more going on inside her head than showed?'

'Oh yes.'

'More mental energy than physical?'

'Oh yes.'

'Yes. Anything else you noticed?'

'She laughed a lot. I mean it was a sad story, really, and painful too, but she smiled and laughed a surprising amount.'

'More, you think, than she would probably have done had it been a speech from a play?'

'Oh yes.'

'Yes. But it enhanced the sadness of the story, didn't it, that she didn't give in to it all the time?'

'Oh yes.'

'We laugh more in everyday life than we tend to in plays. Anything else? Did you think she was telling the story to that particular listener?'

'I did,' answered the listener, quickly.

'But she didn't look at you all the time, did she?'

'Oh no, but that was because she was so full of her story.'

'Anything else? What about her movements?'

'Her gestures? Well, they were all so natural.'

'Of course. They *were* natural. But in what way?'

'Well, they weren't too much. They seemed to accompany what was going on in her head. I mean when she said the baby was tiny she didn't sort of measure the baby, but she did a little, vague, movement bringing her hands slightly closer to each other.'

'Yes. The gestures were an echo of what was going on in her mind. Not an accurate description. Like when she said she'd had to traipse through the snow; she just did a to-ing and fro-ing with her shoulders, and you could feel the trudging, tiring steps.'

'Yes, and what I liked was the way she sometimes corrected herself.'

'Yes,' laughed the class, remembering.

'I mean, when she said, "I was twenty-three, oh no, I wasn't, I was twenty-four, just, it was just after my birthday," it was wonderful: she did it so quickly, and threw it away, and laughed.'

'Did you think, if that had been in a play, it would have been sufficiently entertaining? One would possibly have been tempted to put some moves in, I suppose, and there would have been no harm in that.'

'No, in fact I nearly got up once but then I thought no, he said sit,' said the girl.

The class laughed again.

'But even as it was, would it have been entertaining enough?'

'Oh yes.'

'Why?'

'Because it was so true.'

That was the first girl. Then the second got up. For her the task was slightly different because she knew what we would be looking for. Would this make her self-conscious? Curiously, it didn't seem to. Nor, curiously, does it ever. Occasionally I ask the volunteer to leave the room before telling their story, and ask the class to look for something specific which the performer will not know about, like the varying rhythms of speech, or the times when they look their listener full in the eye, or the revelations of their personality and attitudes yielded by the story and the way they tell it.

Try this exercise for yourself. Tell your stories to real or imaginary people. Place them in chairs so you know where they are.

All this is easy enough to do, because you know what you are talking about and have vivid pictures in your mind. In everyday life the thoughts come first, the words follow. In plays, because they have to be written down, the words come first. We have to work backwards, therefore, to support them with thoughts and pictures.

Try one or two of the following three speeches. Learn them and perform them, and see what happens as you get to know them really well and supply them with more and more background. No characterisation is needed. It's just you, talking to someone.

1. We sat there for ages at the top of the Downs. It was evening, and very still, and we looked out over the low-lying fields. We couldn't quite see the sea. We'd had a nice day, had lunch with some friends in a pub called . . . oh . . . er . . . I think it was called the Fox and Plough. I don't know. Doesn't sound right. It was nice. Beautiful garden, terribly hot today so we sat on a terrace which had a sort of translucent roof-thing over it. Sarah was very funny, telling us stories about Noël Coward, how he never liked to be seen, even by his closest friends, until he was bathed and shaved and groomed and dressed. Or half-dressed, trousers and shirt and tie and then a dressing-gown. I was glad of today, because I'd been feeling low . . . don't know why . . . just sort of vaguely miserable. Well, not so vaguely, perhaps. But . . . low. Yes. Funny. Anyway. We just sat there, amazed at the view. It got quite chilly, because it was about seven o'clock and the sun was getting low. But we'd had a good day. I think Jo enjoyed it too.

2. We spent Christmas that year at a small hotel in Buxton. It seemed convenient because I was working at Sheffield and only had Christmas Day off. We were doing our usual musical play for children and had given a performance on Christmas Eve and had two on Boxing Day. Anyway father came over for me and we drove to Buxton quite quickly, through Baslow, I think, and Bakewell. It was a very dark night, and we had to keep dipping the lights as cars passed. It was quite warm in the car and I'd got my presents all wrapped up in a box I'd got from the local greengrocers in Sheffield. It was on the back seat, and I occasionally looked round to see if it was all right. It was about . . . oh, well after midnight when we arrived. Mother and sister had gone to bed and father was tired so he went up straight

away. I stayed up a little while, talking to the owners, I've forgotten their names now, er . . . oh, it'll come to me. We had a drink, said Happy Christmas, and I was shown my room. I crept about so as not to waken anybody. I had a single bed which was against a wall, and there was a washbasin in the far corner by the window. I undressed quickly, had a wash and cleaned my teeth, and went to sleep. The following morning I was wakened by a tapping, quite loud, on the wall by my bed. 'Wake up,' I heard my mother say. 'Time to get up. It's eight o'clock.' Some more tapping. 'Are you awake?' So I tapped back, said, 'OK, OK,' and the tapping stopped. I looked at my watch and it was just after eight so I got up rather grumpily, I could have done with another hour, and went down for breakfast. 'Why did you wake me up?' I said to my mother. 'I didn't,' she said. 'You did. I heard you. You said it was eight o'clock and it was.' 'It wasn't me,' she said. 'Was it you?' I said, turning to my sister. 'No,' she said. 'Anyway,' said my mother, 'it couldn't have been any of us because we're on a different floor. We're on the second, and you're on the third.' 'How odd,' I said. And after breakfast I went upstairs to have a look at the room next to mine. It was locked, and it didn't have a number on the door. And when I asked the owner he said, 'Oh we never use that room, it's always locked. We keep our junk in there.' I never got to the bottom of it, but I know I hadn't dreamt it . . .

3. After the funeral everybody came home. It was a relief to drive back at normal speed instead of that ritual slowness which made the journey there seem endless. Pointless, really, just done for tradition's sake. Holding up the traffic because they're not supposed to pass, and everybody in the street stopping to stare. Why point it out to everybody, I thought. But, as I said, the journey back was better, and there were about thirty people, and we'd worked all morning cutting up the meats, and making the salads, and doing the bread and butter, and covering it with a wet handkerchief so it wouldn't go dry. We'd got quite a lot of drink in and people could have what they liked. We were a solemn lot as we traipsed into the house, and people said things like, 'Oh it's very sad, isn't it?' and 'We shall miss him, you

know.' But I felt a curious kind of elation. He'd been so terribly ill and he didn't want any more of it and had said so and, well, I don't know, I was a bit mixed up, really. But I wasn't . . . downcast or anything like that and anyway, here we were, having a party. So all we could do was make the party go. Well, the drink went straight to Auntie Renie's head and she became very jolly, talking about her family and what they'd all been up to, and this seemed to catch on, this jollity, and everybody said how nice the food was and we really shouldn't have gone to all this trouble; and when we were all sitting round having coffee and talking in little groups, Auntie Nellie, who comes from Halifax, suddenly said rather loudly so everybody stopped talking and listened to her, 'Oh, you know, I shouldn't say this, but it's been a really good do. It's been really enjoyable. And I think your father would have liked that.' And everybody went quiet, thinking about him for a little while.

You could make up similar stories of your own. If you do, try to recall the experience in as great detail as possible. Don't try to feel, merely recall the detail. If you've got a recorder and a microphone you could tell a story into it, learn it and perform it, keeping the tape as a guide as to how it originally sounded when it was fresh and spontaneous, because freshness and spontaneity are of course what this exercise is all about.

Pay Attention

Two speeches now, to concentrate your attention not so much on the substance of what you are saying as on whom you are saying it to.

You are addressing two people, Peter and Paul. They are on either side of you, downstage of you. Choose good moments for looking at Peter, good ones for Paul, and good ones for using the space between them. Easy enough, obvious really, to find them in Speech A, where the direction of each thought is implied by the sentences. Speech A tells you how to do the exercise. Speech B is less clear, but should be as clearly marked by you as the first.

   1. Yes, Peter, yes. I *think* so. What do you think, Paul? Do you think Peter's right? I'm in two minds about it, really.

On the one hand I see your point, Peter, but on the other I'm not sure. Oh Paul, come on, you must have an opinion. I wish I knew what to do. What shall I do? Paul?

2. I know what I'll do: I'll go and see someone else ... someone I knew a long time ago. He should be able to help. Funny, isn't it, when you *need* help it doesn't seem to be forthcoming? Well, one day anyway. One day it'll all be sorted out. Yes, I'll go and see Patrick, I think. Do you remember him? It's ... oh ... five years since I've seen him. He lives in Wandsworth now.

Try the same exercise (talking to more than one person, more than two if you like, and using the spaces between them) with other speeches that you know, or perhaps with the speeches in the previous exercise.

Divide Your Attention

Now, use those same speeches to practise dividing your attention between talking to someone and doing something else at the same time, like:

> sharpening a pencil,
> making yourself up,
> polishing shoes,
> washing up,
> knitting,
> eating,
> drinking,
> reading a newspaper,
> going for a walk,
> driving a car,
> being a passenger in a car, looking at the view,
> looking out of a window,
> looking out of a window, waiting for someone.

I like this exercise because it tells you so much. It tells you the places in the speech where you must give it your whole attention and stop doing the other task (except driving, of course!) for a moment. It tells you the peaks, therefore. It sways the speech, gives it its ups and downs.

But when you are doing it, remember that the other task must be done. It is important to get that pencil sharpened. And sharpened properly: if the content of your speech is full of passionate emotion, beware of taking it out on the pencil, otherwise you'll break the lead. I once saw an actor taking it out on a pair of shoes he was supposed to be polishing: he was getting very worked up about something, and because the brush and the shoes were getting equally worked up, you knew that the shoes weren't being polished properly. They were just smothered in the stuff. So it all looked ridiculous.

What's Your Continuity?

'Continuity' is the connection of things: one minute with the next, one day with the next. It is an underlying mood, induced by the sort of person you have become and the circumstances you find yourself in. If, for example, things have become very bad for you, your continuity will be one of depression; but that does not mean that everything you do within that continuity is necessarily depressed. A cup of tea can taste nicer than on a happy day, an affectionate word can be more welcome, a joke more of a release. The fact that you are depressed makes certain things better.

It's like the sea. The continuity is the water underneath. The water underneath and the surface are of course one and the same thing but they appear to be different and have different qualities. There could be no surface without the water underneath. And the underneath is vast and changes only slowly. The surface is smooth or choppy, and always changing. It is the surface which is pelted by the rain, warmed by the sun, whipped up by the wind; it is on the surface, too, that traffic moves.

Or, really, it's more like a river. There is the water underneath and there is the surface. It is the surface which is cut through by the ships (the people who cut through you); it is the surface which is influenced by the weather (all those external things which influence you), which sparkles in the sunshine and which is darkened by the shadows of bridges (your minor ups and downs). But a river is going somewhere, and the water underneath and the water on the surface travel together, widening and deepening as they go.

It is essential to find the flow of your continuity through a part. It is what unifies it, binds it together, prevents it from being a mere assemblage of bits and pieces. 'How could she laugh like *that* when she's feeling like *that*?' we can often ask of someone's jerky performance. It isn't that she laughed which we query, it is the way she laughed, which seemed unconnected with what had happened previously.

In a poorly written play, one without depth or imagination, or with a poorly written part, one which is nothing more than a pawn in the author's story-telling game, you will have to invent your own continuity in order to give it any life at all.

Refer again to the three speeches at the end of the exercise For Talking (pp. 126–28). Try doing them with different continuities. In speech 1, how low are you? Why? Low enough not to snap out of it despite a good day? Or happy enough to have forgotten the temporary low spirits, finding them now hard to imagine, like a cold when you're better.

In speech 2 how dismissive are you of the mysteries of the tapping on the wall? Or has it remained an intriguing reminder of your belief that 'there are more things in heaven and earth . . .'?

In speech 3 you can choose between various underlying moods: dislike of the rituals of cortèges and funerals, sadness at the loss of a parent in spite of laughs at the party, or relief that the painful days of a terminal illness are over and surely it's better now to celebrate the life than to mourn the death.

For Relationships

Use the same speeches, or any others that you know (and knowing them is important: you will get far less from these exercises if you just read them), and do them as though you are speaking to:

> your little child,
> your teenage son,
> your best friend,
> someone to whom you are newly attracted,

your lover,
your family,
your boss,
a stranger.

For Intentions

What do you intend to achieve by what you are doing? Try the same speeches with the following intentions:

to entertain your guests at a dinner party;

to make someone, whom you suspect doesn't like you, sympathise with you;

to have the last word with someone: you've got to go, you're in a hurry, and this must be the end of the conversation;

to recall the events for a psychiatrist, in the hopes that it will clarify for him your attitudes and opinions;

to talk frankly to someone you hardly know in the hopes that they will be prepared to reveal more about themselves;

to make conversation, trying to get your mind off something which is really worrying you: to cheer yourself up;

to convince a detective, who had accused you of being somewhere else on that particular day, that you were not lying;

to cheer up someone dear to you who is very ill in hospital.

Use Your Imagination

This exercise is not as frivolous, nor in some cases as easy to do, as it may look.

Mary had a little lamb
Whose fleece was white as snow,
And everywhere that Mary went
The lamb was sure to go.

It followed her to school one day,
Which was against the rule:

It made the children laugh and play
To see the lamb at school.

Try this nursery rhyme in the following ways:

as if you can't quite remember it: you have only just learnt it;

as if you are making conversation to a stranger, in any place, while waiting for someone else to turn up;

as a sermon about Mary and Jesus;

as cocktail-party chat;

as cocktail-party chat when some piece of your clothing – a belt, braces, a suspender belt – has broken;

as cocktail-party chat: a very full cocktail-party, this, so you have to stand close to people and shout;

as if you've got the giggles about something else (like you do in plays);

as if you are drunk;

as part of an electioneering address by a junior education minister;

as if talking to someone you love, but you haven't told them yet;

as a voice-over for a television commercial for wool;

as if to a foreigner with very little knowledge of English;

as if to tell a young girl why she can't take *her* pet animal to school;

as if you are the director of a film to be called *Mary*, telling the story to an actor up for the small part of the headmaster;

as if, in the course of an interview for a part you badly want, you are telling the director the story of the last film you were in;

as if talking to someone who is wearing a toupee for the first time and you're determined not to look at it;

as if you are a guide showing people round an art gallery; you are describing a picture of Mary and her lamb at school; you've had the job for five years and it's the end of a gruelling day;

as if you are a Sunday-school teacher taking the toddlers' class;

as if the lamb has just died;

as if Mary has just died;

as if you are a television newscaster reading an obituary about Mary, using an auto-cue.

Improvisation

The classes I used to take in improvisation at RADA were some of the most exciting the students and I ever experienced, and when the two participants became really involved in the story the rest of us would sit riveted, wondering what they would do and how it was going to turn out and what emotions would be forthcoming. We watched them with penetrating eyes, and afterwards discussed details of the feelings, the actions and the development of the story, with the relish of knowing we had observed, and therefore, in the heat of it all, discovered new facets of human behaviour.

It had been Anne Kimbell, an American actress who had studied under Lee Strasberg at the Actors Studio in New York, who told me how to set an improvisation. 'Arrange it so that the actors start at the moment of inevitable clash,' she said, while we were having tea at Valoti's in Shaftesbury Avenue, after a matinée of *Roar Like a Dove*, which we were both in. 'So limit it to just two people. It works better. It's less complicated. Tell them a long story of their past lives, leading them nearer and nearer to the moment of crisis. Give them enough specific facts to build on, so they don't have to invent any. I mean it makes an improvisation impossible if, for example, one partner in a marriage says to the other, "You know that time when you got out a knife and threatened me with it?" and the other is taken totally by surprise because it wasn't included in the lead-up story. The whole point of choosing a peak moment of clash is that it will then be a question of will against will, and nothing at all to do with making up dialogue. A bad improvisation would be one which was set like this: "So you're waiting outside this movie-house, see, and your girl-friend is late and you look at your watch and think, hell, is she coming or isn't she, and then you notice this girl, also waiting, also impatient, so you go over to her and talk. OK? Let's see what happens." All they would have to do is make up dialogue or, if they've any sense at all, say, "I know, there's a coffee-shop over there, let's go and have a coffee," and exit. Anyway, the winner would be the one who could talk the best. And that's not fair. And it's not what it's about.

'So. A few "don'ts", Peter. Don't set a time limit: let them go on until the situation is resolved or there's a stalemate. Don't let them characterise, because that gets in the way: they start concentrating on it. And don't, as I say, let them invent anything about their past lives. That means your story will have to supply them with a lot of facts, and last for some time. This will establish a mood, too, in the classroom. Don't rush anything, but be sure that when you leave off they've got to solve the problem, right now.'

Here's an abbreviated version of one of the stories I evolved. I tried to include in all of them experiences with which drama students could easily identify: some of them were therefore perilously close to home. I'll call the couple here John and Diana.

To John I would say, 'You are you,' and to Diana, 'You are you. With these differences:'

To John: 'You were born of rich parents, who live in Alderley Edge, a smart outer suburb of Manchester where your father was and still is the Chairman and Managing Director of a successful business, manufacturing medicines and drugs. The firm has been in the family for generations and has never ceased growing. You were brought up in the lovely Cheshire countryside, attended a local prep school and eventually went to Rugby. You were an only child and have always been rather pampered. Your favourite toy had been a model theatre, and you acted quite a lot at school and once with a local dramatic society where you were pronounced "good". So with no other particular talent rising you thought you might as well have a go at being an actor. You'd heard it provided a fairly easy life once you got started, and you knew you had a nice voice and a pleasant appearance. You'd also heard it was an attractive profession socially, especially at a drama school where there were bound to be a lot of pretty girls. Your parents did not object openly to your idea: in fact your mother was quite pleased and enjoyed telling her friends that her son was going to be an actor. So on the strength of your good voice and appearance, and with the aid of plenty of coaching, you got into RADA. Once there, you just managed to get by: you were not highly regarded vocationally, but socially and sexually you were as successful as you had anticipated. You were a popular boy.'

To Diana: 'Your parents were less well-off and you have a younger brother, Jonathan, who also wants to be an actor but who, so far, after many attempts, has failed to get into a drama school. He is beginning to feel he must be hopeless and may well soon opt for a course at a teaching college so that he can teach English, which is his next favourite subject. If he does so he will be following in your father's footsteps, as he is the senior English master at the comprehensive school at Enfield which you attended. You were very successful there, being clever at nearly everything without having to work too hard: this was because you found most of the subjects, from maths to athletics, so interesting that it took the slog out of it all. You converted enjoyment into success. You were the leading light of the dramatic society and when, each year, it produced the set 'O'-level Shakespeare, you were Viola, Portia and, eventually, Lady Macbeth. You knew, as everybody knew, that you were going to be an actress. You auditioned for RADA and got in.'

To both: 'I can tell you this summary of your lives before you met because obviously you will have told each other. You met at RADA, you were in the same class, you found each other attractive but did not have an immediate affair: your friendship grew slowly and deepened slowly; and only eventually did you realise you were very much in love. You married while you were still there, in your final term. You, Diana, moved into John's flat, which was adequate (the rent being paid by his father) and in the University area of Bloomsbury. You were idyllically happy. As far as your careers at RADA were concerned yours, John, was unremarkable, but yours, Diana, went from strength to strength: you won several prizes and at the annual competition, attended by casting directors, agents and others, you were snapped up by a top agent, Julian Belfrage, of Leading Artists Ltd, and you immediately landed a leading role in a television series, starring Ian Holm and Denholm Elliott, called *The Well*. Your photograph appeared on the cover of the *Radio Times* with your two co-stars and you scored a major personal success when the series was shown.

You, John, got nothing from the same competition. No

agent seemed interested: and when you rang round you were unable to speak to any of them personally. Secretaries intervened. You wrote letters and got some replies, the most encouraging being from the casting director of Granada Television who said he would bear you in mind whenever he was casting a new play or series. As yet, though, there was no work, and Diana was out all day rehearsing or recording, and sometimes staying away for days on end, filming the outside sequences for *The Well* in Hampshire. You looked after the flat, did the shopping, cooked the meals and washed up.

'From *The Well* you received several offers, Diana, and you asked John for his advice. You always got him to read any scripts which arrived and growingly you relied on his judgment. You agreed that the most attractive of the immediate offers was a sequence of four separate two-hour plays for television in the *Thriller* series for London Weekend. This also involved a considerable amount of filming away from home, and very long hours.

'You were still happy together and glad of the albeit curtailed times when you were both at home. Work for you, John, remained hard to get, although you did have a tiny part in one episode of a Granada series called *Tales of Hadrian's Wall*. Happily your time away, when you lived at home at Alderley Edge, coincided with Diana's filming for *Thriller*.

'You both realised that the conventional husband-and-wife roles were being reversed. Diana was the bread-winner, out all day, obsessed with work, delighting in it, but getting tougher in the process. You said to him one evening, "I don't want to get hard but, really, if you don't stand up for yourself people ride rough-shod over you: I mean, if it's a bad line I ask for it to be changed, and if I don't like a move I say so." Your confidence was growing and you received a lot of praise.

'Your confidence, John, was withering, and you surprised yourself one evening by confessing to Diana that if you got a part now you'd be terrified of being inadequate in it. "I think I must be hopeless," you said, "otherwise people would want me . . ."

'After *Thriller*, Diana, you had a film-test for a starring role in *Dark Angels*, which was to be Michael Caine's new picture. This was about a year ago. You got the part. Nothing, you felt, could stop you now. The flat in Bloomsbury was suddenly no longer adequate and together, before the film started, you looked for somewhere else to live and found a pleasant unpretentious house with a large garden in Weybridge. A mortgage was easily forthcoming on the strength of Diana's earnings, and you both enjoyed choosing curtains and carpets and furnishings, and arranging it all. You had a very happy two months together, undisturbed by work, though sometimes, when John started in the garden or did an extra job in the kitchen, you Diana, would disappear upstairs, to do some learning. And when the telephone rang, as it often did, it was nearly always for you.

'Filming started. First of all there were six weeks in the south of France, followed by four months at Pinewood for which you had to be up at six o'clock most mornings, arriving back at around seven-thirty most evenings. John always had dinner ready for you. You acquired a daily woman, who comes three mornings a week, and, at your instigation, John, a dog, a Yorkshire terrier called Hunter. You take him for walks every day.

'Diana was beginning to think that a certain amount of entertaining was now a necessary accompaniment to her work, so friends from the studio were occasionally brought back for dinner. Prepared, of course, by John.

'After *Dark Angels*, which finished shooting about four months ago, there was a lull in Diana's work. But there were invitations to First Nights, film premieres, and lunches at grand hotels. These gave you, John, no pleasure at all and you said so, but you insisted, Diana, that they were important, very good for publicity and, as you said to him, "Who knows, something good may well come of it all for you? And, anyway, it's fun."

'Your new film is called *The Bright Day* and for the first time you have top billing. Your co-star is your old friend Ian Holm. Just before production starts you have a serious talk one night about children, and you make it quite clear, Diana, that now is the wrong time to start a family. You could not afford the time off required for the pregnancy, and you would not have the time, either, to look after a young child as a mother should. "We can afford a nanny," said John, "and I can do a lot of the looking after that has to be done."

'"But what happens if you get a job?" said Diana. "And anyway I don't want to have a nanny looking after my child."

'*The Bright Day* started shooting six weeks ago and Diana's routine is again a gruelling one.

'A week ago a letter arrived for you, John, from your father. He said he wanted to talk to you and asked that you visit them for a few days.'

At this point I ask John to leave the room so that I can talk to Diana alone.

'When John is away, and you wonder what his visit up north is all about, you realise that you still love him a great deal. You are surprised how much you miss him. He has become your home. And for you the arrangement is perfect. You wish he were happier and had more work but at least he is no competition for you and his softness and your ambition go well together in your eyes. You are regarded as a happy couple enjoying a happy marriage and you know that this is good for your career. You would acknowledge, if pressed, that sometimes his diffidence and reticence in public irritate you, but you do everything you can to hide that. You would acknowledge, if pressed further, that your rapid success carries strain somewhere within it and that you are not necessarily happier or easier to live with because of it. Are you becoming hard? Are you becoming selfish? No, you cry convincingly, not selfish, not at all: after all, I'm paying for him. You have been tempted, from time to time, to sleep with other men, especially when filming away from home, but have so far resisted the temptation. It is a growing possibility that you will yield to it one day; John is wonderful to you in many ways, but he is not exciting any more and grows less so in your eyes.

'While he is away you are sent a play to read. It is called *First and Foremost*, it is by Simon Gray, the part is excellent, though one of a team, and an impressive list of names for the cast is being approached by the director Harold Pinter. It would do you good, you know; your first love is still the theatre. A six-week pre-London tour is envisaged and, from your reading of the play, it should be an enormous success when it arrives in the West End. Julian Belfrage has told you that you will have a good salary but that you will have to agree to a nine-month run in London. You are very tempted indeed, especially as it will give you, once it has opened, far more time at home. This is good news. You can't wait to tell John about it and get him to read it and ask his opinion. Michael Codron, who is putting it on, has already telephoned to ask what your reaction is. You stalled, saying you hadn't quite finished reading it yet. It's obvious he's anxious for a quick reply.'

Then I ask Diana to leave the room and send John in.

'You are very dissatisfied, John. You're not exactly jealous but you hate the role you have come to play, that of the one who looks after the house and garden, who does most of the shopping and is always in the background. Even the move to Weybridge has not helped: in fact it's made matters worse because it's taken you further away from your old RADA mates and any other friends you made while you were there. You are lonely, and feel out of it all; the people who come to your house are her friends and not yours. You still love her, though she is not as sweet and loving as she used to be. Her obsession with her career is making her hard, in your view, and self-sufficient. You do not see how the marriage can last. You want children and you need to be the master. You suspect she has been unfaithful to you, especially when she went to the south of France, but the subject has never come up and you have no proof at all.

'You tell your mother and father quite a bit about all this. Your father, in return, tells you he is retiring in a year: he asked you to come home to discuss the possibility of your taking over the firm. It would involve spending the coming year preparing for it by studying each department from the chemists' to the accountants'. The job would carry a large salary, to be agreed, which would be increased generously from time to time and which would enable you to live at least as well as in Weybridge. You would of course have to move to the Manchester area, choosing, no doubt, one of the smarter outer suburbs. Not necessarily Alderley Edge.

'It all seems exactly what you want. You already have a considerable knowledge of and interest in pharmaceutics, on account of hearing so much about them when you were a boy. You have always known secretly that your father was a little disappointed when you opted for the stage, while he and your mother have known for sometime that you are unhappy about the lack of work. For Diana, well, it would be a very hard decision for her to agree to move up north. Her career would be impossible. But this could carry many advantages: you could raise a family, she would become something of a legend, and she would, you are sure of it, revert to her old self again, because you are equally sure that if she persists in her career she will harden beyond endurance, grow less happy rather than more, and probably become promiscuous. And you couldn't bear that. You have remained utterly faithful to her throughout your married years. She may well regard the whole idea as an impossibly dreary alternative to her present mode of living, but you are sure that with the extra care and attention and love you would give her she would not find it nearly as dull as she may expect. And it needn't be the end of her career. She could work from time to time. But your present role-playing is impossible, your attitude to it will deteriorate rather than improve, and you would like to be the breadwinner.

'Your father has said he would like an answer very soon. In fact he has said, "When you've talked it over with Diana, ring me." The train journey back to Euston and on to Weybridge seems endless.'

Diana comes back into the room. The time of day is established (Diana home first from the studios, John back at, say, eight-thirty p.m.) and the two of them plan the room together: which room it is, where the doors are, what furniture there is, what it looks like. Are there any drinks? Newspapers? Books? What lights are on, and is there a telephone? It's better to have props than to mime, but the important thing is to agree what there is.

Then, with a final reminder that there is no time limit and a reiterated warning against inventing any further details of the past, John leaves the room to give Diana a minute or two to be alone at home. When he is ready he returns and the improvisation begins.

For those who perform, it is an unforgettable experience; for those who watch, an engrossing, even educating, play.

Telephone Conversations

This and the next two exercises are again for two people and it is probably best to start by improvising them. However, you will not reap the benefit they can give unless you then write down what you say, or at any rate consolidate the words in your minds so that you can repeat them exactly, as you would in a play. Do not characterise: just be yourselves, and make the conversations as trivial as you like.

So, for this one: improvise, then write and learn, the two sides of a telephone conversation. Include in it:

talking at the same time as each other,
interrupting each other,
laughing at something the other person has said,
being distracted by someone else or something in the room you are in.

Perform the entire conversation together, if possible using two prop telephones.

Then perform the two sides separately. What adjustments do you have to make so that your part of the conversation is *entertaining* enough on its own? Certainly you will want to speed up what the other person says, because he has now become a silence. But not too much. Do you want to make your listening more active? Perhaps a little. But not too much.

This is one of my favourite exercises because you learn, merely by doing it, all you need to know about telephone conversations. They're easy. It's such a pity they are so often done badly.

Getting About

Improvise, write and learn your own scene to incorporate a lot of moves hither and thither. The kitchen, with all its activities, is a nice room for this, although it could be more general housework or preparing a room for a party or anything like that. Use as many objects as you can and, by turning your attention as early as you can from one thing to the next, do the scene as quickly as possible. Make a rule: no pauses!

I won't write a whole scene, because you will want one to fit where you are and what you've got and what you want to do. But here's a brief example of the sort of thing I mean:

> (*It's her kitchen. He is the visitor. She is cutting some bread.*)
>
> SHE: Darling, you lay the table will you? The knives and forks are there (*she goes slightly towards where they are*),

the mats are over there (*ditto*), and you'll find the salt and pepper in that cupboard (*she starts to return to the bread, while he gets the knives and forks*). Hell, the bacon needs turning (*she goes to the oven*).

HE: I'll do it (*he makes for the oven*).

SHE: No no, it's all right. I can manage. What are you doing there?

HE: Looking for the salt and pepper.

SHE: No, it's not that cupboard, it's that one.

HE: Oh sorry. Look, the eggs are sticking. I'll do that.

SHE: All right, thanks. Kitchen utensils in that drawer.

It's good to be nimble when you've got to be, and get those feet going round the room.

Standing Around

Improvise, write, learn and perform a duologue for standing around, the way people do. Circle round each other a bit, as people do when they talk at street corners. Take it outside, and do it at a street corner! Or on a walk. Or in a queue. Or in a room. Don't hold anything and don't hide your hands.

Bad Habits

This is a check-list of the more common bad habits. They are only bad, incidentally, if they are indeed habits and you do them, therefore, too much or too often. The best remedy is to acknowledge the habit and refuse to allow yourself to indulge in it *at all* for some time, until you realise how much better you are without it. So here's the list, with some suggestions for exercises:

Fidgeting.

Go through, right through, the exercises called Start From Scratch, and Do Everything Separately.

Perpetual use of restricted gestures: cramped, and from the elbows only.

Say 'I open my arms like a cross.' During 'I open my arms,' raise both arms, parallel and forwards, fully extended, to shoulder-height: and during 'like a cross', open them fully sideways, like a cross, still at shoulder-height.

Repeating the same gesture too often, especially if it isn't a good one anyway.	Enlarge your vocabulary of gestures.
Fading out at the ends of sentences, or fading in at the beginnings.	Say any nursery rhyme so that each line is consistently loud from its first to its last word, but change the volume for each new line: '(*very loud*) Mary had a little lamb (*whisper*) Whose fleece was white as snow, (*medium loud*) And everywhere that Mary went (*quietly*) The lamb was sure to go.'
Going blank at the ends of sentences.	Again use a nursery rhyme, but this time put enormous pauses between each line, and carry the thought, and therefore the expression, of the line you have just uttered, right through the pause. 'Mary had a little lamb (*pause, pause, pause, think of the lamb, think of the lamb, think of the lamb, pause, pause*) Whose fleece was white as snow (*pause, pause, think of the snow, think of the fleece, pause, pause, pause*) . . .' And so on.
Being too regularly intense, which is often accompanied by being too wide-eyed.	Relax in a chair or sofa, as you might on a psychiatrist's couch, and do known

speeches, perhaps from the part you are now studying, as though dreaming them, through half-closed eyes, without ever looking at the person addressed. Talk to him as it were, through the ceiling.

Blinking.

Wrinkling the forehead too much.

Using nods of the head for emphasis.

Joining the first word of the next sentence to the end of the present sentence, pausing, and repeating it: 'I went home. I . . . I didn't feel very well. I . . . I wanted to lie down; and . . . and have a good cry. So . . . So when I got home I went upstairs. And . . . And I lay on my bed and . . . and cried.'

Repeating the first words of a sentence: 'But but I don't understand you.' After after I'd done that . . .'

Stopping at all the full stops.

Running sentences into each other too glibly.

Coming in on cue too glibly.

Listen, right up to the final consonant. Remember: you have to pretend you've never heard it before.

Dipping your eyes on the turn from one character to another, especially on the stage when they are on either side of you.

Do the Pay Attention exercise (pp. 128–9) and keep your eyes up as you turn between Peter and Paul.

Being unable to take inflections.

Everyone knows that giving inflections is rather frowned upon nowadays, but directors often have to have recourse to it, as it's a quick way of getting results. When a radio play has to be recorded in a day, or a commercial in fifteen minutes, there's precious little time for lengthy reasonings. It is dreadfully shaming, on such occasions, if you can neither hear nor repeat an inflection, and you'll just have to work at it. And it isn't nearly so bad a way of directing as some people think: it is shorthand, after all, and avoids tedious explanations which are often more harming than helpful.

Talking to the audience instead of to the other characters.

Being a ham.

Being a hack.

Never, never say, 'Well, as long as they pay me . . .'

Special Skills

If you've got any, you might as well make the most of them, as you never know when they will come in useful and indeed be a contributing reason for getting a job.

The Spotlight now sends us all an Artists' Accomplishments Form with a daunting list of little boxes to tick if you can do, and do well, what it says. Foreign languages and accents, dialects, types of dancing, singing, sports ('please insert ONLY if you are of above average ability') and Special Skills ('e.g. Flying, Juggling, Mime and any other unusual qualifications of high standard').

I would add, as very desirable skills, on which the landing of a part can often depend: horse-riding, driving, swimming and all sorts of fighting. Never say you can do something when you can't, and come clean straight away if you see that a part requires, say, that you drive a car and you're a non-driver (if the director really wants you he'll be able to accommodate your inability, but if you don't tell him in advance so that he can plan what to do about it, he'll just be cross); and be sure that, if you claim to be able to do a regional accent, it is an accurate one, belonging to a place or a county, and not just vaguely Scottish, north country, or posh.

Have Party Pieces Ready

Eric Portman said, 'Any actor worth his salt will have some party pieces ready.' We are entertainers, after all, and are often asked to get up and do something, either at a house party or at a charity function. It's nicer to be able to say yes than no. It's easier.

So why not search for and learn one or two? It's a change from searching for and learning audition speeches, which I'll come on to now.

Auditions

When someone comes on to a stage or into a room, you notice first of all what they look like, then what they sound like, and then you wonder if they are any good or not.

There are two kinds of auditions: those at which you will be asked to perform speeches you have learnt and those at which you are asked to read for a particular part.

You will certainly need audition speeches if you want to get into a drama school or a permanent repertory company; but any director casting a play or film might well ask you to show him a piece or two you have prepared.

I think the thing is to keep increasing your stock of pieces whenever you can so that you can pick and choose, and not always have to do the same old thing which can so easily go off and get stale; and when you are choosing your pieces to be sure to cast yourself well. Use them to show the director what you are like. Let one contrast well with another, but don't attempt to be versatile, unless you think versatility is your strong point. Variety, not versatility.

The best audition speeches are those which are self-sufficient, needing little preamble, avoiding, therefore, this sort of introduction: 'Well, you see, the thing is this character has just come back from a party, which she didn't enjoy very much, and when she got home she was surprised to find a note waiting for her, and in this note it said a friend of hers was very ill and would she go round as soon as possible, but then there was a knock on the door, and it was the woman from the upstairs flat who was in a desperate state so this character just had to spend some time with her, all the while knowing that her friend was waiting for her . . .'

No. A self-sufficient speech. A memory. A story. Everyone loves a story. It doesn't have to be amusing, but it's no bad thing to get a laugh or two. It doesn't *have* to be from a play. It can be a poem, a piece of narrative from a novel or from the Bible, or a speech of your own which you've composed and learnt.

If it is from a play, know the play and not just the speech. Know where it comes in the play and what the story is at that point.

Here is a most arbitrary list of plays which contain ideal audition material:

Make and Break by Michael Frayn,
Duet for One by Tom Kempinski,
Season's Greetings by Alan Ayckbourn,
Way Upstream by Alan Ayckbourn,
Intimate Exchanges by Alan Ayckbourn,
Henceforward by Alan Ayckbourn,
The Dresser by Ronald Harwood,
The Real Inspector Hound by Tom Stoppard,
Night and Day by Tom Stoppard,
The Real Thing by Tom Stoppard,
Travesties by Tom Stoppard,
The Deep Blue Sea by Terence Rattigan,
The Beastly Beatitudes of Balthazar B by J. P. Donleavy,
Tonight at 8.30 by Noël Coward,
Dear Octopus by Dodie Smith,
After the Rain by John Bowen,
Not Quite Jerusalem by Paul Kember,
A Man for All Seasons by Robert Bolt,
Murder in the Cathedral by T. S. Eliot,
Can You Hear Me at the Back? by Brian Clark,
The Caretaker by Harold Pinter,
The Homecoming by Harold Pinter,
Strindberg by Colin Wilson,
Plenty by David Hare,
A Map of the World by David Hare,
Teeth 'n' Smiles by David Hare,
Equus by Peter Shaffer,
The Royal Hunt of the Sun by Peter Shaffer,
The Public Eye by Peter Shaffer,
Bent by Martin Sherman,
Destiny by David Edgar,
Made in Bangkok by Anthony Minghella,
Camille by Pam Gems,

Beside Herself by Sarah Daniels,
Another Country by Julian Mitchell,
Red Devils Trilogy by Debbie Horsfield,

and most of the plays by Christopher Hampton, Peter Nichols, Joe Orton, John Osborne, Arnold Wesker, Hugh Whitemore and Simon Gray. Then of course there are the classic authors: Shakespeare (nice things in the less frequently performed comedies), Shaw (*The Apple Cart* has a lot to offer), Chekhov (*The Seagull, Uncle Vanya* and *The Bear* are happy hunting grounds), and the great Americans if you want to do an accent: Tennessee Williams, Edward Albee and Arthur Miller.

I'm sure I've left myself open to charges beginning, 'But what about . . .?' and 'Fancy including . . .!' But the plays are those I happen to have read or seen, and the authors are those I admire.

When someone comes on to a stage or into a room, you notice first of all what they look like, then what they sound like, and then you wonder if they are any good or not.

So when you've chosen your audition speech, prepare it properly. The director will suss out fairly soon whether you've worked on it or not and will deduce from that whether you work hard or not in general. Direct it well, or have someone direct it for you. Put some moves in, whatever it is. If you don't, the director will wonder why, and suspect it's because you are not very good at moving about. Recently I saw an audition speech done by someone who I was told afterwards was extremely talented, but I'd thought he probably wasn't because he'd done the whole thing in a monotone and had sat slumped, in profile, all the time. Well, this might have been all right if it had been part of a performance of the entire play, and it's nice to know that actors *can* sit still and be slumped in profile and talk in a monotone. But an audition speech is a vehicle for showing what you can do, and it will help the director if he hears something of the range of your voice and sees your body in different positions. And it's in an audition speech that you really ought to upstage any other characters so that the director can see your face.

The presentation of your pieces is as important as the choice of them, and I'm amazed that so many people will risk mugging something up at the last minute and trotting it out without care or work. Believe me, it shows. There is no point in being seen unless you are seen to your advantage.

Beware of relying too much on props or on arranging furniture, as this is time-consuming and boring, though certainly you can put a chair or two and a table, which ought always to be there, where you want them to be, preferably at the same time as announcing what the piece is. In short, get on with it; and have alternative productions in your mind in case of lack of furniture or space. A young actor told me that he now tries to choose pieces which are as apt as possible for the place he finds himself in: he had sunk with embarrassment, apparently, shouting a big, declamatory piece of Shakespeare in a tiny room. This is another advantage of having several things up your sleeve: some best for a stage in a large theatre, others for a poky little room.

When someone comes on to a stage or into a room, you notice first of all what they look like, then what they sound like, and then you wonder if they are any good or not.

Many a director nowadays chooses not to ask you to do prepared speeches, but relies instead on interviewing you. He may, or he may not, ask you to read something from the part he is considering you for. Try not to object, in your mind, to the form of audition he chooses: it really is up to him. He may well have heard in advance of your reputation – he will have asked around – and will therefore want to see you only to have a look at you and to hear you speak, to see if you match in any way his conception of the part. He will be weighing you up with the other people he is considering for the other parts, to see if you will coalesce. He will also be wondering if you are likely to be a good company-member, if you are easy to get on with and unlikely to cause trouble. If he asks you to read a scene with him, he may give you some notes and ask you to read it again. He will be watching to see how you respond to his direction.

So it's good to go for an interview in as good a mood as possible; and in a good talking-mood too, having done some talking, to yourself or to others, before you go; and in a good listening-mood. Really listen to what he says. It's so easy to half-listen when you're nervous. If you give your full attention to what he says it will help alleviate your nerves and you'll be able to have a proper conversation: you will be revealing yourself more than you think, and without trying too hard.

Try not to have rules about whether or not you should have a sight of the script beforehand if you have to read from it (remembering that a little knowledge can be a dangerous thing); and if you know in advance what the part is, don't go dressed exactly as you think you ought to look, because that will smell of trying too hard and relying too much on the clothes. M'm, clever, the director might think, not necessarily admiringly. On the other hand, as a well-known director said, if the part is that of a nun, it's silly to go with an exotic hair-do and a skirt with a split up the sides. Go with some sort of approximation to the look of the part, but only some.

In his book *Conversations with Ayckbourn*, Ian Watson quotes Ayckbourn, the Director of the Stephen Joseph Theatre at Scarborough, thus:

> Robin Herford (my Associate Director) and I go to endless trouble when we audition.
>
> I'm talking about actors particularly, and of course they are the most delicate. What you cannot tell is how an actor will socialise. You look and hope he isn't a heavy drinker; and you check with a few people, and you look at the references, but ultimately you employ him because you like the look of him and because he looks as if he can act. I have little faith in auditions, and I loathe those big workshop sessions that go on for days. It's an awful thing to say, but I tend to like people when they walk in the door. And, of course, this occasionally leads to disasters; we've had some extremely inferior actors in the company from time to time; we've had actors who've drunk; and we've had some that have been so anti-social and so unpleasant that people longed to get rid of them, because you are in fact asking people to live in each other's pockets for twelve hours a day, and in a very small concern of eight, nine actors with a communal men's, communal women's dressing room. So it's tricky, and obviously we make mistakes. You can't hope they'll all love each other: what you can hope is that you can gather people together who, although they may well see each other's errors, respect each other as artists.

They are a nuisance, are auditions. But they are here, and they are here to stay. Some are well run; some are hideous: crowded, rushed, demeaning. 'If this is the way they do it, I'm not sure I want the job anyway,' one is tempted to say. All one asks for is a little time, a little courtesy and a little attention.

A friend told me recently of an audition he had attended at The Warehouse in Earlham Street. After the appointment had been made, he was sent a speech from a play the company was about to produce, together with a note that it was to be read and not learned by heart. He was asked to have one speech of his own choice ready, and was also supplied, to his great surprise, with copious information about the company: its aims and its fields of activity.

He arrived at the agreed time. The director came out to the waiting area and said, 'I'm extremely sorry, but we are running a little late. Why don't you go for a coffee somewhere and come back in about fifteen minutes?' During the audition the director was attentive, encouraging and thorough. 'I'd like you to read our speech again,' he said. 'At least you've solved it, which most people haven't managed to do because it's so difficult. Very good. The only thing is, the emotional pitch you achieved at the end is really how you should have started it. So do you mind doing it again, starting more or less where you left off and rising from there? Very good, though.' And he muttered encouraging remarks while the rising was attempted. Afterwards he said that if there were a recall it would be within three days. In fact, my friend did not get the part. But the director rang him at home two days after the audition to tell him so, to thank him for the trouble he'd taken and to say, again, how impressed he had been.

The company was the Actors Touring Company. If only all auditions were held like that!

Nevertheless, the idea is of course, to get the job; it can be very dispiriting when you don't, especially if you've put a lot of hope into it. I've tried to console myself when I've failed an audition by saying, 'Well he obviously didn't think I was the best for the part so it's just as well I haven't got it: rehearsals would have been awkward and I'd have sensed his displeasure and lost confidence, so I'm probably well out of it.'

But it doesn't really work. At least not for long.

Attitudes

I realise I've got thus far without having yet found an answer to that question put to me in the Hayward Gallery: 'It's all very well if you've got work, but it doesn't tell you anything about how to get it, does it?' I was reminded of this all over again the other day, when a girl said to me, 'I just wish someone would write a book telling an out-of-work actress how to get a job.'

Well, Clive Swift's book, *The Job of Acting*, is full of advice about letters and contacts and agents and auditions and photographs and all the paraphernalia we need to try to sell ourselves to prospective employers.

But I have noticed that there are many actors and actresses, far more than I had supposed, who, for some incomprehensible reason, do not do their best when they *get* a job, and who therefore *ensure* that their present employer will not want to work with them again. 'I could never recommend him to anybody,' said a company manager to me about a lazy, unreliable, undisciplined and boring actor who wasn't much fun off-stage either.

So this is going to be a very po-faced little chapter indeed, all about good behaviour and trying hard. Why throw away what opportunities you get?

There are obvious things like always being early and never being late for rehearsals or performances. Take your work seriously; but don't talk about your performance unless you have to, don't brag, don't bitch unless you've absolutely got to, and don't take up a disproportionate amount of the director's time. Look as if you're enjoying it even when you are not, and be nice and kind and funny and helpful, and if you've got a good idea, say it. And try not to judge the others too much.

Yes. Try not to judge the others too much. It's so easy to have double standards: to be mercilessly critical in your heart about the others, when all the time you are making excuses for your own lapses and lacks. It's so easy to think like this:

'Of course today is the day of the read-through and of course one is not expected to give a performance at the first reading. Actually, someone said to me once that he thought people who give good first readings are extremely suspect, and will probably go off as rehearsals proceed; they are probably facile, I remember he said. So although I know my reading must sound flat and boring, and as though I've done no work on it at all, which is *not* true, everyone will know that it is just the first reading and not to be taken too much notice of.'

Or: 'Of course this is the day when we are given moves by the director, and everyone will know that that is what I'm concentrating on, and not on the acting, though he has irritated me several times by saying how such and such a speech should go, but really, first things first, let's get the moves done and *then* concentrate on the acting. Left to myself I'll be able to work on my speeches, thank you very much. I made it quite clear, albeit *very* subtly, that I was trying to concentrate on the moves which, my God, are very odd and absolutely no help at all.'

Or: 'Of course this is the day when we do it without books for the first time, and everyone will know just how awkward such a day can be. I don't really know it yet, I'm struggling for the words, and I'm making it quite clear that I am struggling by drying more than I need to. And another difficulty is that whereas I've always had the book to hold before, today I haven't. And I don't *quite* know yet what to do with my hands. Or where to look. I always had the book to look at before. That's why I'm either staring the other actors out or looking at the floor.'

Or: 'Of course the trouble is my part is just not well written. In fact I think it's the worst part in the play. In all fairness to the author I have to say I didn't think so at first; but first impressions are necessarily superficial: and since then I've tried to plumb the depths only to find there aren't any. There's no real character there, and there are impossible switches of mood. And the actual words I have to speak, well I mean I try to think of alternatives but I can't because the author's words stick, good or bad. Mostly bad. Anyway I'll have to tell people I'm finding it awkward because then they'll know what a problem I've got trying to be good in this awful part.'

Or: 'Of course everyone will know that the reason why my performance is not as good as it ought to be is that the director is so hopeless. I mean he's all right with some of the others and I agree with what he says about Brenda Browning because she's so dreadful; but as far as I'm concerned he doesn't understand me. He doesn't understand what I need at any given time; he doesn't understand the phases that I go through: for instance, I'm feeling my way gradually into this appalling character and he doesn't help me at all with his little picky notes. What I need, and he should know this, is gentle guidance and encouragement. I'll have to have a word with some of the others, especially those who I can see are also worried, so that they know exactly what I'm up against.'

Or: 'Of course everyone will know that Dafydd Dryden is an appalling actor and just impossible to act with, and unfortunately all my best scenes are with him. He gives nothing and he doesn't listen either, and the reason why our scenes fall so flat is that he is no bloody good.'

Or: 'Of course it's the dress rehearsal and I have to say I'm completely thrown. The furniture is not at all where the stage management put it in the rehearsal room, and how they expect us to act on that sofa I really don't know: I mean you just sink down and disappear in it. And it's impossible to get up out of it. We had hard wooden chairs at rehearsal and no one warned us it would be like this. Also my clothes don't fit properly and the pockets are not where I asked them to be. Anyone who is fool enough to go out front and watch will know how completely thrown I am.'

Or: 'Of course now it's the First Night and I'm really desperately nervous.'

Or: 'Of course we're on tour now and this theatre is VAST compared to the one last week. It's hopeless to be expected to adjust without a proper rehearsal. Anyway, everyone will know that the reason why I'm shouting is that I haven't quite got the measure of it yet.'

Or: 'Of course I've been playing this play for far too long. I try to keep it fresh but it's an uphill struggle. But everyone will know and make allowances.'

But they won't, will they?

Oh, we do have extraordinary attitudes towards each other sometimes. A Very Famous American actor, who has ambitions to be called great as well as famous, confessed of his ambivalent feelings towards the people he was acting with. On the one hand he wanted to be the best, and therefore feared that if anyone else was too good they would constitute a threat to his supremacy; on the other hand he knew he ought to be surrounded by splendid performers because the product would be better and more likely to be successful, and he would shine all the more.

I suspect we've all got a bit of that in us. I know I have. It's very odd. Why do we so easily think we are in a competition instead of a play?

To restore a proper perspective, and to keep our attitudes clear, it would be no bad thing to ask ourselves from time to time, 'Why should there be plays? What good do they do? What's so special about them, that we devote our lives to performing them? Is there anything they give to audiences which couldn't be obtained from books, newspapers, music, the visual arts, lectures, after-dinner speeches, conversation, church services, documentaries, talks, sitcoms, *Call My Bluff, Round Britain Quiz, This Is Your Life* or *Desert Island Discs?*'

Although we would all acknowledge there is a lot of overlap between the pleasures from plays and those from all the other things, the answer must be 'yes', and 'yes' several times over. You will have your own favourite 'yesses'. One of mine is: 'Yes,' because of the laughs. Eight hundred people in a theatre roaring away at the stories, dilemmas and jokes (not just jokes, as from a variety performer, but stories and dilemmas too) supplied so freely by Alan Ayckbourn, Tom Stoppard, Michael Frayn and the other funny ones, are sharing a delightful experience made all the more delightful because it is shared. Laughter is catching, and they laugh more loudly and more often than they could possibly have done had they seen it on their own; and this intensification, this enlargement of their reactions makes a play memorable and life-enhancing. Any serious content pierces more profoundly because it has been cloaked in laughter.

And 'yes', because when a play is so momentous that it becomes an event, drawing the audience into its world, into the story and characters, suspending disbelief as far as disbelief can ever be suspended – as happened in recent years at *Nicholas Nickleby* at the Aldwych, *Peter Pan* at the Barbican, *Duet for One* at the Duke of York's, *All My Sons* at Wyndham's and *The Rivals, Lorenzaccio* and *Translations* at the National – when the audience responds without reserve to the immediacy and presence of what is happening on the stage, there can be no feeling like it in the world.

My favourite 'yes', however, comes from television. In all programmes, other than plays, the performers are putting on a public face. They are aware of the camera and, through the camera, of the millions of viewers they are addressing. Newsreaders have a public face: composed, dignified, a slight smile for good news, a warning seriousness for bad. Panel-game players grin to the camera as they say, 'Good evening', and laugh more glamorously than they would bother to at home. Variety performers – well, they really do have a public face: nothing can cloud their jollity, their enveloping smiles, their manic energy. Even people being interviewed or appearing in a documentary know that they are being photographed and are altered because of it. A friend of mine, Mischa Scorer, who makes documentary films for television, said to me, 'the trouble is that the presence of the camera changes what is happening: you would like to photograph those kids as they *really* arrive at school, as they *really* behave in the classroom, as they *really* play up to the teacher; you would like to photograph that Arab at his vegetable stall in Cairo as he really is, but you can't. You have altered him: he is self-conscious and he puts on a public face.'

Plays are the one area left for privateness. Actors are the only people who have to pretend that there is no camera there. This does, I think give them a particular responsibility: they are there to show the private face, to show what it's like to be that sort of person, what it's like to be angry, selfish, generous, in love, ecstatic, depressed, lonely, excited, exhausted, ill – whatever the play demands. They are there to show what life, with all its suffering and all its joy, is really like, so that the audience can say, 'Yes, that is it . . . yes, I recognise that . . . yes, that is what it's like.' That is the stuff of drama; that is why there should be plays.

How Do You Work On A Part?

The idea for this chapter came from a conversation with Gerald Harper, who said, 'What I'd like to get from a book about acting is something about how to work. I still don't really know how to work on a part or how to rehearse it. And I certainly don't know how other people work or rehearse.'

Oh, I thought afterwards. Right then. I'll ask.

Judi Dench

I asked Judi Dench, who is married to Michael Williams, on Friday 21 January, 1983. She was then appearing in two plays in the repertory of the National Theatre: *The Importance of Being Earnest* by Oscar Wilde and *A Kind of Alaska*, one of a double bill of plays called *Other Places*, by Harold Pinter.

JD   The bit I like most about acting is when I'm asked to play a part, because I don't like rehearsing it and I don't like doing it and I'm sad when it's over. That's a joke in a way, but in a way it's related to a tremendous truth. When I've been offered a part I feel as if I'm standing on a great hill. I never read up about it: I mean I barely read the play. I prefer, as in the case of *The Promise* and *The Wolf*, which Frank Hauser directed, that he should come for supper and, while I'm preparing it and we're having a glass of wine, he tells me the story of the play in my kitchen. I like being told the story in somebody else's words.

     I'll tell you what I know now, as certainly as I know I'm sitting in this mustardy chair. I know that if, for example, I have to get up impossibly early for filming, I can wake at the required time, have my bath and get dressed to go. In the same way, if I'm giving a dinner party, there's something in me, not fabricated, not imagined in any way at all, like a bell which I actually hear go off and which I know means it's the moment when I've got to go down and start cooking so that I can finish exactly at the moment I need to. If ever this goes awry it's because something unforeseen has happened like a telephone call which goes on for a long time or I've smashed a plate or something like that, but it's never because I've started late, because I always have this person inside. I also do the crossword, the *Telegraph,* and in the morning I look at the crossword but I don't fill any in, and I can think, yes I know that, yes, yes, yes. I'll read the rest and then I'll put the crossword down. And in the evening, when I come back, I can fill in over half, because this person who wakes me up at the required time has also been doing the crossword during the day.

Now once I've heard the story of the play, if it appeals to this person who's inside me I think, oh yes, I'll do that. Of course it's got a lot to do with the director.

Having been offered the part – you don't mind my going on like this do you? I'm feeling quite lucid this morning, more lucid than usual.

PB   Please . . .

JD   Having been offered the part I just feel as if I'm standing on this great . . . you know the opening shot of *The Sound of Music?* Well I'm standing on that green, Swiss hill and I'm looking down into the most enormous forest. Now when I say I don't ever refer to anything (if it's a classic) that anyone else has ever done with it, it's because I think that if I do that (I suppose it's rather arrogant of me) it'll get in the way of an instinctive reaction, and I'm only a creature of impulse and instinct. Only. I'm no creature of intellect whatsoever.

So during this period, which might be weeks or months or whatever, this person inside obviously never stops working.

When rehearsals start, when I first talk about the play, it's only then that I enter the forest. I go down the hill and I'm in the forest; and although I know it's all trees I can't tell which tree is which.

PB Do you not do any deliberate homework at all before
    rehearsals start?
JD No. None at all.
PB So your pre-rehearsal work is subliminal?
JD Yes. I didn't know for a long time that it happened like
    that but I realise now that it does: that there is a kind
    of subliminal thing inside me that must start thinking
    about it. And being in *The Importance of Being Earnest*
    proved that conclusively. What happened there was I
    said I couldn't be in it because of a holiday we'd
    planned, so Peter Hall said, 'Well, you can have your
    holiday because you're not in Act Two.' So after three
    weeks of rehearsal Michael and I packed our tent and
    went off to the West of Scotland where I had two divine
    weeks of never sleeping for one single night, because by
    then (a) I didn't know the lines, (b) I didn't know how
    to play it and (c) they were all rehearsing back in
    London. I couldn't bear it. But . . . When I came back
    we did a run-through that afternoon and Peter said to
    me afterwards, 'Perhaps I should tell everyone to go off
    for two weeks into their tents.' And I swear to you, I'd
    taken the script, but I'd never even opened the cover.
    I'd never touched it. But I wouldn't have gone without
    it. And the night we came back from the holiday I
    opened the script and went through it before I went to
    sleep. I think you shouldn't look elsewhere.
PB Elsewhere than in the play itself, you mean?
JD Yes, I think that in every play there are signposts that
    you find, either what you say, what somebody else says
    about you or the way somebody else behaves towards
    you.
PB Did you, for example, get the idea of Lady Bracknell's
    being quite so conscious of fashion from that bit where
    you criticise the young girl's dress?
JD Yes. The French maid. Lady Bracknell says, 'Only an
    experienced French maid produces a really marvellous
    effect in a very brief space of time.' And I think this is
    because she's got that person back at Upper Grosvenor
    Street. And also I think she wears glasses because
    Gwendolen says, 'Mama has brought me up to be
    extremely short-sighted,' and I don't think Lady

Bracknell would bring a very presentable girl up to wear glasses if she didn't actually have to wear them herself. John Bury's original designs for Lady Bracknell's clothes made her a very rigorous, very fat lady in glasses with a kind of up-turned po on her head. And I said to Peter, 'Oh! Is that what we're going to do?' and he said, 'No I don't think so.' And I said, 'I mean she wants a bird on the hat, doesn't she? There has to be a bird, and the hat has to be worn at a slight angle, to one side?' I was rather relieved when I saw Sir Laurence on that telly saying he had to see what the character looked like. I have to do that. Once I have seen, and know just what she looks like, then that's out of the way, it's done, and I can get on to the meat of it.

PB When you come back after rehearsal do you do homework then?

JD No, never. It drives Michael mad.

PB So you work only in the rehearsal room, and a bit of this thing going on inside?

JD A lot. A lot of that. I think there's a lot of that. But I can do anything else I like. I don't have to look at the lines.

PB Do you like to discuss your part, and the way it is developing, with the director?

JD No, I don't like doing that. And I never ever talk about it to Michael. I might ask him some very oblique question indeed, but he won't even know it's about the play: I have to dress it up a bit; because I have a feeling that we have a sort of valve inside us, and even if I let out just a tiny thing it's gone, it's escaped. I'd rather keep it in, like compressed air.

PB How obedient are you to your director? Say, for example, with moves. If he gives you moves do you do them? Or do you like to be left alone?

JD I like to be given some guidance about it: but I've got so used now to the RSC way of working where you're told where everything is and you move it yourself but have help if you need it.

PB I thought your revelations of the nicer side of Lady Bracknell were very interesting. I've never seen that before.

JD   That's Peter Hall really. He said, 'They're not just
       cardboard characters, penny-plain and tuppence-
       coloured, saying very witty things. They say them
       because they think they ought to say them, or they
       think it's outrageous to say them, or they think it's
       covering up some other emotion.'

PB   What happens when you find yourself disagreeing with
       a director?

JD   Well, I'll always try to do what he says. But sometimes
       I find something so against my instinct that if I try to
       live with it it's like wearing a hair-shirt. So then I
       might say, 'Could I show you something else? Could I
       just show you?' And usually, now . . . The RSC way of
       working, with all of us finding out a way, is ideal for
       me: I love it, and I love it when other actors suddenly
       do something. Trevor Nunn makes me feel free. He did
       in *The Winter's Tale* and in *Juno and the Paycock* too.

PB   Talking of *Juno and the Paycock* I remember your first
       entrance particularly: you came into the house and you
       were going to do something but you didn't do it and
       you went to do something else. Do you like doing things
       like that? Do you like things like hesitation and
       changing your mind and darting about: the mess of
       everyday life?

JD   Absolutely.

PB   The Irish accent seemed to do a lot for you.

JD   I whispered in that. I whispered for all the rehearsal
       period. I was so frightened with all those Irish actors
       around; and eventually Trevor came to me and said,
       'You're going to have to commit.'

PB   Do you find one thing, like an accent, or the kind of
       things which Geoffrey Hutchings sometimes does with
       a physical mannerism, or Anna Massey's leaning
       forward a bit in *The Importance*; do you find one thing
       can open doors for you?

JD   The best one thing I ever had was during the holiday in
       Scotland. We visited Inveraray. And I looked at the
       castle. It was a windy, wet day and I remembered the
       whole incident of the Duchess of Argyll and the Duke of
       Argyll; but it wasn't till the final week of the holiday,
       the last few days, that I thought, I know just who I'm

going to base Lady Bracknell on: Margaret, Duchess of Argyll. She is a great society beauty and had been a very lovely debutante; and there was the scandal, you know . . . And I thought, that's who I'm going to base her on.

PB   How set are your performances? Do you like changing things?

JD   Yes. And I think, ooh, gracious, gracious; and that happens a lot in *Other Places*. It's totally free, like no play I've ever done. It's because of Pinter's writing. Once I start that fifty minutes I'm like a mouse on a wheel: I'm on a track that I can't get off; it won't let go of me, it's like something pulling me into a cage. I've never felt it so strongly in a play before. I mean you know how rigorous *The Importance* is: symmetrical, beautifully orchestrated, and within that orchestration there are a few places you can go, but not many. But in the Pinter, the places you can go are legion. So if I have notes after one performance, they simply wouldn't apply to the next. So I've never had notes, ever. It's always changing.

PB   Do you let it change in performance or do you sometimes think in advance what you might like to change?

JD   Never. Never in advance.

PB   Do you get less satisfaction from the comparative exactness of Lady Bracknell?

JD   No. No I don't. In a way I don't get any satisfaction from the Pinter play. I just feel very tired at the end of it. It's very rare now, much rarer than it was when I was younger and didn't know the pitfalls so much, that I come off the stage and feel: well that's the best I can do up to this present moment. Until tomorrow. But I haven't had that feeling for years. I had it last for one night, one night only, in *Juno and the Paycock*. And I came out and I thought: that is all I can do with that – for the time being.

PB   Do you ever give a mechanical performance?

JD   No. No. I don't. I don't think anybody can, really.

PB   People do, though, don't they?

JD   Well I think pride takes over in a way. I think: oh, my God, I mustn't let the side down.

PB   How important to you is being in voice, and do you do any work on it before you go to the theatre?

JD   No. If you've got a voice like mine you're never in voice. When I have a cold people don't notice. I never knew I had this voice until I first heard it and I said, 'That's not me.' No. The only voice exercises I do are in my bath beforehand – I have the luxury of a bath at the National – and I lie in the bath every night, and I do a lot of Clifford Turner, you know – niminy piminy – before Lady Bracknell. At the final dress rehearsal, we were allowed to ask a few friends to it, and after the line 'He seems to have great confidence in the opinion of his physicians' I said, 'Hoorallypallyleeleeleelee-pooblyooblyoobly', or some such rubbish. And it got a belter of a laugh. And we shrieked.

PB   How important do you think the off-stage life of an actress is? I don't mean keeping up appearances, looking after yourself in that way, but looking after yourself as a person, because everything that you are shows?

JD   Michael says that you can't ever be more on a stage than you are as a person in life. I used to disagree with him. But now I think he's quite right.

PB   Do you like to get to know the company you are acting with well, off-stage as well as on?

JD   Oh yes. I like to check up on people. I like to know about them. It's kind of essential. I'm always very unconfident and shy of meeting actors I don't know. I can bluff it out. But I actually don't like it. Therefore, as at Stratford, when a new company comes together, you've got twelve weeks to do two plays. But that twelve weeks I believe contains six weeks of just getting to know and relax with everybody so that eventually you are able to remove every bit of clothing, and laugh at yourself and everybody else. If you're going to be inhibited in front of everybody and not dare to make a fool of yourself then you will never get to anything. Unless you can push the boat out too far, there's no point in calling it back.

Alec McCowen

I interviewed Alec McCowen on Friday 28 January 1983 at his flat in Kensington. He was not in a run of a play at the time, but was giving intermittent performances of *The Gospel According to St. Mark* at the Queen Elizabeth Hall; and he always seems to have a lot of ideas coming up to the boil.

AMcC   I guess I'm much more prepared now when I go to a first rehearsal than I used to be. It depends on the director, though: if it's a director I trust then maybe I won't do anything like as much work, but if it's a director I don't know, or I'm not sure I can totally trust, I will do a good deal of preparation; also, as I get older, there's simply the memory factor, and I do like to become fairly acquainted with the words before rehearsals start. For instance, for the play about Hitler, *The Portage to San Cristobal of AH* which I did a year ago, I had learnt the whole of a twenty-five minute speech in advance because I thought it would take the entire period of rehearsal to, as you might say, put the expressions in.

PB   You had a different voice for that performance. It can be dangerous when actors change their voices, because so often it doesn't come off. With you it did. Where did that low, guttural voice come from?

AMcC   I didn't set out to change my voice; it just happened. It startled me, and people used to say 'Doesn't it hurt your throat?' It didn't, I suppose, because it happened naturally. I think it became confirmed when I saw a film clip of Hitler not long before we opened and I noticed, above all else, that his voice came not from his chest, nor from his stomach, but from his bowels. But I didn't do an impersonation, and couldn't 'put it on' now. Most of the work I do now (I didn't used to do this) is concerned almost entirely with understanding: understanding what the play is, and what the part is in my own terms. I have to understand the situations and the other characters totally within my own experience. Because I cannot *imagine* what it is like being a king or a pope or Hitler or whatever it is I'm playing, I have to relate it to things within myself. When I was a young actor I disguised myself: I dressed up and hid myself under make-up and costumes and funny walks and funny voices and everything, and this went on for years and years. But then there came a point . . . well, it's a journey isn't it? A long, long journey. I met Vivian Matalon and he influenced me greatly. And now, as I say, I just work for understanding, and search for total clarity. I find this releases me physically: I mean if there's any nervousness, if there's any confusion, if there's any unsureness about what I'm doing, there's going to be tension and then my body won't do what it's told.

PB   So you like to go to the first rehearsal prepared with this rather penetrating understanding of the play and your part in it?

AMcC   Yes; yet I find the first rehearsal the most terrifying part of the job. I always dread it.

PB   On account of meeting the people?

AMcC   No, on account of exposing myself for the first time. I don't know what it is that makes me so extraordinarily self-conscious after so many years, but I am; I'm like a teenager among adults: I think I'm going to be found out in some way when I open my mouth. Yes. The beginning is the most terrifying of all. And the next terrifying thing is letting go. Especially if it is a part which requires extremes of behaviour. I find all that much more terrifying now than First Nights.

PB   What do you expect from a director?

AMcC   I like him to have done a certain amount of work before rehearsals start, certainly in the physical sense, so he has some idea of how a play should look. Then there's something to work on. Otherwise the rehearsals become anarchic, and I hate that because one starts being directed by the actors with the loudest voices: 'Why doesn't he do this?' and, 'If I go there, then he can be there,' and that sort of thing. I can't rehearse under those conditions. It's agony if actors start directing each other.

PB   Are you ever tempted to do it yourself?

AMcC   Oh yes. I'm tempted. Often. But I try to resist it. Perhaps I try in devious ways, like slipping in an idea quietly in the coffee break. I like a director who gives a good deal of help at the beginning but who also gives a good deal of freedom for one, two or three weeks, by which time I will have explored all sorts of avenues, all sorts of ways of doing it; and by, say, the fourth week of rehearsal I'll have no perspective. That is when I need a director to say, 'No, not that one, that one. The way you were doing it the second week was the best.' I need a selecting man, a selecting genius, I suppose.

PB   Have you ever found one?

AMcC   Well, in recent work I found Michael Rudman superb with *The Browning Version* at the National. His best notes were his last ones; maybe for other actors it would have thrown them, that he would suddenly come up at the last minute and say, 'You do not need that pause, you don't need to strive so hard for that effect, you don't need to make that point so clearly, trust this, trust the other.' He was marvellously selective. And very sensitive.

PB   Do you ever get stuck with a part?

AMcC   Oh yes, often.

PB   What do you do?

AMcC   Well . . . I've had great help in the past from what Vivian Matalon used to call 'as ifs'. They can be so remote from the play itself that anybody knowing what was going on in my head would be extremely startled. I found the Fool in *King Lear* a most difficult part because the lines are practically incomprehensible nowadays and because we're not quite sure what a Fool is. He's not Morecambe and Wise. There's no counterpart today. I couldn't get near the part. It was gobbledygook. Or it was until I found an 'as if', which was simply recalling myself as a small boy, when my father, who was the 'as if' for King Lear, would come home from work tired, angry, spiky, often very bad-tempered, and I used to keep him sweet; I used to amuse him, and tried

to stop the row with my mother about the food
being late or not what he wanted or whatever. I
would cavort about and make him laugh. It's
strange how vivid childhood memories are: I work
from them a great deal. And once I'd remembered
that, the part lost all its stress for me. The struggle
went out of it.

And I found Malvolio, when I did it in the BBC
Television Shakespeare series, difficult because I
had too much of a mental picture of this stately,
pompous, slow-moving person . . .

PB   Because of performances of it you'd seen?

AMcC   Well it started at school. We were taught that
Malvolio is like this, Hamlet is like that. It was a
sort of brain-washing. And so, when we were
rehearsing, I knew my Malvolio was a cliché-
character and I couldn't find any life in it. Until I
realised two things. First of all that he's a servant
and he must be a good servant: he's got a very good
job. That wasn't much help though. The second
thing was an 'as if'. And I remembered it when I
was thinking about his relationship with Olivia. I
remembered working with Vivien Leigh in *Antony
and Cleopatra* in New York. She was the most
beautiful, glamorous woman I've ever met or
worked for; and there were a few of us young actors
in the company and we all were behaving in a most
ridiculous fashion trying to please Vivien Leigh,
trying to get her to smile at us, trying to get a few
words from her. So before going on in *Twelfth Night*
I would do this substitution: that I was going on to
get the approval, to get the love, of Vivien Leigh.
And immediately the whole rhythm changed: from
being a slow, stately, pompous man, I became fussy,
and would rush to get the chair in place for her,
rush to get the cushion and plump it up, and push
back other people and not let them get near her. So
thinking of Vivien Leigh brought the part to life. I
had been a messenger in *Antony and Cleopatra* and I
had one marvellous scene directly with Vivien
Leigh, in which I had to tell her that Antony had

married. And she had to slap my face. She was a very technical actress and she required me to be in exactly the same place and to say the lines in exactly the same manner at every performance, and once or twice I was hauled over the coals for being an inch out of position. And the night I ducked when she hit me . . . well, I'd seen this bracelet she was wearing had slipped down to her wrist and I knew I was going to get really smashed in the chops, so I ducked; and of course I got hell from Vivien Leigh. Quite rightly I suppose. But I was so stupidly besotted with her that although I was working with her I would wait at the Stage Door to see her leave the building. So she was an enormous help to me in *Twelfth Night* years later.

PB   Any more 'as ifs' you've used?

AMcC   Well yes. This is a geographical one. I don't think I was particularly good as Hamlet . . . I couldn't get a line on it which suited me, and I was too old for it . . .

PB   In Birmingham, was this?

AMcC   Yes and that was the great point about it. I was basing my performance chiefly on the line 'Denmark is a prison', because I think Hamlet had escaped from that prison, he'd got to university at Wittenberg, and I think the enforced return to Denmark was immensely galling to him. I think he had a contempt for Denmark, for the Court, for nearly everybody in the play. They were small-town people, they were suburban, and he was trapped in this prison. Well I did *Hamlet* after playing on Broadway for nine months in *Hadrian VII*; and to return to Birmingham, the old, dirty Birmingham Rep., in the drizzle, and to leave the theatre totally unrecognised after all the fuss of New York, all the glamour: this helped me very much as an 'as if' in playing Hamlet. Denmark was Birmingham.

PB   When you're in a long run, do you change much?

AMcC   Well, I have about five different versions which I will call upon to stop me from getting stale. They still don't, but nevertheless . . . I will have an

evening when I think solely about my relationship
with the other actors, to remind me not to go over
the top and that I'm actually talking to the people
on the stage with me. Or I will ask myself, 'What is
the verb for what I am doing? Am I flirting with
somebody, am I intimidating somebody?' and so on.
Or I think of the intentions: I think of what I want
to achieve. My favourite version, though, which I
can't use too often, is what I call the 'fourth-wall'
version, when I spend the entire performance
shutting out the audience, and giving myself total
freedom, as if I'm in a room, alone, where there's no
temptation to be good. No temptation to be
impressive. It's marvellously releasing.

PB   It sounds as if getting stale is a hurdle for you. Is it
hard, keeping fresh?

AMcC   Harder and harder now, yes, because as I get older,
the thought of doing things over and over again
makes me angry. I mean, it's a way of earning a
living, but I feel I'm putting my head in the sand. I
resent it, and I think the resentment creeps into my
work now, to its detriment.

PB   What's your worst failing?

AMcC   Just being phoney. Phoneyness. I love acting badly.
Who is to say what is good or what is bad, but I
would love to be a completely technical, calculating
actor who was just enjoying himself. It's painful
that to act well is just sheer hard work, and not very
enjoyable. Except at the moment of discovery.

Edward Petherbridge

Edward Petherbridge came to my home to talk on Monday
31 January 1983. He had just finished playing Feste in *Twelfth
Night* for a tour of the Far East culminating in a short season
at the Warehouse, Earlham Street. Emily Richard, his wife,
had played Viola in the same production; and in the famed
production of *Nicholas Nickleby* she had been Nicholas's sister
Kate, while Edward was Newman Noggs.

EP   It's such a social thing, being an actor. It's so easy to
      get impatient, but you have to try, and not let the grit
      of people's differences or their selfishnesses or their
      hang-ups get in the way, while you're busy dealing with
      a hang-up of your own, perhaps, and building up your
      working relationship with the director. And it's not
      unknown for *that* to be a minefield.

PB   Do you do much work before rehearsals start? Do you
      like to go well prepared?

EP   I do. I do like to. But I often don't. I sit and think. In
      the bus or in the car. I think it's very bad to turn up
      without having read anything about the period if it's a
      period play, or the background if it's specialised in any
      way. Sometimes observation of real people in particular
      jobs or situations is necessary beforehand. I like to have
      some coherent vision to contribute even if it's going to
      be modified in rehearsal.

PB   So you like to do as much research as you can?

EP   Oh yes. Of course with a few directors, Trevor Nunn
      for instance, research is contained within the rehearsal
      period as well. For example, for *Three Sisters* we did
      individual projects. He gave each of us a subject, like
      life in Moscow, or life in Perm, which was the town we
      chose, because it was a long way from Moscow: I mean
      it's important to know how far away it is and how hard
      it is to get to Moscow from there. It's about five
      hundred miles, I think. Or more; I forget now. Other
      subjects were travel, education, the army, religion,
      living conditions, local industries. When we had all
      read up our particular subject, we came back and
      shared it. And of course it's a very good way not only of
      building up a background to the play, but of getting to
      know everybody you'll be acting with.

PB   If there is a book about it, for example there was a book
      about Newman Noggs, would you read it?

EP   That example is a bit difficult, because, yes, there was a
      book about Newman Noggs, I think: unfortunately he
      called it *Nicholas Nickleby*. It was immensely useful. It
      must have been torture for David Edgar, who did the
      adaptation, because everybody kept saying, 'Well, of

course, in the book . . .' There it all was, chapter and verse.

PB   Did you make any specific requests for things which David Edgar hadn't included?

EP   Well, one I can remember. When Nicholas gets back from Yorkshire, penniless, having beaten Squeers and befriended Smike, Noggs starts to give him advice about caution and moderation – then suddenly bangs the table and says, 'Damn it, I'm proud of you! I'd have done the same thing myself!' Very illuminating about Noggs, although the scene wasn't long enough to merit setting a table so I banged a chair.

PB   Did you do projects, as you had done for *Three Sisters*?

EP   Oh yes. We had a very long run-up to the rehearsal period, because we didn't have a play to start with. About six weeks, we had.

PB   What was your project?

EP   For *Nicholas Nickleby* we did it in pairs, so there were twenty projects. I did mine with Emily. We researched the theatre of 1838, because of the Crummles company. We took lots and lots of photographs of old prints of actors and theatres and plans and things, and then made them into slides, and found some music which was right, and some facts and figures, and gave a twenty-five minute magic-lantern show.

PB   But neither of you played one of the actors.

EP   No. The parts hadn't been assigned yet. I thought I might be one of them, but I wasn't.

PB   How did your characterisation of Newman Noggs arrive?

EP   There were many sources. The famous drawings of Phiz gave me an image. They were caricatures of course, but I thought if I can capture some of the reality inside the caricature, it would be a good thing to do and luckily I was the right kind of shape to do it: I mean long and thin. And then there was all his history, suggested here and there in the book and barely hinted at in the play. David Edgar's dramatic telegrams were a marvellous exercise in economy. And then . . . I suppose the imaginative part was imagining him in his attic on his own, before he'd met Nicholas, or even after he'd met him. Newman Noggs spent hours in his little room, having his drink, fanning the four or five coals in his grate and feeling cold, and thinking about his past or trying to forget it. And I had to ask myself: how does he get from one minute to the next? How does he put up with it? Does he switch off, and does he think about other things? How did he cope with being so solitary, not only when he was alone, but at work too. Thinking about all that helped with his physical attitude: how he stood, how he was, how he stood inside his body.

PB Did you have a red nose? Was that because of drink?

EP Yes . . . no, it was because of a little bit of lake I put there . . . yes, he was described as having a red nose. I worried about that red nose because of the clown suggestion in it; all these things can become clichés. Then I had to think: find what the cliché is, then try to discover the truth that underlies the cliché, and then do it so that the audience can't even see the cliché. I call this process 'making it organic', so they can't see the joins and I can't feel them either.

PB How much are you influenced by your interest in mime?

EP A lot. Though I have a kind of dread about this because a caustic American actor said to me, when he'd seen *Nickleby* in New York, 'I take it that you've studied mime, judging from your performance.' I didn't like that. It ought not have shown up as a style, though I am certainly interested in acting styles which use obvious artifice.

I've just been to China and watched nine- to sixteen-year-old children being taught how to act. At the Peking Opera everything is traditional and is still being handed on intact despite the Cultural Revolution: the way they hold their hands, tilt their heads, the way they take a step, hold their feet. Every single thing is taught; and the exercises they are given are to do with fighting, singing, speaking and dancing. They achieve a completely received technique which takes care of . . . their eyebrows, everything. And yet they imbued what they were doing with a great deal of personal involvement. When we came into the room, with interpreters and all, they were in the middle of a scene and they didn't falter because of us: their concentration was so complete. I do like the kind of theatre which depends on great artifice, on stylisation, on the extremes that the performer can be called upon to come up with.

PB   What is the furthest extreme you have gone to in your acting?

EP   I was once in a production by Tyrone Guthrie of *Volpone*. And many of the characters in that play are named after animals: Volpone, the fox, and Voltore, the vulture, which was me. I was sent off to the zoo in Regents Park to look at vultures. And I thought, my God, this is just up my street on account of my interest in movement; and ages before I'd played animals and things at theatre school a little bit, and here I was, going to look at a real vulture, and to try to speak Ben Jonson as a vulture. It proved to be very difficult. I mean, Guthrie was in love with what I was doing physically and he used to say things like, 'Fly up on to the bed,' you know, with Volpone lying in it, 'go on, fly on to it!' But he didn't like the voice. 'You're not sepulchral enough for a vulture,' he said. And of course Ben Jonson is very difficult: you can understand it, just, when you read it, but you can't understand it when you're actually saying it. At least that's what I found, especially when I was trying to combine a human being with a vulture so that the join wouldn't show.

One of the things I liked about working with Guthrie was that he had a real sense of fun and he would prod us all to go over the top which is one of the things I usually don't like doing. I like restraint. It's been the undoing of me a lot of the time.

PB   Why has it been the undoing of you?

EP   Laurence Olivier said to me, just as I was about to leave the National Theatre, 'You're very subtle and unusual, but I'd like to see you come out more. Raise the flag more.'

PB   Do you think you ought to come out more?

EP   I've always thought it important that if you can you should suggest rather than emphasise, so that you don't

tell the audience what you're doing, you let them have
fun discovering it. I've thought that ever since I was at
drama school. I don't know where I got it from.
Perhaps, in the past, that has made me afraid of the
bold statement sometimes, and bold statements are
necessary because without them subtlety has nothing to
show up against.

PB Do you ever feel inadequate? What do you do when
things go wrong? Do you have remedies?

EP I think remedies are very important. I had a difficult
time when I was rehearsing Vershinin in *Three Sisters*: a
crisis of confidence. I felt eighteen most of the time.
Absurd. As well as having a thing about looking
younger than I was because of what people had said, I
had a thing about being thin. And Vershinin's a
colonel, for God's sake, in the Russian army.

PB And the remedies?

EP The remedy was to say to myself: Look. You've only
got this equipment. That's what you've got to do it
with. They did ask you. They haven't suggested
recasting. So. Now then. You must not concentrate on
these difficulties. You must not let the rehearsal period
and then the performances be marred by allowing these
worries to take root and become destructive. You must
take a Zen attitude, to live in the moment. *You* (because
they've chosen you), *you* come in, you say these things
and you look at that woman and you say, my goodness
you remind me of so-and-so, and you say, what a
wonderful room. You go from one thing to another.
One by one. Just the things you have to do. Don't
worry about how you're looking or how you stand
(though of course these things are important). Just
concentrate on feeling happy. As if you've invited the
audience to a party. Even if you're a bit wrong, only if
you are happy and confident can you be acceptable or
useful to an audience.

PB You act quickly. Do you do that deliberately?

EP Yes. I think I've always acted fast. I remember Olivier,
again, saying, not to me but to someone else, 'You
mustn't waste the audience's time.'

PB You said that things like how you stand and how you look are important. Do you still do much work off-stage to get these, and perhaps more inner things, right?

EP I have bouts of doing things: I'll jog for a bit, or swim for a bit; I've even lifted weights for a bit. I'll do some old movement exercises or voice exercises for a bit. Topping up, really. It's awful, isn't it, because it sounds as if one is a prize garden, which one is continually weeding and hoeing and putting compost on.

PB But actors and actresses are stared at, aren't they? And isn't all this part of feeling happy on the stage?

EP Yes. One is one's own instrument; and intellectually and emotionally and in every way one has to be a good vessel for all the things one has to do.

PB Are there untrodden paths you'd like to tread?

EP I think one goes to rehearsals with the backlog of all the things one has ever done before. I mean I know why they've cast me and I know what they expect. And nine times out of ten I'll give them what they expect. I'd love to surprise them.

PB How?

EP Well. I suppose I've played what is laughingly known as a large range of parts. And I suppose really I'd like to get away from all these eccentrics: clapped-out, benign creatures, clowns, intellectuals, poetic lovers, scholars. Recently I played an ordinary chap in a television play. An ordinary chap in the present. I liked that. And I'd like to do more plays which are about now, and about the problems which are to do with living in *this* world, and where I could come on dressed as I am now, maybe, and be natural. Though to be natural is just another kind of artifice.

Anna Massey

Anna Massey came to talk to me at home on 9 February 1983. Like Judi Dench she was at that time appearing in *The Importance of Being Earnest* and *Other Places* at the National Theatre.

AM   Vivian Matalon was a great influence on me. His
     theories changed my attitude to work and to
     rehearsing. He kept saying, 'Don't be general: be
     specific.'

PB   What do you think he meant by that?

AM   Well, after meeting him I was lucky enough to be
     directed by Max Stafford-Clark in the Irish version of
     The Seagull at the Royal Court Theatre and Max put
     into practice what Vivian had said. He told us to 'play
     the action' of a line and not to 'demonstrate' it. You
     can have a simple line like, 'I love you.' Then you have
     to decide, within the context of the play, what you want
     to *do*, what the *action* is behind the line: in this case it
     could be to seduce, to provoke; there are lots of verbs to
     choose from. And in the early rehearsals for *The Seagull*
     Max used to take passages of the play, and ask us to
     say what the verb was before each line. We all did it. I
     mean, say my character was Anna and you're Peter: I
     get up and say 'Anna provokes Peter,' and then say the
     line.

PB   You obviously react strongly to directors. Was Max
     Stafford-Clark an ideal one for you?

AM   A milestone. He took away a lot of the wasteful fret I
     often get into in rehearsals. After a while we stopped
     saying the actions and just did them and let in a lot of
     other things, but at least we knew what we were doing.
     We could all see the scenes from everybody's point of
     view, so it led to good teamwork and stopped anybody
     from giving a solo performance. It also made us
     economical, and I like economy. It helped us, when we
     came to perform the play, to keep it fresh. I swear it
     was as fresh at the end of the run as it had been at the
     beginning.

PB   Do you say 'I' or 'she' when you talk about your part?

AM   Vivian Matalon says you must say 'I'. I'm sure you
     should. The part has to become *you*. What was it John
     Gielgud said? – 'Ninety per cent of you is there
     anyway.'

PB   Do you like to do your own placing?

AM   It depends on the director. Max Stafford-Clark sort of
     says he doesn't know how to do it, but of course he

does. If everything's going right he shouldn't have to say, 'Sit on that sofa,' or 'Get up on that line.' It should just happen; and Max made us so aware of our relationships with each other – including the man who brought on my suitcase: I knew exactly what I thought of him and he of me – that all the moves came out of the actors. I like that, especially since I think actors are unselfish. On the whole.

PB   How do you start to work on a part?

AM   Well, first of all I read the play to decide whether I want to play the part or not. This is the most important read because my instinct's at work. Actually I didn't do that for Miss Prism, because everybody said when I was offered it, oh what a good part for you, oh you'll be very good. So I said yes. Then I read it and thought, I can't do it. It's not me at all. What have I let myself in for? I mean Miss Prism is eccentric and I'm not. Well, not in the same way. I mean, I'm not a born eccentric like Margaret Rutherford was. Margaret Rutherford didn't have to act eccentricity: it was something she brought on with her. So the first thing I had to do was pretend the play had never been done before and Margaret Rutherford had never been Miss Prism. Actually of course the word 'eccentric' is a generality and not much help. It's like saying a character is mad, or ill or whatever. You have to work out what these generalities mean. So I worked out a biography. I do that with every part.

PB   Before rehearsals start?

AM   Oh yes. Always. I like to know what my parents were like, and whether I have brothers or sisters. And I cast them. From old friends, new friends, people I've seen in the street. Then I can see them. In my mind's eye. Images. I like to know the house where I was born, the school I went to and, most definitely, where the play takes place.

PB   So what was Miss Prism's biography?

AM   I worked out a story which made me fifty-two. I'm too young for the part, you see. And I worked out the youngest I could be was fifty-two. In the play there's a line, 'An injury received from the upsetting of a Gower

Street omnibus,' so I worked out that I went to college in Gower Street and fell in love with a German student: I was writing my novel at the time, and became a governess when I was twenty-two. I was born in Leamington and I made Patrick Moore my father. My mother had died because I couldn't think of a mother. And because we all talk so much about Germany in the play I thought that I had spent quite a lot of time in Heidelberg, because I'd been there once; so I cast myself as a governess there.

PB   Teaching foreign students? Is that what made you speak so precisely?

AM   I don't know. You see when I work out these biographies I don't know what the result will be. I don't play the result. For example, my son came to the play and said, 'I love the voice.' And I said, 'What do you mean, the voice?' And he said, 'It's so high.' But I didn't, honestly, know that it had happened.

PB   Where did the slight stoop come from?

AM   The corsets I had to wear.

PB   And the dainty step?

AM   From a walk in Holland Park with a friend when we talked a lot about the play.

PB   I've been listening to you today, and on the telephone, and I've noticed that you speak more quickly and flowingly in everyday life than you tend to in plays. Do you do that because you think actors and actresses have a duty to protect the language, and speak very clearly?

AM   Daniel used to say I over-enunciate. Of course I'm often cast in parts which demand quite precise English. Harold Pinter, for example, writes very precisely. In *Family Voices* I have to say: 'I hear your father's step on the stair. I hear his cough. But his step and his cough fade. He does not open the door.' It's not naturalistic dialogue. But maybe we do it with too much reverence.

PB   Do you agree with Daniel?

AM   I suppose I do. There are only a few more performances to go of *A Kind of Alaska*: perhaps I shall work on it in that. Could stop the reverence coming out. It might have something to do with a fear of

fluffing. I used to have that a lot. It's less now, thank
heavens.

PB   Yes I have that too. Especially on those nights when
you have to be careful, like First Nights, or friends in
front. Do you like to know when friends are out front?

AM   Oh no. I absolutely hate it.

PB   Why?

AM   It distracts me from the world of the play. It can be a
block, preventing me from entering that world.

PB   We start, in our childhood, by showing off, don't we?
That's why we become actors. But then it changes and
we can become shy and self-conscious. Did you start by
showing off?

AM   Oh yes. And the first play I did, *The Reluctant Debutante*,
I just thought, on the opening night on tour, oh this is
heaven; and then the Tuesday night the same; and then
on the Wednesday afternoon I dried, and I thought, oh
I don't like doing this, I don't think I'll bother to come
to London. And then I started getting nervous and
realised that doors don't always open, and things go
wrong.

PB   What do you do when things go wrong?

AM   Well, I write myself a lot of notes after performances. I
set myself goals.

PB   Such as?

AM   Hands stiller. At the drop of a hat I can be conducting
an orchestra.

PB   And?

AM   Lightness. It's so easy to force things in a long run. In
The Importance I lost a very big laugh, and I said to Paul
Rogers, 'Why have I lost that laugh?' and he said, 'I
don't know, you seem to be doing it in exactly the same
way.' So I gave myself notes: lighter, spontaneity – I
often write that word down – often to no avail – and I
suddenly remembered what I'd done at the first
preview. The line was 'I think, dear Doctor, I will have
a stroll with you. I find I have a headache after all.'
This after I've just denied having a headache. And I
remembered I used to do it with such joy, almost a
little skip, and that's funny.

PB   And how had you been doing it when you lost your laugh?

AM   Very sadly. As though I had a headache.

PB   And where did that hilarious walk towards Lady Bracknell in the last act come from? It's so bold. When you approach her with your head turned right round the other way?

AM   That came during the previews. One night I just felt it's as though I'm being drawn to somebody and I don't want to look at her.

PB   What had you done before?

AM   Just walked with my head down.

PB   And did you get a laugh the first time you tried the new way?

AM   No.

PB   But it was a hoot the night I saw it.

AM   Oh, sometimes it gets a round. It varies colossally.

PB   When you're on television, do you like to watch yourself?

AM   No, I hate it.

PB   Why?

AM   I think I'll catch myself not listening properly or something, or that I'll be acting too much, or being jerky. It's the same really, I suppose, as my dread of people being out front. I've got this dread of criticism. Especially from people I admire. They have to have my respect and admiration and then I dread their being out front. Part of me shies away from the notes they may give me, but part of me is grateful because I can learn from them. And there's something in there that I haven't quite sorted out.

PB   Do you enjoy acting more now than you used to?

AM   I've always had a love-hate relationship with it; in the seventies, about the time of Simon Gray's *Spoiled*, which I was in at the Haymarket, and David Hare's *Slag*, I felt seriously like giving the whole thing up. I had such a fear about acting in the theatre that I thought, well, I can't do it, there's no enjoyment left, I can't bear it, I'll just do television. But the fear came with me to television. So I went to an analyst.

PB   Was it self-consciousness that made you dislike it so much?

AM   No. It was panic.

PB   About what?

AM   Well, panic seizes everything up. It's like frozen, blocked drains. Nothing happens. Everything freezes. I suppose it was self-consciousness. Yes. I didn't know it at the time.

PB   How did this affect your acting?

AM   I was at my unhappiest when I took over from Penelope Keith in *Donkeys' Years*. I mean, the fact of taking over didn't help; but no director in the world at that time, 1977, would have got through to me. I was very resistant.

PB   To directors?

AM   To everything: to life. What your life is like affects your acting. I think your approach to life is what is going to come out as your approach to art. I'm happier in life now so I'm a happier actress.

PB   Do you work on life?

AM   Yes. And on acting, all the time. I think it's very very hard. And I'm not at all like Judi Dench who sometimes says, 'Oh, I can't wait to get on there.' I've never said that in my life.

Wyn Jones

When I interviewed Wyn Jones at home on Wednesday 23 February 1983 I asked him to concentrate on his most recent work: a six-month tour of Alan Ayckbourn's *Sisterly Feelings* preceded by a season of fortnightly rep. at the Leas Pavilion Theatre, Folkestone.

WJ   In a fortnightly rep. a good average working day, well, it'll depend a bit on how late you stayed up the night before – going out for a drink after the show, or learning, or most probably both – but a good average day will start with a couple of hours before rehearsal at ten o'clock to go through the lines you've only just learnt. You don't wake up with them, you see: you've only had one sleep-time on them, so you have to refresh

yourself and go through them. It becomes part of going
to the theatre warmed up and feeling on top of things. I
like to do voice exercises, too, and things like that,
though in digs it's a bit difficult to do too much of a
vocal warm-up on account of the other people there.
And some physical exercises, too: relaxing, stretching
and perhaps going for a quick walk.

But as the season goes on and you get tireder, it's
harder to do all this. You crawl out of bed and just try
to get to rehearsal on time.

PB   For the first rehearsal of each play, did you have a
read-through?

WJ   Oh no. There was no time for that.

PB   Do you think it's right, in a rep., for the director to tell
you what the moves are going to be?

WJ   Absolutely. I think it would be chaos if he didn't.
You'd spend the whole of the first week working out
where you were going. I mean, you might get better
results for yourself, but you'd waste so much rehearsal
time for everybody else. It's especially necessary for the
director to be strict if there are eight people on the
stage; if it's a duologue you can be more approximate
to start with because there can be more give and take.

PB   How long did it take to do the placing?

WJ   We'd block the whole play the first morning. The
Wednesday. Then of course we'd have a matinée and
an evening performance of the current play.

PB   And then how did rehearsals go?

WJ   Well, the next day, the Thursday, we'd know the first
section and break it down, then Friday the next section
and Saturday the next. So the first week was spent
learning the play as best we could. During the second
week, if we rehearsed mornings only, we could use the
free afternoons, apart from matinée days of course, for
going over what we'd rehearsed in the morning but also
for reading the play for the following fortnight.

PB   Did you always have afternoons off? I did when I was
in rep.. If you don't, it's a twelve-hour working day,
isn't it?

WJ   No we didn't always have afternoons off. Usually, but
not always. Because there's so little rehearsal time

many people, including of course the director, are tempted to go on into the afternoon. This happens especially when everybody's enthusiastic about a play, as we all were about Mike Leigh's *Abigail's Party*. We used to go on with that till five or five-thirty. It was far too much. It's a very intense play, all about people driven to their limits; I was Laurence, and, you know, having a heart attack five times in an afternoon, well, it's very tiring. Then I'd go to the digs for tea and a very short nap and go back to do another large part, in *Butterflies Are Free* it was, in the evening. If you over-rehearse you pay for it at the end of the season; and I think you just have to pace yourself so you don't get dog-tired. All I know is that when I got to the smallest part I had during the season I was really relieved to have time off from rehearsal because I wasn't in every scene, and I thought, oh I haven't got to learn a whacking part. I mean it can become just learning after a while. Some people can gauge realistically what can happen in a fortnight. I can't.

PB There are many differences between the life of an actor in a provincial rep. and the life of a freelance in London: you don't live at home, you're working on three plays at once and you can't pick and choose your parts. Do you like the challenge of the inevitable wide range of parts, for some of which you are bound to be miscast?

WJ Absolutely. And if the general opinion seems to be that you've been all right in other plays, you can afford sometimes to be below par: of course you don't want to be bad, but you can more easily accept that you're not going to be good in everything. I try not to give in, or I give in as little as I can. I try not to say, 'Oh, this part isn't me,' and just rely on disguise. Edward in *The Hollow* is a diffident bear of a man, a kind, woolly teddy-bear, very gentle, a bit lumpish, a different class from me, a different age, forty or even forty-five. How was a neurotic, wiry, bouncy twenty-eight-year-old supposed to play this uncle-figure? So I decided to forget all that and think, how can *I* be gentle and

diffident and avuncular at twenty-eight? I didn't want
to spray my hair with grey.

PB   So you went for the qualities rather than any sort of
disguise?

WJ   Yes, although I always like a little bit of disguise. And I
do take great pleasure in working out what I'm going to
wear. And I like to have little things that only I know
about. They're like superstitions; they're like talismens.
They can be little things I do off-stage, as preparation
for it, or on it during the performance. For one part I
liked to carry a book sticking out of my pocket; it was
just a private joke really: it was a book this character
would read, but it was also about the theme of the play.
It was called *The Principles of Freedom in Society*, and at a
matinée I was very pleased to hear someone in the front
row read the title aloud. But it was also a relic of this
character's untidiness; and so for the same part I had
my tie not tied properly, and hair which looked as if it
had been tidied by somebody else but not very well. I
just like to fill my performance, and therefore myself,
with physical things that I know are there like: why a
wedding ring? or why a particular watch or something?

PB   Why a moustache as Laurence in *Abigail's Party*?

WJ   Oh, that was just to make myself look older. I hate
stage moustaches, but in rep. there's no time to grow
one. You close on a Saturday without one and open
three days later with one. So I had to stick one on. And
this meant, because of the spirit-gum, my upper lip had
less mobility than usual. It was a terrific help, because
it made Laurence's smile into a dreadful, sidelong
sneer. He was so sad inside, you see, that he only
smiled out of duty; and this awful triangular mouth was
born at the dress rehearsal.

PB   Was Laurence one of your favourite parts there?

WJ   Yes. When I look back on the whole season I know I
was better in the better plays. *Abigail's Party* is so well
written it just carries you along. No lines are wasted;
and when my instinct really got going I felt that the
whole play was about Laurence not being loved by
Beverly: life was a constant battle for him, and he says,
'Not that life is easy, no, life is hard,' and it *was* hard,

and I connected all this to his indigestion and heart complaint, so the heart attack was inevitable.

PB   Do you find what Mike Leigh calls 'running conditions', like indigestion and a heart complaint, helpful? Do you like to find encapsulations?

WJ   Yes. They're not always easy to find, though. In the poorer plays I just couldn't, and felt vague and in grave danger of losing interest. But when you're proud of a play, not necessarily the production but the play itself, like *Abigail's Party* or *Stage Struck*, and you can believe in what's being said, it's a different world altogether.

PB   But in rep., once a play's on, that's it, isn't it? You've got to start work on the next one?

WJ   Well, you do bits of work. You have to grit your teeth and get on with it.

PB   How much stage management have you done?

WJ   At various times I think I've done nearly all the jobs. I've been on the book, I've done electrics and sound and flies and props and marking the set and building the set and painting the set.

PB   Do you think it's a good thing for actors to have done stage management?

WJ   Only briefly. Only to get an understanding of what it entails.

PB   As an actor, what do you expect of the stage management?

WJ   Mostly that they don't do it grudgingly, but regard themselves as part of the team, part of the play. You want them to be accurate, of course, but more than that to give you support. The person on the book is the most important of all. For example, there are ways of giving prompts: somebody can give you a prompt and at the same time manage to make you feel like an idiot for drying; somebody else might withhold a prompt for a little while because they know you really know it, and then they might give you a key word or something. And if you feel that the person on the book is interested in how the play is forming they become part of creating it.

PB   Do you like to be close to the company socially?

WJ   Yes. Very. Drinks afterwards and jokes. Oh yes.

PB   What did you learn from this particular season?

WJ   Hard to say. The importance of vocal variety and
things like that, basic things; the importance of
everybody supporting each other and caring; but I
suppose for myself I could see the harm that I did when
I hated a play and went around saying so. So I tried to
shut up about the things I didn't like. I mean, it could
be awful: there was one play when we'd go to the pub
afterwards and laugh our heads off about the rubbish
we were doing and that made the next performance
almost impossible to do. It was dreadful. So I thought,
I won't do that again.

PB   After the season was over, you did a national tour of
Sisterly Feelings. Here you had a part which suited you
and which you had accepted in the normal way. But
you had to sustain the role for six months.

WJ   Yes. The longest time, by far, that I've ever had to play
a part.

PB   Did you feel stale as the tour continued?

WJ   No. Oddly enough. No. I realised it was possible to
continue to care, to keep on trying, for a very long time.
That was a surprise. But my first surprise was that
acting with tried and tested people like Peter Sallis,
which I had been a bit scared of, knowing that I was an
unknown actor and would have to prove myself, was
easier than I could possibly have imagined. I found it's
easier to be good if you're with good people.

And there were nights, particularly in my scenes with
Tessa Peake-Jones, when new things happened,
illuminating things, and we thought, oh why have we
never thought of that before? And this was particularly
towards the end of the run.

And there were other nights when I would lose
laughs, and wonder why. I remember vividly a night in
Richmond when I got off to a poorish start, I mean it
all felt like the repetition it was, and I just said to
myself that old cliché, come on, be 'in it' a bit more;
and just saying that made some lost laughs come back.

PB   It does work, doesn't it, telling yourself stories about
the characters or the play before you go on, so you can,
hopefully, be 'in it', as you say?

WJ   Yes, but there's a reverse side to all that. I was terribly
     late once getting to Birmingham on account of missing
     a turning, and even later one night at Cardiff when my
     car broke down. I got to the theatre with two minutes
     to spare. They were two of the best performances I ever
     gave. Especially the Cardiff one.

PB   Have you any theories about that? Could it be because
     you're on a high of excitement when you arrive, full of
     adrenalin, there's no worry, no preconception of
     possible failure that night?

WJ   Yes. The wings are dark, the stage is light, and you
     switch on your familiar world. After the turmoil of the
     journey you know where you are. Yes. It can be quite
     exciting when it happens suddenly.

PB   What were the hardest things about touring?

WJ   Oh, the usual things when confidence goes. Bad nights.
     Just got to grin and bear them.

PB   What did you get most out of the experience of playing
     the same part for six months?

WJ   Well, it was interesting largely because it was a
     comedy, and people in different towns laughed in
     different ways and at different times.
         During the rep. season I've told you about one of the
     directors said, 'Oh you're going to hate this part
     because you can't be nice Wyn Jones in it. You do like
     to be liked, don't you?' And another time he said, 'Oh,
     come on, you're not playing Jesus Christ in this.' And
     this took me very much by surprise because the
     characters I had liked playing most were the
     unsympathetic ones. Of course I'd tried to identify with
     them and see things from their point of view. But
     latterly I have realised how much I do like to be liked.

PB   Was it *Sisterly Feelings* which pointed that out to you?

WJ   Yes. I always have a soft spot for whoever I am playing
     and I had a particularly soft spot for Stafford T.
     Wilkins. And the nights when the audience's laughter
     was affectionate laughter, when I felt they loved the
     character as much as I did, well, those were the best
     nights. I mean, there's obedient laughter and there's
     uninhibited, unreserved laughter which isn't only to do
     with a funny line or a funny situation, it's to do with an

actor or actress you like, and are willing to respond to readily. There are comedians that you like and comedians that you don't. They tell the same joke, and you laugh at the one and not at the other.

PS 1991. A DIRECTOR'S VIEW

I interviewed Wyn Jones again on Monday 25 February 1991, almost exactly eight years after our previous conversation. In the interim he had become a director and was no longer an actor.

WJ   It wasn't really a new ambition to be a director, because I had directed at university, and in an amateur group before that. After that I didn't think about it much, but the ambition was always there somewhere.

Anyway. After over a year of unemployment, which affected me a great deal, trying to come to terms with it, I was given the opportunity to go back to Folkestone both to act in and direct alternate plays. Part of me thought I was getting nowhere, going back there after all that time; but part of me thought, well, I'm untrained as a director, just as I was untrained as an actor, and here at last is a chance to try it out. You see, I didn't know if I would suit it, or indeed if it would suit me.

PB   And did it?

WJ   Well, it seemed to. I mean to start with I overprepared like mad, working out 'sit on that word,' 'move DR to sofa,' you know, rep. moves. But what spurred me on was that actors responded to me, seemed to like working with me. As time went on I realised I was enjoying it more and more. The thing I loved about it was that I was able to concentrate on other people and not on myself.

PB   How long did you stay there?

WJ   Two years. Two seasons.

PB   After that did you act again?

WJ   Not so as you'd notice.

PB   So what did you do?

WJ   With Robert Daws and Amanda Drewry I set up a
      company called Southern Lights. And you know how I
      said before that I'd done all those peripheral things like
      electrics and sound and flies and props? Well, none of
      that was wasted; and the same thing has applied since
      then, because setting up a company, going into the
      dark, we had to do everything ourselves: I mean none
      of us had any business skills or knew about printing,
      posters, distributing them, advertising, casting,
      contracts. We had to explore so many areas involved in
      putting on a play, with help from literary agents and
      casting directors. It was very interesting. And of course
      more people are doing it nowadays, taking control into
      their own hands. Through necessity, often.

PB   You presented plays at the New End Theatre in
      Hampstead, didn't you?

WJ   Yes. Of course the difference here was that I could
      choose the plays, and thereby find out more about my
      strengths and weaknesses. I found out that I could do
      intimate, psychologically detailed, realistic plays far
      better than zany comedies or black farces.

PB   It was a remarkable season, with Githa Sowerby's
      wonderful play *Rutherford and Son* being the standout
      success.

WJ   Yes. From that I got my first freelance job, at the
      Theatre Royal, Plymouth. And of course the big
      difference here was that I didn't have to do all those
      things which have to be done when you're running a
      small fringe company. They have workshops and
      people and a publicity office. All I had to do was cast
      the play and rehearse it and get it on. Luxury.

PB   Let's talk, then, about casting and rehearsing. This
      chapter is called *How Do You Work On A Part?* and I'd
      like to ask you for a director's view. What do you look
      for in actors when you are casting and rehearsing?
      Casting first . . .

WJ   Well, I hope that an actor will be technically well-
      graced, able to do good acting things, and those things
      which we all delight in . . .

PB   . . . You do take great pains with casting, don't you?

WJ   Yes I do. I take great pains to cast actors who, in my view, are the rightest for the part: actors in whom I can see glimmerings of a connection with the part. I look for interesting people, not just people who act well. People who can be people, not just actors on a stage. And people who I think *I* can connect with, too. People who want to do the play. I get feelings after interviews that I would like to work with this person, and usually it's not a one-way feeling. As Simon Rouse was leaving after an interview for *Rat in the Skull* at Plymouth, he just said, 'I'm really keen to do this part, you know,' and went . . .

PB   Do you ask around?

WJ   Yes.

PB   It's interesting that prepared audition speeches are very much on the way out now, isn't it?

WJ   Yes, I don't like them. Eamonn Walker wanted to do one and I said, 'Don't.' But he went ahead and did it and was so wonderful I offered him the part.

PB   Yes . . . so where are you? But actors have to accept what directors choose to do at a casting session, don't they? It's well known that at the National Theatre at present one director wants a chat only, whereas another doesn't want to chat at all, but wants a reading.

WJ   I meet and read. The two things are important. It's nothing to do with sight-reading or with people who don't read well, but you can tell so much from a reading.

PB   Let's talk now about rehearsing. I think one area where this book is dated now is in its references to the director initiating rehearsals by giving moves which he has predetermined. There's such a reference in your previous interview, and in the chapter called *Attitudes*.

   I remember when I was rehearsing for a play recently there was quite an altercation between the director and one of the actors. The director said, 'How are you going to do this speech? I mean it needs far more energy and conviction. You are talking about big issues here.'

   And the actor, who was of a certain age, said, 'I

thought we were doing moves today. I'll give you the acting when I know what the moves are.'

The director replied. 'I can't give you moves until I see something of what you intend to do.'

They both got quite cross. After the rehearsal I explained to the director that that is how actors used to think.

What do you do? What do you start with?

WJ Well, a read-through. Actually I think it's good to have a read-through in advance of the rehearsals. Or at least a meeting. And if it can't be everybody together, I like to meet for a coffee or a drink. But then, yes, on the first day, a read-through. You've got to break the ice somehow, because everybody finds first days difficult. Including the director. Then I often do a second read-through, but make it a walk-through, which is to say the furniture is here or there, and just see where people want to move, see what their instincts tell them to do; and sometimes you find that they are relating to each other much more, though not performing yet, and that's valuable. In early days too I like to ask questions about each character's past.

PB Do you do the blocking early?

WJ It varies. When I did *The Price* in Plymouth, we spent the first week sitting round a table, breaking down the text into beats, and me saying, 'What does this beat mean?' I hadn't planned to do it like that, and there were some anxious actors by the end of the week because they were used to getting up and moving it on the floor. But it was money in the bank for later.

And in Stephen Jeffreys' *Hard Times* in Cheltenham, where four actors shared over twenty parts, we spent a long time over characterisation and did a lot of improvising, so we were still plotting at the last minute.

But sometimes it can be quite quick. We did *Rutherford and Son* in two days. Not planned by me, at least not in too much detail – I mean I had ideas – but people used to try things and I'd say, 'Oh that's good, well don't you move there, and if you try sitting over there,' you know, using the stage; and while all this was

going on I would try and select the best positions for
the furniture and the best places for the actors.

PB   What do you hope for from the actors in rehearsals?

WJ   Oh, an openness, a commitment, a readiness to take
risks. At an early rehearsal of *Rutherford and Son* Pauline
Letts, who was playing the old aunt, did her first
improvisation ever. She whispered, 'Oh, is this an
improvisation? Oh God, I'm terrified.' She sat in a chair
with her script, but I took it gently out of her hands, and
she improvised the scene and wiped the floor with the two
young actresses who'd done improvisations at drama
school. She was the truest, the funniest and the cleverest,
and she retained all the things she discovered that
afternoon. She was wonderful.

But the director has to be as open as he hopes the
actors will be, and not foist on people things they don't
want to do. Ewan Hooper, in the same play, didn't
want to do improvisation-type things. He said, 'I don't
believe in all that.' So nothing was foisted on him and
he was brilliant.

What I really hope for is that an actor will connect
with a part on the deepest emotional level possible, and
will allow that emotion to crack through his rational
defences. When an actor is possessed by a part, well,
it's a great bonus. In *Rat in the Skull* Gerardine Hinds
was inspired by the part. She was the soul of Ireland in
it. Not with the head, with the heart. She couldn't have
given more to the play.

PB   As rehearsals progress, presumably you become more
picky and technical, tidying it all up?

WJ   Yes. I like to start with things which cause emotion –
history, facts, intentions, wants – I like to start
emotionally and end technically. A director is an editor
as much as anything: you start off as an enabler and
then you pare down. You try to feed their confidence
and hopefully earn their trust. It's give and take.

Alison Steadman

When I interviewed Alison Steadman on Friday 25 February
1983, I asked her to concentrate, to the exclusion of everything

else, on how she worked with her husband, Mike Leigh, on her part as Beverly in his play *Abigail's Party*. I had known nothing, until that winter morning at home, about Mike Leigh's method of making a play, even though he had been a student at RADA while I was still taking classes there. I didn't connect, until after the interview, his use of improvisation with mine (explained earlier in this book), possibly because he goes so much further than I had in its application. I had been amazed at his plays, *Abigail's Party* and *Goose-Pimples*: how deep they were, how extreme, how savage and how funny. But what Alison Steadman had to tell me was an eye-opener: I didn't know things like this happened.

AS   For *Abigail's Party* Mike chose five actors: three women and two men. He had said to me, 'I'm going to do a play and I'd like you to be in it. I don't know what you'll be doing: you might do a small part, you might be the central character, I don't know. But are you willing to take that risk?' So, I said yes. Then he said to me, and to all the others, separately, 'I'd like you to make a list of people that you know, either very well or just acquaintances, that aren't in the theatre, that are in this age-group,' – in my case it was something between, I don't know, twenty-eight and thirty-five, – 'and within this certain class of society.'

PB   Does he always specify that?

AS   Usually.

PB   How did he define it in this case?

AS   I can't remember exactly but probably lower middle class or working class. So I made a list and I talked about them, and when I'd described them he said, 'Right. I want you to think about and work on that particular woman.'

    She was someone I didn't know terribly well: I knew her family and a few things about her but I didn't know much detail. Nevertheless she was the jumping-off point, the springboard. It's not to say that from then on I wanted to impersonate her: she was the start. Mike calls it, 'The first mark on the canvas. You've got to start somewhere. When you paint a picture you've got to begin. And once you've made the first mark you can make the second.'

Anyway. After that we all met for the first day's rehearsal. We had eight weeks, with a week of previews, and people said, '*God*, what a length of *time*!', but really, when there's not a word written yet, it's no time at all. Anyway. We all met and sat there and smiled at each other and were very apprehensive. After that we all, individually, had a session with Mike, and we each spent the next ten days or a fortnight working alone with him. First of all being that person alone. He said to me, 'Where is she living?'

'At home with her parents.'

'Does she have her own room?'

'Yes.'

'Right. Here's her room. Let's say her parents are out, or on holiday, and she's alone. What happens? Would she read magazines?'

And so you start making decisions that give you your base.

'Does she work?' he said.

'Yes.'

'What kind of job does she have?'

'Er . . . well . . . she's very fashion conscious, very make-up conscious, maybe she would work in a chemist's shop, selling make-up.'

'Right,' said Mike. 'Now: it's a day when she's at home and she's alone in her room.'

He sits in a corner. Very quietly. Forget about him. No pressure. Be that person. No need to do anything. Actors are so used to performing they tend to want to do a lot: make a lot of telephone calls or a cake. But that's not the job in hand, which is merely to be that person, feel like that person. What mood is she in? What day is it? It's a Saturday morning, and it's raining outside. She's on her own, she's not going out that night, she's not seeing any friends. How does she feel that day?

So that's the beginning. Then a little chat with Mike, who will stop it at some point. There's no one else in the room to watch, so you don't have to start performing and being good. I mean, sometimes it's awful: you don't feel right and you get self-conscious; but eventually a little life does begin to grow and suddenly you think, oh I am somebody different, I am beginning to think like another person and not like the actress Alison Steadman saying to herself, 'I know, I'll do this bit like this because it will be right.' And then there's bringing clothes to rehearsal. We had by now established that this particular woman was preoccupied by her appearance and her make-up and her hair, and so for rehearsal . . .

PB   Still alone?

AS   . . . Oh yes. In private. I was never told what was happening with the others.

PB   And always in a rehearsal room?

AS   Oh yes. Mike and I talked hardly at all about it at home. It wouldn't work.

PB   How many hours a week each?

AS   I suppose I'd have about five shortish sessions. The rest of the time I'd do some research. For instance, we decided that ultimately her job would be a beautician, you know, a down-market . . . well, she'd call herself a beautician, in fact she was selling make-up in a big store in the West End. So I got in touch with a cosmetics company, I think it was called Clinique, or some such name, and asked if I could meet a personnel woman who would tell me what training Beverly would have had and what money she'd earn.

We had by now decided to call her Beverly, and when I was chatting to this woman the phone went and she answered it and said, 'Oh hello, Beverly!' And afterwards she said, 'She's one of my girls, she's been out on the circuit.' They tour around the big stores. So I spent the next few days wandering around John Lewis and Selfridges, just watching the girls: the way they dressed, how they behaved and spoke; and gradually things were beginning to grow, without actually saying, 'Ah that's a good idea: I could do that.' None of that. And then, a wonderful thing happened, because there was this girl doing a demonstration, making up a woman, and there was a crowd round and she'd got a little microphone tucked in the corner of her mouth, so I just stood and watched. And I got so much: her style, her manner, everything, the whole performance, because of course she was giving a performance. So I went back to rehearsal with much more information.

Then Mike set up an improvisation with Tim Stern, who was to play Laurence. Ultimately the two characters were married, but this impro. was about the first time they met. Also of course it was the first time I spoke as Beverly, and this voice came out. I still didn't know anything about the other three people or what Mike had been doing with them, and really I wasn't interested to know: I was getting so involved with Beverly and her life, and by the time I met Tim I knew so much about her that I could answer any question about her that he might ask me: 'Are your parents alive?' and I knew. So our conversation was backed by a great deal of information, which prevents that awful thing of someone saying (as can happen in ill-prepared improvisations), 'Oh isn't it cold today?' when you'd been thinking it's hot. I'm not saying all our impro.'s were good. Sometimes they were very boring. And long.

PB   How does Mike initiate an improvisation?

AS   For instance, this first one: he said to me, 'Right. Get ready. Go into character. It's Monday morning, it's eight-thirty and she's going off to her new job. I want you to go outside and walk down to the tube. Then turn round, and when you come out of the tube station, come back here and this will be your new office, and when you walk into the office, if you see anyone else, they are in character.' Well, for this first impro. I wasn't sure who I'd meet, but it was Tim Stern. It was Laurence. It was gradually established that Laurence invited Beverly out. Obviously a lot of the stuff we accelerated forwards, so we had chats with Mike, and he'd say, 'Well, he's asked her out: where would they go?'

And Laurence would say, 'For a meal.'

And Mike would say, 'If we suggested that to Beverly, how would she react?' I mean we talked things through, and in an hour you can have a six-week

relationship: you don't have to act everything. But I
knew for example that she wouldn't want to go to a
Wimpy Bar, she'd want a bistro.

Then one day Mike said, 'Right, they get married.'

And Tim's face fell and he said, 'No, I can't bear it.'

But Mike said, 'They get married. Now. Would it be
a white wedding, would the parents be there, would it
be a registry office? What would it be?'

So we talked the wedding through and we'd got them
married then.

Mike said, 'Where will they live? He's got a flat:
would she move in?' And we decided she would, but
then she decided she didn't like it, so they moved to
another flat; so we leapt it on, did a lot of
improvisations in this new flat, like: 'She's at home,
she's got home from work, it's six o'clock, she's
preparing the evening meal, or not, as the case may be.
Go into character.' We'd set up a room with pots and
pans and things, even a practical television.

Then Laurence would come home and say things
like, 'Where's the food?'

And she'd say, 'Oh sorry, I haven't had a chance to
shop.' And gradually it built up that they were at
loggerheads most of the time because she was so
preoccupied with everything except domestic things
that it drove him up the wall. She became very
dissatisfied with this new flat, so eventually they bought
a house in Chigwell, Essex.

PB   How long had you been rehearsing by now?

AS   About five weeks. And in that time we'd gone from
making the list of women to being married and living in
a semi in Chigwell. Mike told us about the street, how
on one side the houses were 'thirties semi's and on the
other they were brand new. He told us who else lived in
the street, and that the people over the road were the
Macdonalds; and it all became very real. We'd add
new layers: did Beverly want a baby? – 'No, no way' –
did Laurence? – 'No, never.'

PB   Did Laurence have his heart condition by now?

AS   No.

PB   Oh!

AS   No. Beverly never knew about his heart condition.

PB   Did he know?

AS   No. As far as I was aware. He had certain symptoms,
     but it was always heartburn or overwork or something.

     One day Mike said to me, 'I want you to go into
     character, and I want you to go out and do some
     shopping.' Well, we were rehearsing near Regents Park
     in a church hall and there were some shops not far
     away. He said, 'I want you to go to the shops, in
     character, and then come back.'

PB   In Beverly's clothes?

AS   Oh yes, with all the gear on. I mean it's the funniest
     thing to walk along a street as somebody else. Anyway
     off I went, and I saw Thelma Whiteley. Now I knew
     she was in the play: I didn't know what she was
     playing, but I knew she was another character, because
     she didn't look like Thelma Whiteley. So, I saw her and
     I sort of smiled as Beverly would, and Thelma just
     nodded to me and that was all that happened. And this
     went on for days: we kept seeing each other in the
     street, nodding and smiling. And something in me kept
     thinking, as an actress I should obviously be moving
     this on and talking to this other character, but I
     thought I can't because that's not what she would do.
     So I thought, no, go on trusting and keep to the truth
     and do what you're told, and don't think, well it would
     make the play better if I did this or that. Do what she
     would do and you can't go wrong. You can only go
     wrong if you start not following the rules. Anyway,
     eventually Beverly talked to this character, who was
     called Sue in the play, and said, 'If you're ever passing
     do pop in for a coffee,' because she was the sort of
     neighbour that Beverly would like to be friends with: a
     nice, middle class lady; and she also wanted to show off
     her home.

     And then it was established that Laurence and
     Beverly did their weekly shop at Sainsbury's. We
     actually went to Sainsbury's a few times, in
     character . . .

PB   Didn't you giggle?

AS   Not yet. We hadn't got to the giggling bit yet. But on
     one occasion Mike said, 'Right. Go off in the car to
     Sainsbury's. Drive along so-and-so road . . .' (in fact
     we went down to Finchley Road and used that
     Sainsbury's) '. . . park the car, go in, get all your
     shopping, and bring it back.' The only thing was when
     we went shopping we couldn't buy Beverly's stuff – you
     know, it would be twenty quid down the drain – so
     Mike said we could compromise.
         Anyway on the way we saw Sue standing at a bus
     stop. So I said, 'Oh Laurence, stop, there's Sue!' It
     turned out her car had broken down, and she was going
     shopping. Mike had set the whole thing up and had
     said to her, 'Your car's broken down, you've got to go
     shopping, and you've got to go on a bus.' So she got in
     and we all went off to Sainsbury's in character. We did
     the shopping, and when we were standing in the
     checkout queue Tim saw a friend of his, an actor. And
     this friend said, 'Tim, Tim, hello,' and waved to him.
     Of course Tim didn't want to ignore the bloke
     completely, but he didn't want to break the whole thing
     up, so he just kind of grunted and nodded. And this
     bloke couldn't understand why Tim was being so rude
     to him. Anyway. Back we went; and this impro. went
     on for a long time: Sue came in for coffee, and we put
     the shopping away and chatted. When we'd finished
     Mike said, 'The Ideal Home Exhibition is on at the
     moment. Would she like to go?' And I said, 'Yes,
     definitely.' And he said to Tim, 'Would Laurence want
     to go?' and Tim said, 'No, he wouldn't be very keen,
     but if she forced him he'd go.' So the next day we went,
     in character, to the Ideal Home Exhibition and spent
     the whole day there.
PB   Was Mike there too?
AS   No. He had watched us in Sainsbury's, but he was
     rehearsing someone else on this day. It turned out to be
     one of the best days, really, because it established so
     much about their relationship. Beverly's life was only
     furniture, cosmetics, clothes and sex, so of course she
     was in paradise: I mean there were heart-shaped baths
     and things like that; and they were arguing over

everything and he would say, 'You have no TASTE',
and 'I wouldn't have that in my house.' And in fact the
painting that Beverly brings down at the end of
Abigail's Party, the one with the swan with a naked man
standing on it, was at the Ideal Home Exhibition, and
Beverly said, 'Can we buy that picture?' and we had a
terrible row about it. When we got back we told Mike
about it and I said, 'She'd go back and buy it.' Mike
said, 'Let's leave that for now,' and then he told us that
the Macdonalds over the road were moving out, and a
new couple had bought the house. How would Beverly
react to this? So I said, 'Well she'd watch all the
furniture that was going in, and she'd spend a long
time just watching them, weighing them up.' Mike
said, 'They're a young couple with no family.'

Next day he said, 'Go into character and you're at
home. It's six-thirty in the evening. Laurence is out
with one of his clients.' And there was a knock at the
door. I didn't know who it was going to be. So I opened
the door and Janine Duvitski was standing there, as
Angela, and she said, 'I hope I'm not disturbing you
but I just wanted to say hello because we've just moved
in.' So I said, 'Oh. No. Come in.' and we did an impro.

It had been established that Beverly had watched
them a lot and had taken a fancy to Tony, the husband,
and had been trying to work out an opportunity for
getting them over there for a nice social evening. So
Beverly said to Angela, 'Would you and your husband
like to come over one evening for drinks?' Well we did
an impro. of that and then we did another one when
Sue called, and Sue told Beverly about her teenage
daughter Abigail who was having a party at home that
Saturday night. Now, without Mike saying anything,
Beverly quickly said, 'Well, why don't you pop down
here and have the evening with us?' So it was agreed
that we should have an evening when the three of them
would arrive. The rehearsal room was set up with a
record-player and drinks and food. Whatever I said
Beverly would provide was brought in by the stage
management.

PB   Had you chosen the furniture by now?

AS　We were still working with rehearsal furniture, but we knew what it would be. Of course, while all this was going on, Mike was working with the designer, Tanya McCallin.

PB　And you now had a full stage management?

AS　Yes. They were around. As we needed things like coffee and tea they brought them. Gradually we were building it up.

PB　And were the drinks real for this improvisation?

AS　Yes. For the only time. It lasted four hours. It was wonderful. The next day Mike, who was monitoring it very carefully now, said, 'We've got to put a play together. After all this nonsense we've been doing for weeks, we've now got to construct a play.' And he said, for the first time, 'The play will take place in Laurence and Beverly's house on a Saturday evening, the night of Abigail's party.' So we started with Beverly alone, and he said, 'It's seven-thirty in the evening. Laurence isn't home yet. What would she have done by way of preparation for the party?' And so we started to construct the events, still using improvisation. But Mike would stop us now, and say, 'Let's go back to the beginning, and when Laurence arrives don't shout at him,' and he'd give us lines to speak now and build a scene as any writer would.

PB　Writing it down the while?

AS　No. Making notes, distilling what happens, paring it down. But when we started putting the play together I laughed till I cried. For a fortnight I couldn't stop. It was disgraceful: I was sure Mike would lose his temper. But I couldn't help it: it was so desperate, so awful, and so hysterically funny. Particularly when Sue came in, and we were so rude to her . . . I mean it was like throwing custard-pies at the woman. Anyway, I simmered down, and as we went on, with Mike giving us more and more lines, it was curiously easy to do, so secure we all were in our characters. But when we'd finished working through the play it lasted four hours. We'd got the basic construction, and knew when the audience had to be given this or that information; now we had to go back to the beginning and really refine, and cut out bits. And when we'd got about three-quarters of the way through Mike set up an improvisation, and he said to me, 'And this is where the picture comes in.' And I said, 'The picture?' And he said, 'Yes, the picture she saw at the Ideal Home Exhibition.' And I said, 'Oh yes,' and he said, 'She's bought it. It's upstairs in the bedroom.' You see in improvisations Mike sometimes uses the technique of asking people to leave the room so they don't know some information they shouldn't know.

PB   Yes.

AS   Well. We did this impro. and Laurence said, 'You bring that picture down, Bev, and I'll kill you.' And I walked out and actually said the line, 'Drop dead!' We were at Hampstead Theatre by this time, working in the set, and the picture was in the dressing-room. And when I came back there was Laurence on the floor. I was terribly thrown. There he was, dying on the floor and it was . . . an extraordinary moment because of this total panic.

PB   Had Mike said it to him that day?

AS   I don't know. I don't know. Obviously this condition was known to Beverly only as she would know about it in everyday life. What had been established privately between Mike and Tim I don't know, but presumably, yes, they had talked a lot about how far his condition had gone; and it was Mike, not Tim, who said, 'On this day, at this time, you have a heart attack.' So we all dealt with it as our characters would. It was terribly upsetting; the rehearsal had been fun and we'd been laughing and enjoying ourselves and suddenly it was awful. It was quite a heavy morning, as I recall, and it upset Tim Stern a lot. He actually cried when the impro. had finished. He was crying for Laurence, for his character: that we do these awful things to each other. They were destroying each other, locked in this room, drinking like mad; and this is what society had produced: a man who had no choice, who was trapped by all these things. I mean, nothing was said, but we all just knew it was awful, this whole thing of these people we were playing. But the important thing is, that that was just the impro.. We still had to construct the scene itself.

PB But no script?

AS No script. That was done well after we'd opened.

PB So how did you set your performances, so you could repeat them?

AS Well, by going back to the beginning, and rehearsing each section; somehow you learn it and know it.

PB Did the performances of it vary a great deal?

AS No. Exactly the same.

PB Words and all?

AS Words and all. You play it like any play. You begin to know where the laughs are, how to time them.

PB It was remarkably fresh on television too.

AS M'm. It was very difficult to do because it was never made for television. Suddenly to be in the studio alone, with no audience, and with all the pressures, was not so good. It was still fun to do, I suppose, but not the same as on the stage.

PB When you appear in other people's plays, written-down plays, do you find them comparatively boring?

AS No, not really. It depends on the script. What I do know, though, is I'm happiest when I'm furthest away from myself.

Patience Collier

I visited Patience Collier at her home in Kensington at two-thirty p.m. on Thursday 3 March 1983. She had just opened in *Lent* by Michael Wilcox at the Lyric Studio Theatre, Hammersmith. At three-thirty when we'd finished, and I'd switched off my pocket-sized cassette-recorder, she said she was going to rest and was already getting nervous for that evening's performance. I had promised I would take no more than an hour of her time, and left at three-thirty-five, after having said goodbye to Alice, her eighty-four-year-old cook-housekeeper.

PC I've discovered a new word. Pith. An actor or an actress should have inside them the pith of the part they are playing. Now, if you are a woman of many parts, and I suppose I think I am, it means that I can play a murderess, or a beauty, or a mousey little person in the village, and they will all have the pith that's inside me. I mean, they can have my nose and be a beauty, because the beauty is in my head. And that's not sentimental, you know. I think I look quite pretty as Mrs Blake, this woman I'm playing now. And it's strange that I can use the word 'pretty' about myself with my phizog.

PB   Pretty, yet frail.

PC   Well I'm frail because my face is frail now.

PB   But you look frailer. Very pale.

PC   I don't put any make-up on. But what I do is, before I put on my wig, I dust my face and neck with Johnson's Baby Powder, and on my lips I put a non-colour colour, which gives them a shape and prevents them from looking dry and crinkled.

PB   How did you start?

PC   Well, you know this play is partly autobiographical, all about Michael Wilcox's days at prep school, and so I said to him did he know this woman, and he said, yes she was my grandmother, and I said, have you got a picture of her anywhere, and he said, yes, and he brought it; and she had a square face and looked like Flora Robson. She also had soft, pretty, idiotic white hair and it was so untidy always, he said, that the family used to go about catching the kirby grips. I had to get this sort of person, a mixture of softness and discipline, into me. Now, in the photograph she was wearing a two-piece, made of navy-blue and white foulard, a fashionable material of the time, so I said to Christopher Fettes, who was going to direct it, 'I can't do this part unless you let Cosprops dress me.' He said, 'We can't afford them and they won't do us.' I said, 'Yes they will, they'll do me: let me get on the telephone.' So I rang John Bright and said, 'Look, John, I'm stuck; I don't want to do a part unless I can have a navy-blue and white foulard two-piece and a navy-blue plain hat. If you can find them, I can do this part; I can't otherwise because anything else will be too smart, too vulgar or whatever.' The following Tuesday I went to him, and he had it hanging there.

PB   You have to ask for a lot in the theatre, don't you?

PC   Oh yes. You have to. It's not like filming. There you
don't have to ask for anything. You see I don't like
economising in any way, and in films they don't. If they
want a diamond necklace they get a diamond necklace:
they get everything and money isn't considered. They
get it because the director wants it and tells them to get
it. Anyway, for this play I went as usual to Wig
Creations, and I said to David, 'Don't *make* me a wig,'
and I always say this, 'find me an old wig out of a
drawer which you can clean and re-front, but it must
be soft enough to be on to . . . to be *in* to my head.' And
then I thought to myself, I know what shoes I've got to
wear, and I got my great big brown-and-white shoe-
bag filled with shoes which I'd stolen, over the years,
from the RSC (but Peter Hall and Trevor Nunn knew
about this), and I found these white summer shoes
which are so uncomfortable that I thought I can't walk
better for this part than in these shoes because they're
so uncomfortable. I wear them for hurt. So I haven't
got to think about how to walk. The walk is done. The
stick is my mother-in-law's which she left here.

PB   And the voice is yours, isn't it?

PC   Oh, absolutely. And also it's mine not trying to be old,
because I don't believe old people sound old. But fear
of making an 'acting' noise with an upper-class accent,
because it is quite upper class, made me too quiet to
start with, and the director said, 'You must be
tougher,' and somebody who came to see the first dress
rehearsal said, 'You need some more decibels: you're
being too modest.'

PB   Did you go louder?

PC   Oh yes. One decibel up.

PB   You're the only person I've talked to for this book who
has just done a First Night. How did you feel?

PC   Unready. I'm still unready. You see I haven't studied
this play as I usually do; I haven't done it nearly so
thoroughly.

PB   Why?

PC   No time. I've been spoilt at the RSC and the National
with eleven weeks or nine weeks for rehearsal, and

that's what I like: to have time to find out what the author's attitude was when writing the play, what the person I was to play was like as a child, how she grew up to be the adult she's become. I suppose I did this most for *The Government Inspector*, when I was the Mayor's wife, that idiot; and when I thought about it I got this child into my head who went in for Butlin's Holiday Camps' baby competitions; she was not particularly pretty, but had hair that was gold and sharp, with curls, and I could hear her mum and dad and her auntie and uncle all saying, 'Oh, isn't our Annie loovely?' 'Don't her hair shine?' Dreadful voices, a dreadful accent. She was that sort of little girl: harsh, but loved by all these people. So I said to Peter Hall, 'Can I do this part with this sort of voice?' and he said, 'Absolutely: you keep on with that dreadful Butlin child.' And later, he said, 'Now put it into the accent we're going to use,' and this accent had no 't's' or 'r's', so I said 'Pi'usburg', not 'Petersburg': that sort of thing. And I kept the child's voice and the child's laugh for a time, and later Peter Hall said, 'Now, keep this timbre, but grow up into a harshness: throw away the child.' And with that harshness came the shape of my neck, and my mouth; but this was a long study, you see. And that woman, mutton dressed as lamb, became an inevitability. That's how I like to work.

PB   You give the impression, because of the sort of actress you are and the sort of person you are, that once your performance is set, that's how it stays. Is that right?

PC   No of course not. For instance I've just been practising a little moment where I think I spell it out too much.

PB   So if you want to change anything, you work it out at home and put the revised version into your performance that night?

PC   Yes. And nobody'll know but me.

PB   But apart from that you wouldn't risk a change on the spur of the moment?

PC   Never, never, never. Such a thing could not possibly happen to me, ever, to the end of the world.

PB   You've done a lot of radio. How do you approach a part when it's the voice only that you can use?

PC Well I like radio because I can do voices. When they did a feature programme with eight women they used Betty Hardy and me for the eight: bus conductresses, beggars, nannies in the park and ladies at the hairdressers. But acting for radio has taught me an enormous amount about words, which I would never have known if I hadn't done it.

PB Such as?

PC Well it taught me about people's listenability.

PB What does that mean?

PC Well . . . if you lived with Alice you'd know she doesn't hear anything I say, however clearly I say it. I mean if I say, 'Alice, I think today, the best thing to do is to buy a white loaf,' she'll say, 'M'm,' and I know she hasn't heard because she's been looking out of the window, and then she'll say, 'What did you say?' and I have to say it all over again and she'll say, 'Oh yes. Right ho.'

    Now if you are on the radio, you say things with pauses behind them. You say: 'Darling, when you go to the shops, get me a white loaf, will you?' and you do a tiny pause, before the word 'white'. And you whistle the 'wh'. And if you say, 'Try not to make mistakes this morning,' there's a funny thing behind an 'm'. There are things behind words, you see, which shouldn't be made big but should be there.

PB Say your line is, 'It's hot today,' how far do you like to go into the feeling of heat, which perhaps you wouldn't bother to do if you could be seen?

PC It depends what the heat is doing to you. It can be hurting you, relieving you, or tantalising you, and you put that in. There's no limit to what you can do with words.

PB Do you write on your script?

PC Write? I can't see the script. There's only one person who wrote more on her script than me and that was Edith Evans. She underlined all her own words in red, and every cue with green, and every cue-light with a green asterisk. I've always done those things too; I draw funny pictures like waves to remind me of how a line should be inflected. Not proper things, but things I

know about. A mess. I do what suits me, when I want
to. No rules. I love radio.

PB   You've hinted you like filming too.

PC   Oh films are wonderful because you can take three
years to say, 'How do you do,' or 'Come in!' Yes, I love
filming.

PB   What is it that you like about it? Doing it in little bits?

PC   No: the fuss that is made of me. My ego is in a joy.
First of all, for a close-up in a film which is important,
you have the biggest, closest light on your face that can
exist on earth without killing you. Then, everybody is
attending to you, powdering, patting, combing,
pinning, minding, not because they love you, but
because they've got to do it. It's all the time they spend
on you that I love: the wig-fitting and the make-up and
the clothes.

You see, at the age of eighteen months I experienced
my first 'audience reaction'. I was sitting on my
mother's drawing-room carpet with a white sheet
thrown over it, and in front of me were spread currants,
raisins and sultanas, and three jars; and my mother
said, 'Now, darling, try to separate those three things,
the currants, raisins and sultanas.' And I knew that my
finger-tips were being watched by elderly ladies in furs
and crêpe de Chine, and they said, 'Isn't she sweet?'
'Isn't she a clever little girl?' and 'You've got a
treasure, Eva.' They were talking to my mother, but I
remembered what they said, and then forgot. But years
later, when I was in the revue, *Living for Pleasure*, at the
Garrick Theatre, and I was doing my solo number,
'I'm the lady who sits at the loo at the Ritz', dressed in
pitch black, with all the lights on me, I remembered the
little girl in white all over again. It was 'audience
reaction' which made me have to be an actress, I
suppose.

PB   Which directors have influenced you most?

PC   Oh . . . I've worked with so many . . . but I suppose I
can't imagine what life was like before Joan Littlewood.

PB   In what way?

PC   Well, she taught me things I never thought existed.

PB   Such as?

PC   Well, for instance, she asked me to play Mrs Gilchrist
       in her production of *The Hostage* in New York. In the
       week before I flew out there I went to Stratford East
       and learned all the songs and dances; and when I
       arrived in New York, I went to a fiendish rehearsal
       room off Broadway, and Joan was there, and I walked
       in, and although we hadn't seen each other for years
       she didn't say good morning, she didn't say thank you
       for coming, she didn't say hello; she said, 'Patience,'
       and I walked over to where she was talking to other
       people. 'Patience. Now. I've watched you for many
       years and as far as I can see you get a lot of things
       right. Your diction's very good, your accents are very
       good, your walks are very good, your clothes are
       miraculous, you always know your lines, you're always
       on time and you're a hard worker. Have you ever
       thought about love?' And I said, 'What do you mean?'
       and she said, 'Have you ever thought about the
       audience loving you and you loving them?' I said,
       'Well, no, never,' and she said, 'Well, this is what
       you've got to learn this time. I'll teach you.'

PB   And did she?

PC   Oh yes. I couldn't do my present part without Joan.
       Without the years-ago Joan. In *The Hostage* I had to
       sing a solo in a spotlight, and she said, 'Now, don't
       have a singing lesson. I'm sure you've got a pretty
       voice.' And she said, 'Look how you're standing! Your
       bottom's out at the back: pull it in, stick out your
       breasts and give yourself to the audience. Don't beg,
       don't lean forward, let them come to you, welcome
       them with open arms, and sing,

              "Only a box of matches
               Across the Irish sea." '

And she said, 'When you do this, the audience in the
front stalls will be like beds of asparagus. You'll feel
like a young virgin, teasing them away. And you'll sing
like a genius.' And I did. I had never before been on a
stage with no nerves, no fears, no inhibitions. I loved it.
I loved getting ready. I loved the warm-ups, I loved the
character, I loved the audiences in New York. Joan

Littlewood taught me to reach. To reach people. Or rather, to bring the audience to me.

PS 1991.   Patience Collier died on 13 July 1987. Nicholas de Jongh wrote in *The Guardian*: 'She was fierce and fiery, quick and quirky, as much at home as a Jacobean bawd or a Russian conjuror, as a grand upper middle class English Lady, wearing disdain to the manner born. Patience Collier was one of those stringently unsentimental and acute actresses in which the profession is generally lacking. Her candour and her quickness could be alarming but it was impressive as well. And in her late years, she mined new veins of pathos.'

Roger Rees

I interviewed Roger Rees on Tuesday 8 March. He was then well into a long run of *The Real Thing* by Tom Stoppard, at the Strand Theatre.

RR   Oh, I panicked a great deal during the rehearsals for *The Real Thing*. Peter Wood expected a lot and he was quite right; but the rehearsal period was very short – only three weeks – and every day words were being changed, speeches were being changed, or put in different places, and I felt I was just being pushed along; and all the time I was trying to find this man, this writer, who starts very eccentrically, being rude to everyone, and then becomes a sort of redeemable creature that you want to hug, someone who is not brittle any more.

PB   Do you often panic?

RR   It's a feeling that's been with me for a long time. I was a choirboy at our local church in Balham and we were going to sing at Southwark Cathedral, and I was going to sing a solo: 'Once in Royal David's City'. And after school that day, I went, and got as far as the door, and I didn't go in. I walked off down the road. Someone else had to sing it. Just because I was scared. I walked and walked. There's still a great strain in what I do and I think that's probably why it comes out in such a

nervous way. I even find walking about difficult; and
sometimes when I have a long speech I feel
embarrassed, so I do it as quickly as I can just to get it
over with and let somebody else do something. I think
that's why I act so quickly. I am embracing fear. When
I was a boy I found it hard to throw myself
wholeheartedly into things because I was even then an
observer. I watched. And I find now that if I have to do
anything extremely physical or frightening on the stage,
I am able to stand completely outside myself, really
look at myself, almost see myself from the back of the
auditorium. And I hate it. It makes me feel po-faced
and unadventurous; and that's why sometimes I do
physical things which are quite wrong, quite
embarrassing; but I have to do them just for *my* sake.
It's me fighting against myself, and I think that's what
acting is about. I don't want just to be safe, or just to
be careful. I'm prepared to be embarrassing. David
Threlfall, who was Smike in *Nicholas Nickleby*, said to
me, 'You do light-bulb acting.'

PB   What did he mean?

RR   Well, that I go, 'Whish, whish, whow,' you know,
putting in the light bulb, 'whow', it's the twist of the
hand, the added thing. It's like jumping or dancing. If
I elect to put my hands in my pockets I thrust them in
like this, or if I sit I hunch myself up in the chair or
something like that. It's an elaboration, a decoration on
top.

PB   Do you do these things in order to be interesting?

RR   I don't think just to say the words is exciting. So, yes I
do.

PB   John Hurt told me this morning that he's sick of
naturalism. 'We are entertainers, after all,' he said,
'and we need a sort of heightened naturalism.' Do you
agree?

RR   Yes. Yes I do.

PB   You do act very physically . . .

RR   Yes I know.

PB   . . . for example at the end of each part of *Nicholas
Nickleby*: there was a great yearning and love for Smike
at the end of Part I and for the crippled boy at the end

of Part II, and you expressed these feelings with yearning movements. Not like the movements which a dancer might make, but going that way.

RR   Yes. That's what I'm afraid of. I don't want it to look like a dance. And yet I feel words need assistance. I feel the story-telling needs assistance. When Smike said to Nicholas, 'You are my home,' I turned away from him and looked up at the sky. Thelma Whiteley said to me, 'Why do you do that? Do you need it?' And I thought I did . . . I could explain it as a sort of Christian thing, but that was the moment I made the decision to take him with me.

PB   Yes, those sort of things are rather your trademark, aren't they? Those and speed.

RR   I suppose so. When I was Roderigo and Emrys James was Iago my mother said, 'That Emrys James, he wasn't jerky, was he?' But I can't really call it jerky any more because I've chosen to use the febrile side of my nature. I *am* influenced by dance. Or perhaps by rhythms – rhythms of the body, rhythms of speech. A sort of musicality. I think the first thing I caught when I read *The Real Thing* was the rhythms of Tom Stoppard's jokes. I think for any part which I have I should use everything I can: so I include everything. Maybe it's too like a bargain basement in the end. In *The Real Thing* I like to try to express Henry's unhappiness very physically and I move about all over the place. I guess other actors wouldn't do that; they would do it just with the words. But I can't keep my hands in my pockets, as it were. I suppose a lot of it is wanting to be . . .

PB   . . . Wanting to be exciting?

RR   . . . because I want the audience to feel a kind of excitement. I love it, when I'm in the audience, to feel actors' passions coming across to me. So when I'm acting I feel I should just go out there and . . . I mean plays are written about special days, aren't they, not about any old day?

PB   Do your performances become very set?

RR   Not at all. I like to vary. As long as the intentions remain the same. My understudy said to me the other day, with great surprise: 'Someone told me you change things in performance.' But I like to. I'd be crazy by now if I didn't. Stoppard is quite hard to do, and requires a great deal of physical energy. It's like digging a hole in the road every night.

PB   Are you sometimes afraid of becoming too mannered?

RR   Yes. I have to watch it. I don't like watching mannered actors, because I can't listen to them; and the only way to act really well is to tell a story properly. I find it boring and unsatisfying when the story isn't told, when people occlude what the part they are playing wants to say by doing things which other people have applauded them for over the years, by merely parading themselves and their mannerisms.

PB   Do you work out your performances at home?

RR   Not at all. Things happen at rehearsal and I either accept them or reject them. If ever I work out something at home I usually don't have the gall to suggest it. And sometimes if I think in advance of something funny I'd like to say, and wait for an opportunity to say it, it never comes out right. I can always say it on the stairs afterwards but then it's too late. Anything I prepare becomes arid. And anyway, preparation like that suggests there's something perfect about what you want to achieve, and I don't think it's like that: it's more like a plant, or a piece of fruit which grows and you say, oh this is ready to eat now, but as you say that it can go off as well. I think it's death when you say to yourself, oh yes, isn't that a great moment? And you try to reproduce it. I mean, our job *is* to reproduce, isn't it? But you don't feel the same every night, the audience is different every night, so you can only approximate.

PB   You've just played Oswald in *Ghosts* on the radio, haven't you? How do you react to last-minute notes from the director?

RR   I'm a very obedient soul, I think, and I rather like last-minute notes.

PB   Do you like the mechanics of radio?

RR   Oh yes. It becomes, 'Who can turn the page best?' doesn't it? Siân Phillips was very clever at it, and she'd keep her script in front of me, while I was turning my page over my shoulder, so I could go on reading. I mean it's not natural to talk with a big piece of paper in your hand, and your neck craned round, is it? And you're talking to a piece of machinery: you're not talking to the person you love or hate. It's all ludicrous really, so you might as well join in. I think my favourite is walking out of a door backwards so you can still speak to the microphone.

PB   Somebody described you as one of our most watchable actors. Do you regard that as a compliment?

RR   I'm not sure. I just feel I should go as far as possible and yet be as rivetingly real as possible. That's what I feel.

Prunella Scales

I interviewed Prunella Scales at her home just by Wandsworth Common on Monday 27 June 1983. She had been in Australia, touring her programme about Queen Victoria, when I was doing the foregoing series of interviews.

PS   I always hope to start with what I can only call a strong feeling for the part. I never know where that feeling comes from. It can come from a person I know or have seen in the street, or from a character I've read about, or even from (and this will seem heresy to some actors) somebody else's performance.

PB   When you read a play for the first time, do you read any of it aloud?

PS   No, never. I make myself read the whole play in silence. It was one of the things dinned into us at the Old Vic School: 'An actor's first duty is to the play.' After reading the play I always want to talk to the author. Often an author can tell you where a character was born, and when, what her childhood was like, even what she looks or sounds like. Often authors can't or won't talk, of course, either because they believe in letting you flounder, or because they're dead.

    Quite often, usually after a week or so of rehearsals, I write out a rough list of dates in the character's life:

date of birth, date of leaving school, date of marriage, date of parents' death, etc . . . Then I can work out what songs they've heard in their childhood, what world events they've lived through, what books they are likely to have read, what fashions they've seen, what dances they've learnt, all of which can be helpful from time to time.

PB   The voice of a part is very important to you, isn't it?

PS   I'm never happy until I have found the physical individuality of a part, which includes the voice, I suppose. I've got quite a useful, strong and variable voice, and quite a good ear both for regional dialects and for mannerisms of speech, which is probably just as well because I'm not very versatile physically: I'm quite short and I haven't got a very useful face. A critic very kindly wrote of me once that the six parts I played in one play were nicely differentiated vocally, but that I couldn't change my face, which was that of a worried hamster.

PB   Do you do homework?

PS   Yes, a lot. Perhaps, because I've got a fairly demanding family, I don't work as hard as I should. But yes, a lot. My eldest son once said to me, 'Mummy, you don't understand about homework,' and I'm afraid I hit him. Quite hard.

PB   Someone said of your performance in Simon Gray's *Quartermaine's Terms* that you managed to be very real and yet comment on the character at the same time. I thought the same about you in Michael Frayn's *Make and Break*. Are you aware of this commenting?

PS   Oh yes. I think this is partly because both those plays were by authors who write with a very delicate balance between, for want of better words, drama and comedy. And therefore there was an implied comment on every character in them. As there is, too, in the plays of Chekhov: he has an oblique view of his characters, he comments on life through them; and I suppose it is the actor's task to realise this: to be truthful, of course, but not entirely subjective.

PB   This whole business of comedy, now. You are notably successful at it. What skills do you rely on?

PS   I think a sense of timing, a sense of comedy, a sense of what is funny about a part, are gifts from God. God or whoever. But you can help them along in various ways, for example with rhythm or with different dynamics. To put it no higher, I think you can get laughs in the theatre by tickling the audience's ears, by surprising them: I mean loud and soft and fast and slow, really. Music can be funny in the same way.

PB   By 'rhythm', do you mean keeping the momentum of a line going, right through to the final word?

PS   I think it's more a question of phrasing. Phrasing and stress. I learned about this through John Gielgud. Janet Suzman told me once that when she was going to play Saint Joan, Gielgud said to her, 'Don't forget that in Shaw, there's only one main stress in every sentence.' And I've found that true not only of Shaw but of almost everything: of colloquial speech, of mannered speech in Restoration comedy, of situation comedy on television. Rationing the stresses like this isn't dull, it's the reverse of dull: it makes speech rapid, shifting and varied, and is very good for comedy. All the best comedians I know – for example Richard Briers, John Cleese, Ronnie Barker – have an enormous feeling for rapid speech, which is not so much their skill in diction, although heaven knows that is considerable, as their feeling for stresses and how few they need to use.

PB   Do you enjoy doing situation comedies?

PS   Oh yes, except that the half-hour episodes come round so quickly, once a week; and in *Fawlty Towers* I never felt ready to do it every Sunday night. But John Cleese gave me great courage. It was rather like working with a live machine-gun which you try to keep pointing away from you. But you feel you've got something to bash against and that's very comforting. Leonard Rossiter's the same.

PB   Earlier in this book, I've tried doing stresses for a bit of King Magnus's long speech, and I found there was often more than one in each sentence.

PS   Oh, I think Gielgud meant that there should be only one *main* stress. I suppose the usual thing is to go for the noun. Like I've just done: 'I suppose the usual

thing is to go for the <u>noun</u>.' If you stress something
that's not a noun you can get character and
eccentricity. For example, if I said, 'the <u>usual</u> thing is
to go for the noun,' I might sound like an intense
actress talking about her work. Or you might stress
every single word. I mean you <u>might/stress/every/</u>
<u>single/word</u>. And that, too, tells you something about
the character. And if you stress prepositions and
conjunctions you will sound like a newsreader or a
sports reporter:

> To be <u>or</u> not to be – that <u>is</u> the question;
> Whether 'tis nobler <u>in</u> the mind to suffer
> The slings <u>and</u> arrows <u>of</u> outrageous fortune,
> Or to take arms <u>against</u> a sea <u>of</u> troubles,
> And <u>by</u> opposing end them?

PB   I wonder why so many of us want to stress too many
words, and speak syllabically? Is it a relic of the
English classic tradition?

PS   I suspect rather it's because we don't listen properly to
the nuances of everyday speech. But even with classical
texts it's easy to overstress. I've found through poetry
readings, for instance, that it's usually better to let
subordinate clauses ride without stress or emphasis.

PB   For example?

PS   Well . . . Shakespeare's sonnet 23:

> As an unperfect actor on the stage
> Who with his fear is put besides his part,
> Or some fierce thing replete with too much rage,
> Whose strength's abundance weakens his own
>   heart;
> So I, for fear of trust, forget to say
> The perfect ceremony of love's rite,
> And in mine own love's strength seem to decay,
> O'ercharg'd with burthen of mine own love's
>   might.

The main sentence there is:

> I . . . forget to say . . . love's rite,
> And in mine own love's strength seem to decay.

And I think it's easy to betray the real sense of the
sonnet unless you put brackets round the rest of it and

just let the words themselves do the work for you.
Without over-colouring.

PB   In the theatre, does playing out-front present any
      problems for you?

PS   Not where I have to talk to the audience directly –
      asides and so on. But in 'private' moments I think I'm
      inclined to refuse my eyes to the audience. I have to
      make myself look out. In a realistic play you have to
      know what you're supposed to be looking at, which is
      not the front row of the upper circle: you're looking
      through a window, or over the countryside, or at the
      fourth wall of the room. If you take care of that it can
      help you to stop feeling frightened of the audience.

PB   Do you enjoy the repetition of a long run?

PS   Yes.

PB   Do you ever get carried away and do different moves
      and things?

PS   No. That is, I'd never change something that affected
      other actors without discussing it first. But sometimes,
      especially in *Queen Victoria*, a great deal of which is
      monologue, when there's a very sympathetic audience
      or for whatever reason, I feel I begin to fly. We none of
      us know why this happens, do we? But new things
      which happen on those nights can be incorporated into
      future performances.

PB   Do you ever fly when you teach as well?

PS   Oh, I don't know, but I love it. I learn so much. Just
      now I'm getting the chance to try a number of things
      at the Actors Centre – I'm doing a new workshop
      tomorrow, on acting for radio. I think the thing which
      sorted me out, for both acting and teaching, and any
      directing which I occasionally do, was working with
      Uta Hagen in New York many, many years ago; and
      still I constantly refer to her book, *Respect for Acting*. She
      evolved a sort of grammar of acting, which is not dry,
      which is nothing but truth and common sense. Harold
      Pinter says, 'Acting is common sense.' John Cleese
      says, 'Acting is common sense.' And John Cleese read
      law at Cambridge, Jonathan Miller is a doctor,
      Chekhov was a doctor. All this has stopped my fear
      that I might be too analytical: it is manifestly untrue

that a cerebral approach necessarily dries up emotion
or spontaneous feeling. Uta Hagen's method of acting,
which is out of Stanislavski, by various American
'method' directors, is simple and sensible.

PB   Can you summarise?

PS   She says the first question you must ask yourself is,
'Who am I?' The second question is, 'What do I want?'
The third is, 'What is the obstacle?' And then, 'What
do I do to overcome the obstacle and achieve what I
want?' Then there are various other things like, 'What
are the conditions? Is it hot or cold? What sort of state
am I in? How do the other people affect what I do?'

PB   An example?

PS   Well. A trivial example. I'm an aide-de-camp and I
have to come in and say to the commanding officer,
'Good morning, sir. Here is the report from Major
Smith. In it you will see that he estimates the enemy
will be with us at approximately eight hundred hours
tomorrow morning.' Now. Who am I? I am Lieutenant
Bloggs. Which probably means that I have been
trained to keep a stiff upper lip and not to show
emotion of any kind. What do I want? (At Uta's classes
you're taught always to look for a *verb*, never for a
quality or an emotion.) I may want to do my duty, or
to avoid showing fear, or perhaps I want my breakfast.
What is the obstacle? Perhaps the CO is in a bad
mood, perhaps I'm frightened of him or of the
impending attack. So what do I do? I probably come in
and mutter the line as quickly as possible and get out.
It'll be over in two seconds but it will be true and at
least it won't be over-acted. If you *try* for emotion, try
to feel, it's a sure way of cutting off emotion altogether.
Acting is doing.

When I was a student at the Old Vic School, Glen
Byam Shaw was one of the directors, and although he
taught me a lot he had an extreme suspicion of
anything which he thought was intellectuality; and I
got myself lumbered, partly, I expect, because I wore
glasses in those days and was fearfully earnest . . . well
. . . he said, 'Oh Prunella, you tackle your work like a
piece of arithmetic,' and I was very frightened of this.

But what I learned from Uta is that there is absolutely
no reason why you shouldn't bring every faculty you
have in life to bear on your work. It will open up
channels, particularly emotional channels. In
Quartermaine's Terms I couldn't stop crying . . .

Samuel West

I interviewed Samuel West at home on Friday 8 March 1991.
We had acted together through most of 1990 in Simon Gray's
play *Hidden Laughter*, on tour, and at the Vaudeville Theatre,
London. He was Nigel Pertwee. Other people mentioned in
the interview are Caroline Harker, who played Nigel's sister
Natalie, Kevin McNally, who played his father Harry, and, of
course, Simon Gray, who directed the play himself.

SW   I began work on Nigel by worrying about the injury.
His leg gored by a bull. That seemed to me the biggest
thing. That and his brain tumour. There's always some
aspect of a part which frightens me before I start
because it's outside my experience. But it's things like
that which push me into researching the part.

PB   Did you do a lot of research, then?

SW   Oh, I got the research bug. And I love that. You really
can't do too much even if only ten per cent is useful. I
mean, the more you do the bigger the ten per cent is.

PB   For example, what did you find out about the leg?

SW   The stage management came up to me with a note, and
said, 'This is the man, Dr Ruskin, who will be making
your calliper, the leg-stiffener which you have to wear.
You've got to go and see him, so why not talk to him
about the facts of it while you're at it?'

So I got to the hospital early and I said to him, 'It
seems to me this is awkward. I mean, the leg is broken,
and yet I have to walk home. The leg is not
permanently injured, but it lasts two years.' I laid out
the facts. I had a list of questions like, 'Would the fall
have affected his brain?' He gave me decent answers
and some literature about what they put in my leg and
I said where would I have had this done and he said
where do you live in the play and I said Honiton and

he said Exeter would have done it and I would have
been laid up for six months.

All that was very useful because if you're young and
you break your leg and you're out of action for six
months it's extremely boring, because you should be
doing A-levels or going on summer holidays. And one
of the things which came out of that was that Nigel was
happy wherever he was. He had his injury for two years
and at the end of that time he was the only still point in
a turning world, I thought.

One of the things I didn't do, and should have done,
was go round Westminster School. I'd said to Simon
where did Nigel go, and he said, not surprisingly,
having been to Westminster, 'I think he went to
Westminster.'

But I did work out which book I was reading at the
beginning of my first scene. It was the summer holidays
and I was beginning to work on my A-levels, so it's a
large set text, because they always give you big, fat set
texts at the beginning of the summer holidays so you've
plenty of time to read them. So I went back to the 1986
A-levels Board and asked what the set texts were for
that year and they said *Bleak House* was one of them, so
I said that sounds good. It helped place school and it
helped place the time of year. I mean it was the
beginning of the summer holidays, so it was a new book
which had just been issued to me, and I opened it at
page 20 or so. If it had been later in the holidays I'd
have opened it a bit further on. It's nothing, it's
nothing special, but it's just something which helps you
get there.

PB   When I watched you reading your book at rehearsals, I
thought why does it create so much atmosphere, that
someone on the stage is reading while other things are
going on? But then I thought it established the garden
and the family and that sort of thing, where people
don't pay attention to each other all the time.

SW   Yes, that was one of the things Simon said early on, at
that Groucho's read-through. He said gardens. He said
being outside and gardens. Caroline Harker and I
would go into that garden next door to the rehearsal

room and place ourselves quite far apart and rehearse; and there's a tone of voice which you get while trying to carry across a larger space than we could have in a theatre, and that was helpful.

PB   Can you remember anything else from those early rehearsals?

SW   Well, after that same read-through I was walking with Caroline to the bus-stop and I suddenly said, on a whim, because there was this question as to whether Natalie was really my sister, or whether she had been adopted, 'I think Natalie ought to be adopted because then Nigel could fancy her.' And Caroline just said, 'Oh.' And I thought, oh, I've gone too far, oh no, that's that relationship screwed up for the rest of the rehearsals: I'm never going to be able to talk to Caroline again.

But then when we got to the first proper rehearsal Simon said to me, 'You know what you've got to do, don't you? It's called lust – well actually it's called incest.' And I thought, yes I was right. Good. That was a bold decision I had made, but I'd immediately backed off it; but then the director said, 'No, go back to that,' so that was OK.

PB   It's interesting that you felt you could go ahead with that, having been given permission to do so by the director. There are other things for which you need his permission, aren't there? The whole business of being upstage or downstage, for instance. I always think it's good when the director says, 'You really should be downstage here,' or 'You really need to be the upstage person here.' It solves it. You never feel guilty after that.

SW   Or overlapping.

PB   Or overlapping. You can then do it. But you need the permission.

SW   Yes you do. It's a relief when directors do that.

PB   Did you have to alter yourself in any way to be Nigel?

SW   I suppose one of the first things I thought was that he was quite like me.

PB   Do you, as I do, prefer parts for which you don't have to alter yourself much? So that you can concentrate on the minutiae of thoughts and feelings and activities, and not at all on disguise?

SW   Yes I do, as I find out more about myself. I mean, we all encompass a great deal, don't we? And I've noticed, with every job, there's always something which makes you a larger person. For example, the part I'm playing at the moment, Steve in *Stanley and the Women* for Central TV, is schizophrenic. Knowing how well he was before, and how like him I was before he became ill, is interesting, but we never see it. And in effect he couldn't be further away from me. I mean he's mad. It's completely different from everything else. It's quite daunting.

     And of course it's on film. Once that scene's done it's done. I really miss rehearsals. I wish there were a bit more time for rehearsals for filming, so that you could meet the people properly, both as actors and characters. You'd be more relaxed.

PB   Yes. I did that once. We had a week. And it saved time and money when filming started.

SW   Yes. I've got a video camera at home and I'm finding it very useful for practising the physical symptoms of schizophrenia. At the moment I'm practising a fit which I have to have. It is a side-effect from a drug and physically quite specific, so rather than leave it till next Tuesday, when I've got to do it, I set up the video camera and play around in front of it. Half an hour at a time. But now that I've checked it in that way, I have to take it away from the camera and just do it. You must know that it's good for the camera, but you mustn't be *doing* it for the camera. You must do it for itself.

PB   How do you approach filming? Do you have technical things which you think you need for it, like not jerking, or keeping both eyes to the camera?

SW   Yes, but I didn't know what those things were until I saw Michael Caine's one-hour video on film acting. Golden rules. 'Don't blink in close-ups. Always be sure you can hit your marks by pacing your walk up to them, like bowlers do to the wicket. If the camera is close to you and follows you as you rise out of a chair, be kind to the cameraman and rise considerably more slowly and smoothly than you would bother to in everyday life. Choose the camera-side eye of the person you're talking to. Don't look from eye to eye. If your eyes drift, let them go across the lens rather than the other way, away from the camera.' Absolutely essential. And he talks about going home the night before, and if you know the room you're going to be in, if you've done scenes in it before – if you don't know you can ask to see it or be told about it – go home and set the furniture up to be the people, and learn it as closely as you can to what you'd like to do with it the following day, so that you are totally at ease with it. And then you can play around with it.

I find myself very much under pressure in front of the camera and at my most vulnerable. The only way I can get rid of that is by knowing absolutely what I am doing.

That is why I am practising this fit, so that I can do it by numbers. And, paradoxically, that way it won't be mechanical. I know what I'm doing and I've tested it. Practised spontaneity.

PB Are there any aspects of acting in general which interest or occupy you at the moment?

SW I'm very interested in things I can't do, physically demanding things: circus and mime and clowning. I mean, not subtle, but overstated and huge and melodramatic things. I admire people who go too far, who made bold decisions and then pull back. I don't: I reach in little bits towards something, encouraged by the director and the cast. I'd love to surprise people more. Surprise people who know me.

PB Anything else?

SW Uta Hagen says always try to make yourself a more beautiful person. That doesn't mean just physically beautiful, it means acquiring skills so that your span gets bigger. You reach more easily and take dangerous decisions more easily.

PB Being in a long run is different from everything else we do, isn't it? It's the only acting we have to do when we are not obsessed by the part and the play. You were

notably good at sustaining your performance in *Hidden
Laughter*. I mean you did more or less the same every
night and yet, at every performance, you were
enormously present. Not remembered, not quoting the
text, but present. In it. Happening now. It's hard to do.
My guess is that you observed the nuances of your
everyday speech minutely – with all the varieties, and
fast bits and slow bits and thinking out bits – so that
you were able to reproduce them at will. Is that right?

SW   Well, that's what I hoped for. The aim is to be like a
documentary, isn't it? I mean you fail, but it's the aim.
It's practised spontaneity again.

PB   I think the only sensible thing for a long run is to
construct a performance which is reasonably set, don't
you? If it isn't it can so easily become lifeless, or go all
over the place, become absurdly complicated and
deteriorate into mere mannerism. No: a set
performance on which you can rely and from which,
hopefully, you can sometimes fly.

SW   Well, I think so. It means the outside's done and you
can concentrate in performance on the inside, which is
anyway more fun, and helps you to keep it feeling fresh.

PB   And it makes the evenings pass more quickly, too. But
we were a happy company, weren't we? That's
important.

SW   Oh yes. Say anything to anybody. It makes a long run
bearable. I always liked it when you noticed when
something new happened – an inflection, a pause, an
attitude – and you came up to me and said so
afterwards. And I'll always remember something that
Kevin McNally said to me one night: 'I may sometimes
go through the motions,' he said, 'but I never stop
thinking about it. If you've got a part, and are lucky
enough to have a good run, night after night, don't stop
having ideas. Don't think that because you've had one
idea about a scene that that's that scene over. Keep
being obsessed.' You can see it in him, that it was
really a part of him, and it was inspiring to hear, and I
took it away.

How Do I Work On A Part?

This is nothing more than a postscript to the previous chapter, which I enjoyed compiling, noticing especially how those I interviewed resorted to images and analogies: Judi Dench's 'green Swiss hill', and 'signposts', Alec McCowen's 'as ifs', Edward Petherbridge's 'prize garden', Anna Massey's 'frozen, blocked drains', Alison Steadman's 'first mark on the canvas' and Roger Rees's 'digging a hole in the road'.

Here's another. In 1958 I moved into a new flat. It was the first time I had more than one room, and my own front door, which I could close. I was in *Roar Like A Dove* at the Phoenix Theatre and had been moaning to Ewan Roberts, who was also in it, about the dreadful basement I had been living in for some time. 'Well, look in the *Evening Standard*,' he said, irritated, 'and do something.' So we looked together, and saw that there was a 'top-floor flat, 32 Bernard Street, WC1. Rent £3.5s a week, entire contents for sale £650'.

'There you are,' said Ewan, 'it's an omen.' The part I had in the play was called Bernard. 'Go for that one.'

'But I haven't got £650. I've only got £300. In the Halifax.'

'Go and see it. If it's perfect you can raise the rest of the money somehow.'

I went; it *was* perfect: two rooms, kitchen and bath, nicely furnished; what's more it was only ten minutes' walk from the theatre, and five minutes from RADA, where I was then taking a lot of classes. Mr and Mrs Ring, who were leaving it, liked me and said I could have the contents for £600. 'Done,' I said, and rang my father to ask for a loan of £300.

And it's here that my analogy begins. Moving into a new flat, I thought, especially into a furnished flat, is like taking on a new part. First of all you see it. And if you like it and the terms are right, you accept it. And that is, as Judi Dench said, the most thrilling part of all. You are on the hill.

Then you go back to your old place and think about the new one. And start worrying. Because, actually, you did not look carefully enough: you let your enthusiasm carry you away. When you come to think of it, there are snags: will you be able to put up with the floors which, you happened to notice but didn't bother about at the time, creaked? Do you really like all that cane furniture? Won't it have to be replaced? Worst of all, what you had absolutely not considered, there is no room in the flat for your baby-grand piano. They'd never get it up the stairs: and because the floor creaks and slopes a bit, and because it wouldn't be fair on the person in the flat underneath, you'll have to sell it. Damn! And where the hell is all the furniture you've already got, which you're definitely not going to sell, going to go? You'll sell the piano because you have to, but everything else matters far too much. There's nothing else for it, you'll have to go back and have another look.

They are nice and let you wander around on your own. 'As long as you like,' they say, 'and we'll keep out of your way; but if you want to ask us anything, please don't hesitate. We know what it's like, moving into a new place. We're having to do the same, of course. So we're all in the same boat, aren't we?' You all laugh, and feel better for it. After all, there is no rush: you don't have to make instant decisions about what you'll get rid of and where your furniture will go. In fact it would be better to wait until you move in, and then see. You'll be able to play around with it then and move things. And the cane furniture isn't quite as bad as you'd thought: when you've put some of your own ornaments on it, and books and things, it could look quite nice.

So you wait, more hopefully, with less panic; and little ideas occur to you from time to time. There's suddenly rather a lot to do, too, in preparation: there's selling the piano, and arranging for a van to take your things, and telling everybody what your new address and telephone number are going to be.

Moving-in day arrives. You hadn't anticipated how tiring it would be, humping the furniture into the van at the old place and, worse, humping it out at the new, with all those stairs to climb. Up and down. Up and down. Eventually the van-man leaves, you close the front door, heave a sigh of relief, look round and see nothing but chaos.

'Christ,' you think, 'what have I done? Look at it! It's dreadful. And I've got to go out soon and do some work. I can't leave it like this.' And you sit down and mope and feel full of despair. You go into the kitchen and try to find their kettle, which is not at all like the one you're used to, and far more awkward because it's got a cover over where you pour the water in, and it's very stiff, this cover, and you'll have to do something about that, but not now: you're too tired. 'Sit down,' you say to yourself, 'have a cup of tea, and don't do any more work on the flat until tomorrow.'

When you come back that night, you think, 'It's not home. It's not home at all. I hate it. I wish I'd never come here. I wish I'd stayed in that basement which was not so bad after all. At least there weren't all these bloody stairs to climb. I mean, I know there was dry rot there and it was dreadful. But at least I wouldn't have had to endure all this.' You have a drink, feel a bit better, go to bed, and just before you go to sleep you think. 'Well, I'll work on it tomorrow. And I'll try not to rush it. I don't want to make mistakes. I want to do it properly. So if I get irritated, I'll stop. I'm glad I stopped today when I did. That little sit-down was a good idea.'

The following morning you work out a scheme. Room by room. There's very little to do in the bathroom, so that can take care of itself. The kitchen must be done, and must be done this morning. 'I must put things away, and remember where I've put them,' you say aloud to yourself, with emphasis. 'Be sensible,' you instruct yourself. Tins there, cups and saucers there, pans there. Sort it out. And while you're about it you might as well sort out the types of tin, so they're not muddled. Soup tins there, Heinz baked beans there, and fish and meat there. This will probably take all morning and then you can clean the floor. Scour it. It's filthy. No point in having tidy cupboards and a filthy floor.

That's enough for today. Tomorrow you'll do the same in the bedroom. You go out to work and come back and it still doesn't feel like home. But there's something to look at at last: there's the kitchen. So you pour yourself a drink and go and sit in the kitchen and feel pleased with yourself. 'It's good, what I did today,' you think. And you stare at it.

The following day you have a first go at the bedroom, and it's all beginning to look a bit more ship-shape. And, more importantly, you're beginning to know it. The kitchen's getting good. You could invite people to look at the kitchen. (Only the kitchen, though, so you won't have people there yet.) But you've spent some hours there now, and you've worked on it, and it's not home yet but it's certainly not depressing any more and there's light at the end of the tunnel.

The only thing is, what are you going to do about the sitting-room? You don't mind the floor, that's minor and you can put up with it; but what are you going to do about the furniture you brought, and the furniture that was there? You start by humping it around all over again, and it's quite fun. Yes: for the first time it's fun. Some arrangements are better than others and eventually you make a few decisions. The sofa must be here because the speakers must be there and if the speakers are there, the turntable must be here. Right. Let's have a look. There's a table too many, one of those you brought. Right. Get rid of it.

What you certainly will get rid of are their ornaments, their little things which you positively do not like. They do not suit you. But in addition to getting rid of things there are one or two new things you will have to buy. A standard lamp would look very nice in that corner, and you need another chair.

So the following day you go out shopping. It's a relief to be outside, and you've decided to take your time. You look in the windows of several furniture shops, but go in only if it looks a likely place. You talk to the assistants and state your requirements and if they come up with something approximating what you want you say you will think about it. What you're really hoping for is that they will have something better than you had anticipated: more useful, prettier or whatever. And then, if it doesn't cost you too much, you say you'll have it. You take it home, and it *is* home now and, oh yes, it fits.

But now you've cleaned it all and know where everything is, it looks a bit bare. The walls are bare. You haven't put any pictures up yet. It isn't ornamented enough. So you play around with the few you've got, decide where to put them, and hang them up.

It's getting good now. As good as you, the flat itself, your things and their things and what you manage to buy, can make it. Now you can show it to people. You start with a few friends; and their presence makes you a bit self-conscious about it and you notice all kinds of little details which aren't quite right yet. You don't point them out, of course, but you see the flaws more readily than the successes. Nevertheless they all exclaim about it and congratulate you. Later in the evening when they've had a bit to drink, they volunteer a suggestion or two which, because you're in such a good mood, you accept with pleasure, saying you'll do something about them the following day.

At last you give a house-warming party. Your flat is teeming with people and the party is a success. Well, if you were to be honest, a qualified success. It was a bit too hot, and you were on edge and a bit too nervous to enjoy it properly. You were too anxious for it to be a success. When you give another party it will be better because you'll be more relaxed about it. You certainly learned from the first one: you noticed the flat felt very different with a lot of people there.

And so the weeks pass, and you live there. You make little improvements from time to time as they occur to you. Nothing drastic. Nothing too big. Of course, sometimes things go wrong and you have to work at them: the fridge breaks down and has to be seen to – you have to get somebody in to do that. Eventually you get a new kettle. But the pressure is off now and these little bits of work and little improvements are no hardship.

Perhaps the worst that can happen, as the weeks become months and the months become years, is that you will get bored with it and not look at it any more, not take any more pride in it. So perhaps then you might buy something new, a new picture, something special: something which will make you look at everything all over again, and bring life back into the place.

I thought of this analogy the day after I had moved into my flat at 32 Bernard Street, and I couldn't wait to get to my next class at RADA to tell them about it. 'Yesterday I moved into a new flat, and I thought, moving into a new flat, especially this particular flat, which is fully furnished, is rather like taking on a new part . . .'

This Is What Happens When You Go Filming

'I think,' said Edward Woodward loudly, when we were sitting in a caravan in the middle of a field, 'that all drama students should be made to sit in a caravan in the middle of a field for a WEEK,' (he is a born raconteur and suddenly hits words with an unexpected fury) 'for a whole WEEK, and never, ever be used. Not once. Oh, they'll be made up and dressed, and the boys will have little white tissues tucked into their necks to protect their collars from their make-up and the girls will sit carefully so as not to crease their skirts too much. And everybody will look in the mirror from time to time to see what they look like and if their hair's still all right. They will trudge across the field to queue for their meals outside the location caterers' vehicle, and carry them (soup in plastic beakers and roast chicken and stewed vegetables on a cardboard plate) back to the caravan. They will eke out the meal for as long as they can; and some fool will volunteer to wallow back to the location caterers with all the dirties, and return with requested fruit, cheese and biscuits, coffees and teas. At the end of the lunch-break they will be called to the make-up bus for a check-up, and be told by the second assistant that, hopefully, if the damp weather holds, they'll be needed for a line-up in about two hours. After four hours have passed the second assistant calls again with a few sheets of new dialogue and panics them all by saying, "The director felt this scene wasn't quite right, so here's an amended version. We hope to be able to shoot it in about half an hour." Two hours later he calls again to say it's a wrap for the day. He gives them their call-sheets for tomorrow, which say they are to be made up and dressed by eight o'clock sharp. But they never, ever, get used.'

That's the trouble with filming: it's either all or nothing. Unless you have a leading role it's mostly nothing. But during the nothing you have to be ready for the all. During the nothing, when an hour feels as long as a day, everyone chats. The actors huddle together and swap stories and roar with laughter, or go very quiet when they start moaning about the lack of organisation, or why were they called so early when everyone knew there was no hope of their being used, and why is this particular bunch of location caterers the worst they've ever come across? Actresses like to slink off occasionally to the make-up bus and chat to the make-up girls, who, after the early-morning rush, are in their own nothing for most of the rest of the day.

I like the huddled groups of talking, in fields or in caravans, especially when the talk is funny. Or a moan. You have to say things from time to time, or you'd go mad.

At least it keeps you from brooding and from going over the lines of your next scene so often that you don't know what they mean any more. I was in a film once – *Patton (Blood and Guts)* – in which I had one line only; and I had to wait in Spain for nearly three months to say it. The line was to Michael Bates (General Montgomery) and I had to go up to him, salute and say, 'Sir, Patton's taken Palermo.' I heaved myself along a Spanish beach for days on end, wondering which word to emphasise: 'Sir, Patton's <u>taken</u> Palermo' (meaning 'we didn't want him to, did we? And now he's gone and done it'); 'Sir, Patton's taken <u>Palermo</u>' (meaning, 'he's got as far as that,' or 'it's the wrong place'); and even, 'Sir, <u>Patton's</u> taken Palermo' (meaning, 'instead of you, sir. It should have been you.') When the day finally arrived I discovered I had to be driven up in a jeep, over very rough ground. Well, in filming everyone shows off, and the driver wanted to show how fast he could drive the jeep and stop it on its stop-marks – bits of batten nailed into the grass. He drove so fast that I leapt into the air and banged my head on an iron bar above me which was there for generals to hold if they had to stand up and inspect troops. My cap came off and fell on to the ground as I got out, so I picked it up, because I knew it would be wrong to salute without wearing it, arrived at Montgomery's desk in the sun and, by now dazed, said plainly, with no emphasis at all, 'Sir, Patton's taken Palermo.'

The director said, 'Cut,' complimented me on the delivery of my line, but told me off for picking up my cap and, thank heavens, told the driver off for driving so fast and said, 'We'll go again.' Take two. Perfect. 'Right, print it.' And that was that. The only thing was, the whole scene was cut from the eventual film.

However, in spite of all the enjoyments of perpetual talking – and people in films never stop – I think my favourite, and probably best, filming days have been those when, during prolonged nothings, I have been able to go off somewhere on my own and get on with something. Reading, usually, or writing. Why waste the time? (Someone said, 'The art of filming is to be there, but not to be seen to be there until you are wanted.' Someone else said, putting it slightly differently, 'The art of filming is never to be noticeably absent or needlessly present.') It's good, this, because you don't waste your energy either; and if you really concentrate on something else you get into that mood of concentration which is the best thing in the world for acting.

Especially for acting in films. Because, when it comes to the 'all', this is what happens; or at least this is what happened on my first day in *Champions*, and as it was a very typical filming day, I'll go through the sequence of events as I can now remember them. We were in the disused Wimbledon Hospital on the south side of the Common. A ward had been refurbished. John Hurt, as Bob Champion, the jockey, was in a bed by a window, and there were extras in all the other beds: some of them had had to have their heads shaved on account of the treatment for cancer they were supposed to be undergoing. The scene was about Edward Woodward, as the trainer of the horse Aldaniti, and me, as its owner, visiting John to see how he was. Edward and I were called into the ward to rehearse it, and John Irvin, the director, came over to us and said, 'Welcome.' They'd just finished the previous scene of the day's schedule and everything was being moved. 'Chippies' were banging away, taking out battens which had been fastened to the floor and removing the miniature railway track which had been laid so that the camera could be wheeled smoothly. 'Sparks' were removing heavy, cumbersome lamps, and everyone was talking.

'Can I have quiet, please,' the director said to the first assistant.

'Quiet everybody, please!' bawled the first assistant, who is the sergeant-major of the unit, and who organises everything and never stops working and planning. 'I said QUIET. We want to REHEARSE this scene.'

'Thank you,' said the director quietly. And then he turned to us and said, 'Now, let's go through this scene gently and see what happens. We'll do it several times.' After the commotion, the hush was very comforting. The director wanted us to feel relaxed and easy, especially as it was our first day. 'Edward and Peter,' he continued, even more quietly, everyone hanging on his every word by now, 'you come through the door, say good afternoon or something to a nurse we'll have leaving the ward as you come in, look round for John's bed, see him, and then approach him and . . . er . . . well, let's see what happens.'

We tried it, got to the bed, and started the dialogue.

'Er,' said the director. 'I think it would be better to start the dialogue before you get to the bed and, Edward, you come this side of Peter and go closer to John; and, Peter, you could perhaps get a chair from the middle of the room, there by that table with the flowers on it, and bring it up to the bed and sit.'

So we started again and this time got through the scene. Two and half pages of dialogue.

'Er . . .' said the director, trying to make it natural for us but realising he had to shoot it, and trying to work out camera-angles and something of the later editing: the cuts from shots including the three of us to two-shots and singles, '. . . Peter, don't go for the chair and don't sit down; and we've got to get some glasses for the champagne somehow, haven't we? There'll be only one tooth-glass on John's bedside table, so, Peter, perhaps when it comes to the champagne bit you could go and get another one from the middle table. Yes, go then. Edward: is there time to open the champagne, do you think?'

'Well, I doubt it. I think it'll have to be prepared a bit. So that I just have to do the final twist of the wire or something.'

'Let's try it again.'

And we did. And then the director had a long muttered

conversation, which we didn't listen to, with the lighting-cameraman and the camera-operator.

The director came back to us. 'Yes,' he said. 'Good. Getting there. But Peter: the going for the glass is very good; but when you've got it, could you bring it closer to Edward while he pours, and then stroll round to the foot of the bed and stay there till the end of the scene. Let's just try that bit.'

We did. 'That better?' the director turned to the lighting-cameraman.

'Much.'

'Right. Let's try the whole scene through once more.' And afterwards he said, 'Good. You can relax now John, Edward and Peter, and for the first shot we'll start on John talking to the nurse, then the camera will swing round following the nurse to the door and you come in, look round and see John. That's as far as we'll go.'

'Right. Relax the artistes,' said Bert, the first assistant – gradually you learn the names – 'and, boys, carry on working. Any idea how long, Ronnie?' This to the lighting-cameraman, Ronnie Taylor, who did *Gandhi*.

'Ooh . . . well, with the camera swinging around we'll see most of the ward . . . ooh . . . an hour and a half, I should think.'

'We'll be ready for you, gentlemen, in an hour and a half. Approximately,' guffawed Bert, who has a voice to drown all others. 'Stand-ins, please!'

We strolled away, talked for a while, realising there was a lot of time to kill, then peeled off to have a look at ourselves in mirrors and go through the words a bit. All sorts of little decisions had to be made, too, about clothes and hair. For continuity. I think people in films often look too neat, too prepared, as though their hair has just been combed and brushed, and make-up newly applied, even after a fairly rough night or a bar-room brawl or a long trek through the mountains. This is partly because there's a department for everything, and each of them wants to display itself as efficient and good: so 'hair' comes up and does it for you, 'make-up' comes up and dabs you or slaps you around with a perfumed wet flannel when you're getting hot, and 'wardrobe' comes up and brushes you down. But it's also partly because untidiness is harder to keep the same. We knew that the scene we were about to do would take the rest of the day. So if your hair is untidy, it has to be untidy in exactly the same way all day. If you have an untidy pocket handkerchief, just flung into your top pocket, it has to be pinned like that, very carefully, because the scene on the screen will last only about a minute and a half; and if it sinks in that time from a flamboyant billow to being hidden entirely in the pocket, and then suddenly bobs up again because someone has noticed, it will look silly. For the same reason ties, which can so easily slip, tend to be tied right into the collar, and trousers and skirts kept neatly pressed.

In the pause now I decided how I could keep my clothes right for continuity, by knowing how each little bit was going to be. My dark blue sweater covered the belt of my trousers by about two inches, and I decided to leave the top two buttons of my green quilted jacket undone, and the bottom one as well. This may seem unnecessarily fussy especially as there is always a continuity girl on hand to notice these things. But it's a nicer feeling if you get it right yourself, and anyway, she can't notice everything, especially when there's little rehearsal.

A year or two before this I had been in another film with Edward Woodward, and in one scene we had had to talk to each other across a dining-table, eating the while. I wouldn't let the director shoot the master (the master is the whole scene, shot usually from one all-seeing angle, showing most of the characters most of the time) until I had worked out what I was going to do with the food: on which line I knifed a potato on to my fork, when I lifted it to my mouth and when I ate it. I wanted to know what I ate, in what amounts, and when, because the master-shot was going to be followed by two two-shots: Edward over my shoulder and me over his, and two singles: Edward alone and me alone.

Edward said, 'I'm surprised you fuss so: there's a girl to do all that.'

'Well . . .' I said.

And I was glad I had fussed, because the closer shots were sure. Poor Edward had to do take after take of his close shots. 'No Edward,' said the girl, 'I'm *sure* you had meat and carrots on your fork and put them in your mouth on that line.'

'Yes,' said the director, compassionately, 'it's worth going again, Edward: I know it's tedious, but when I'm editing I'll probably want to use the master for that bit where you put peas and potatoes in your mouth, and follow it with a cut to you, and if you've suddenly got a whole heap of meat on your fork and cram that in too, I won't be able to use it.'

Oh, I did want to say to Edward, 'Told you so,' but I refrained: he'd have laughed, I know, but perhaps not straightaway.

So when I'd thought about those things and had gone over in my mind the moves the director had given me, to be sure I could do them and feel comfortable with them, I tried to think all over again of the content of the scene. Let's see, I thought, Edward and I have driven up, perhaps had a vodka and tonic and a little lunch in a pub on the way (all this had been suggested to me by the real Nick Embiricos, whom I was trying to portray, when I visited him at his home in Sussex). Then I thought of hospitals and visiting and what I had felt when I had last visited my mother, and later my father. The bright face hiding the concern. I tried to think of this as a real hospital and imagine Nick Embiricos's attitudes to the ailing jockey on whom he relied so much.

One of the topics of earnest conversation this particular morning had been a film shown on television the night before, called *Simon's War*, a documentary about Simon Weston of the Welsh Guards, who had been appallingly burnt and disfigured when the ship which was carrying his regiment to the Falkland Islands was hit by an Exocet missile. There were many scenes in hospital, clinical ones during examinations and operations, and emotional ones when his parents visited him. Everyone who had seen it admitted they had been moved to tears in an abundance which seldom happens. I had blubbed continuously at the misfortune and bravery of the man, at the amount of pain and suffering he had to undergo, and at the strength of his desire to get as well as he could even though he will never be able to have a proper face again.

We had also remembered, of course, that it was a film, that the lighting must have been done, and the rooms arranged and positions decided. John Irvin, who had directed documentaries in Vietnam, said that although the presence of the camera invariably affects what goes on in front of it, it does so less when events and emotions are extreme. Nevertheless, he said, it remains a great temptation for a director to ask for another take if something technical goes wrong, a temptation which Steven Rose, who had so tastefully and lovingly produced *Simon's War*, had obviously avoided.

We had noticed, too, with some despair, the immense gap that still exists between acting and real life. It is our ever present struggle to reduce that gap, by filling our minds with as much background as real-life people have, with as much imagination about the circumstances of a scene (like the shock of the parents when they first saw their broken son, but their determination to be as bright as possible and not to convey their distress to him), with a true spontaneity of speech and with a particular sort of concern with which people who love each other look at each other.

I was thinking about all this and saying to myself, 'if you can be half as good as those parents were last night in their hospital ward, you'll be wonderful,' when the second assistant, whose name was Peter, rushed up and said, 'We're ready for you now, please,' and we made our way back to the ward. The noise and the banging and the talking were as insistent as ever, and it was considerably hotter. White screens had been put up against some of the windows to filter the mixture of sunlight and arc lamps outside. Beds behind the camera had been taken away. There were chalk marks on the floor, one for Edward, one for me, and they were not at all where we had expected them to be. While we were waiting, Edward and I practised arriving on our marks without looking. This can take quite a little while, but it's worth persevering with because then you can forget about the mark altogether and devote yourself to the scene. Then, the dialogue went something like this:

BERT: Keep the noise down. QUIET.
                          Right, Ronnie, are you ready?
RONNIE *(after yet another look through his light meter)*: Ready. Oh,
                          just a minute. One more minute. We
                          need another pup. Quick, boys. Just
                          here. That's right. Shut the left-hand
                          side off a bit . . . er . . . OK.
BERT: All right now, Ronnie?

RONNIE *(muttering, uncertain)*: Right.

BERT *(to the director)*: Right, sir. *(To everyone else)* QUIET. Rehearsing. Keep them quiet in the corridor.

JOHN IRVIN: Right, let's rehearse it, please. Edward and Peter, as soon as the nurse gets to about six feet from the door you enter. Push the swing doors, let the nurse through, get to your marks and look round the room, see John, and walk towards him.

(We go through that part of the scene.)

JOHN IRVIN *(turning to the camera-operator, whose name is Eddie)*: Any problems?

EDDIE: Er . . . Peter didn't arrive on his mark so he was masked a bit by Edward . . . er . . . *(racking his brain about what he had seen through the lens only once so far: the camera-operator is the only person who actually sees what will be shown later on the screen)* and I think Peter was masked also as they came through the door; perhaps he ought to come in first . . . er . . . oh yes, and I think there's a reflection of one of the lights in the glass panel of the right-hand door as Edward opens it.

RONNIE *(abruptly)*: Let's see. Yes. Damn. Damn. Er. Move that pup. It's that pup. Little more. Little more. Open the door again. That's all right.

JOHN IRVIN: So, Peter, get ahead of Edward. And you can both spend longer looking around the ward before you see John. Count of five. I'd rather have too much because then I can cut it. If there's too little I might not be able to do a cut to John when I'm editing, and I think I'd like to. One more rehearsal.

BERT: Quiet. Rehearsing.
                         (We go through it again.)
JOHN IRVIN: Problems?
EDDIE: No. Much better. Er . . . I think
                         Peter and Edward could come in a
                         gnats earlier. It's a bit bunchy.
JOHN IRVIN: OK?
EDWARD AND ME *(together, nervous now, because we are getting so
                         near to our first take in the film)*: Yes.
JOHN IRVIN: Right, let's shoot it.
BERT: Shooting next time.
                         *(Ronnie walks around with his light meter,
                         and the army of make-up and wardrobe
                         dash up to Edward and me to dab and
                         brush. Everybody bursts out talking.
                         Pandemonium. The focus-puller, whose
                         name is Cedric, comes up to us.)*
CEDRIC: Could I see you on your marks
                         please?
                         *(Edward and I walk, still being dabbed
                         and brushed, on to our marks. Cedric
                         measures the distance between our faces and
                         the lens and adjusts a knob on the side of
                         the camera.)*
BERT: Right, Ronnie?
RONNIE: Right.
BERT: Right, John?
JOHN IRVIN: Right.
BERT: Right. Opening positions. Thank
                         you, gentlemen. *(Edward and I are
                         bustled into the corridor)*. Right. Turn
                         over.
SOUND MAN *(with earphones on, and sitting out of the way, hunched
                         over his recording apparatus, and whose
                         name is David)*: Just a minute, there's
                         an aeroplane.
BERT: Relax. Waiting for the aeroplane.
                         (A great hush descends, while we all listen.)
BERT: Say when, David.
DAVID: Right.
BERT: Here we go. Turn over.

DAVID: Sound running.

BERT: Mark it.

CLAPPER-LOADER *(whose name is Jason)*:   143 Take 1. *(He then claps the clapper-board and scampers away and hides.)*

BERT: Background action.

(The extras continue to read, or just lie there, and a nurse walks from one bed to another at the far end of the ward. Bert is responsible for all instructions to the extras.)

JOHN IRVIN: Action.

(And we do that bit of the scene.)

JOHN IRVIN: Cut. Good. A good one.

(He turns to Eddie, and they have a prolonged mutter, which we can't hear.) Once more please. *(He comes up to Edward and me.)* Peter: you're just a little too ahead of Edward now. Edward, keep up with him. We lost you for a moment. I think you could be a little more ill-at-ease, Peter. Not you, Edward. Very good, both of you.

BERT: Right, Eddie? Going again. Turn over.

DAVID: Sound running.

JASON *(not always waiting for 'Mark it')*: 143 Take 2. *(Clap. Scamper. Hide.)*

BERT: QUIET. Background action.

JOHN IRVIN: Action.

(We all do it again.)

JOHN IRVIN: Cut. Good. Eddie?

EDDIE: Er . . . Peter was masked for a moment as they came through the door, and Edward stopped just a gnats too far forward. It was all right though . . . er . . .

JOHN IRVIN: Once more.

BERT: First positions. Thank you
                          gentlemen. Make-up? (*Make-up dab us
                          a bit. The heat is mounting. And the
                          pressure.*)

And so on, through the scene, finishing with the close-ups. John's first, then Edward's, then mine. When it came to mine, John's bed had gone because the camera had to be there, and John sat next to the lens, straining his head towards it to give me the best possible eyeline. The one order which is always given to actors for close-ups is: 'Watch the overlaps.' This is because the microphone is adjusted only for the person who is being photographed, so nobody else's voice must coincide with his. There must be a pause before you speak and a pause after you've spoken. And problems of focus become much more acute. The director said to one of us, 'Oh, yes, you can move your head about if you want to. Plenty of leeway. At least an inch.'

Of course if you've done filming you will know about all this, and I rather hope you will have skipped it. I've put it in because if you *haven't* done filming it can be such a shock: the clamour, the waiting, the repetition, the exactness required, the fuss and distractions of it all. Small parts are harder to do than leading ones: if you have the lead you develop a special relationship with the director, you get to know everyone, and anyway you're always at it: there aren't those confounded and confounding days of waiting.

How to cope with it all? First, be secure with the lines and mechanics of a scene. Then you can forget about lines and mechanics and can concentrate on the story, the situation and the people you are with. Have so much in your mind that you can, at least partially, shut out the babble and work which surround you.

'It's simply a matter of using your imagination,' said John Hurt, one illuminating day. 'Being real is not the aim; imagining and remembering what it's like to be ill, to be frightened of illness, to be in love, to win a race, oh, all these things with all their details, that's what to do. I don't really like using substitutions, 'as ifs', as some people call them. I like to imagine what the character I'm playing wants and feels. Otherwise it's me doing the thinking, not the character. Bob Champion wanted to win the Grand National, and that's what I have to imagine if I'm going to be true to him. I'm not a method actor. I don't believe in it, really,' he said. But we could see the part was taking him over and he was becoming indistinguishable from the real jockeys by whom he was surrounded. It was fascinating to watch him work. We had spent a whole day doing a scene in a crowded restaurant, and with all the people, all the lights, and the smoke-gun which was puffed for 'atmosphere' before every take, there was such an oven of heat towards the end of the day that it was barely tolerable. John shut his eyes against the smoke and the heat and the deafening noise, waiting to do his close-ups. He shut out the room, and concentrated; and when the camera turned it was as though he'd never said the lines before, so fresh they were, and so immediate.

John Irvin said to me that John Hurt has a very special relationship with the camera (Alec Guinness has the same, he said), 'probably because he loves it: it sees more in his face and in his eyes than I can see on the set. He often appears to be doing nothing. But he's not. The camera catches his internal life.'

Years ago there was an interview with Rod Steiger in *The Times*, in which he said, 'When it comes to having to do a lot of takes for a scene I try to think of them not as takes, repeating the same thing each time, but as one more opportunity to explore life in front of the camera.'

Odds And Ends

In a long review of *About Acting* in the *Daily Telegraph*, John Barber wrote '. . . such skills have nothing to do with great acting as I understand it.' And of course he was quite right: if it were possible to give any recipes for great acting then we would all be great actors. But we're not. There are very few. It is interesting, though, that many of the Golden Rules and Helpful Hints which I included in that book came from great actors. And I've often wondered if these extraordinary people aimed to be great, or merely to be good, their greatness coming from gifts of presence, power, personality, or from beauty of face and voice. I quoted from Edith Evans more than from anybody else and I know, because she told me, that her only aim was to be a good actress: truthful, simple, but with considerable dexterity with words and moves. She didn't have a particularly beautiful face, but some inner spirit in her transformed it. She had a most idiosyncratic voice, swooping mellifluously wherever she wanted it to go, but *she* thought her speech was very real and very natural. Some are born great . . . and once they become good, God, as Prunella Scales believes, has done the rest for them.

So here, unabashed, I include some more hints and ideas, collected from various sources, and told, as before, as briefly as possible. It's a bit like playing catch: a ball is thrown in the air towards you: if you like the look of it, you can catch it, and hold it, and keep it, and make it your own; if you don't, you can let it go.

Research

Is it worth reading the novel from which the play or series is made? Is it worth reading up about a real person you're about to play? Is it worth meeting that person if you can, or watching film of them if they are famous? Is it worth finding out about the job your character has and the environment he lives in?

Of course it is. In as much detail as possible. Brian Clark, who wrote the television series *Telford's Change*, said, 'I spent six months researching the whole subject of banking, both international and domestic. That six months accounted for about ten per cent of the scripts. The rest came from my head, as plays do.'

But it was that ten per cent which made all the difference.

What Does Your Character Want?

What is his aim? His principle aim? His super-objective? It was Michael Denison whom I first heard use this question. He said to the author of a new play he was appearing in, 'I don't know what my character wants, and until I know that he will remain a cipher to me. Can you tell me?' Unfortunately the playwright couldn't, although he was able to say quite a lot about the character's function within the play. But that's not the same thing.

What does your character want? It's a good question. You could take it further: what is your character's *obsession*?

Running Conditions

Referred to briefly earlier in this book, this phrase of Mike Leigh's is very helpful, I think. It means, of course, continuing conditions of mind or body affecting, or afflicting, the character you are playing, from, say, inordinate shyness to an itchy leg which you have to keep scratching (there was at least one in *Goose-Pimples*).

I first heard of running conditions when I was playing a character who had a particularly nasty cough. In fact the play implied he was terminally ill. During the rush of rehearsals I found what seemed to me the most convenient times for coughing, either because somebody else referred to it, or I did, or because it helped me leap more easily into sudden tempers, or because it stopped me for a moment from getting on with an urgent task. So I found the places. The only thing was, as I discovered at early previews, I was coughing far too much. The audience couldn't take it. One reviewer said that I had 'a cough that even Garbo in *Camille* might have envied'. It was while I was on tour with the same play (*A Coat of*

Varnish by Ronald Millar) that I was told about Mike Leigh's phrase and I realised that I had not integrated the coughing into the whole performance. My running condition was an appalling chest, which hurt all the time. Not that I had to show that, I just had to know it and feel it. It made me want to control my coughing much more, because coughing was the most painful thing I could do. The upshot of all this was that I coughed much less, and in differing degrees. Much better, everybody said.

Work Till It's Easy

It was while I was on the same tour that I felt a new ease in performing, an ease I had never felt on the stage before. I think this was largely because I had rehearsed the part in March, played it for five intermittent weeks in repertory at the Haymarket Theatre, and then, after a long gap, went with it on tour in the autumn. Gaps are very helpful: the part sinks into your subconscious during the silent weeks, and when you come to re-rehearse, emerges more freshly than you had dared to hope. I think this is because at early rehearsals you are planning what to do. You are being given a lot; you are told where to stand and sit. You spend a lot of time trying to be obedient. When you rehearse after a gap the plan is forgotten: only the story, the situations and the characters remain. If only it were possible always to throw the plan away, to forget it! I was greatly helped in this feeling of ease by being directed by Anthony Quayle and acting two of the major scenes in the play with him. We perpetually surprised each other by new readings and slightly different moves. After a performance one night I said to him, 'Oh, I enjoyed it tonight. We were really acting carelessly.'

And he replied, 'It's a lifetime's work, learning to be careless.'

Vary

People have varying views about varying their performances. But certainly the freshness and ease which I have mentioned are assisted if there is leeway, if the tracks are not too rigidly laid. It's more fun anyway, and helps prevent mechanical acting. There is nothing more boring than mechanical acting: the only thing that is interesting, for an audience, is to be in the presence of people who are thinking and feeling and not just going through the motions. Sometimes the varying can be unpremeditated. The play and the thinking about the play evolve as the performances accumulate. But sometimes, I think, it can be inspiring to carry on to the stage a new attitude, or to concentrate more than usually on some facet of the story or circumstances within the play. Do it tonight, you might say to yourself, for total personal involvement: the story *matters* to you. Do it for the job in hand (a particular favourite of mine). Do it with slightly more urgency, or slightly more awareness of the heat, or cold, or the surroundings. And most of all, do it for the other people: do it for talking and listening. Do it for speed. Do it for a little more variety. Oh, heaps of things. And when physical things change because of these changing attitudes, let them. Mustn't go too far off the rails, though, and must expect a note or two from the director when next he pays a visit.

Think in Pictures

Yes, in colour too. If you talk about a field, see it in your mind's eye. If you talk about an event, see it in your mind's eye.

Don't Play The Character, Play The Situation

You can't think of everything during a performance. That's what rehearsals were for, to get some of the thinking out of the way. After you've been rehearsing and playing a part for some time you can assume quite a lot. Alison Steadman knew Beverly so thoroughly towards the end of the rehearsal period that she could just switch her on. There she would be, ready, in all her outrageous detail. Then, and only then, could she concentrate on the incidents of the play. Don't play the character, play the situation.

Heels and Toes

'Have you noticed, darling,' said Penelope Keith to me one evening while we were both in *Donkeys' Years*, 'have you noticed how some people are heels people and other people are toes people?' I limply replied that I didn't know what she was talking about. 'Well,' she said, heaving herself up a little in her dressing-room chair (I had just arrived at the theatre and was paying her a visit before the show), 'it's simple really, darling, but I think it's frightfully helpful when you're thinking of a character. Heels people are those who . . . you know . . .' (and she stood up to demonstrate it) '. . . sit back on their heels, go backwards like that. Shy, retiring people. Receivers, not givers. You know, backwards, not forwards. But toes people' (and she brightened her voice a little, thinking of them) 'go forward and are springy and . . . giving and . . . outgoing. You know?'

'Oh yes, that is good.' I said.

'M'm,' she said, pleased. 'I think I'm a toes person. What do you think you are?'

'Oh . . .' I said, warily, 'er . . . I'm not sure. A mixture of both, I think. I have my heels moments and my toes moments.'

'Yes,' she said, 'perhaps you're right. But it's helpful, isn't it?'

'Very,' I said.

And it is. Mind you, I think very few people are completely heels or completely toes. But a lot are mostly heels or mostly toes. It's quite nice to work out the heels moments and the toes moments of your character.

Get Rid Of Some Of It

I suppose you could say there are heels and toes playwrights too. The heels playwrights (Chekhov, for example, and in our own time Simon Gray and Alan Ayckbourn) use words which imply a large subtext: they float on top of the meaning rather than explain it, while the toes playwrights (Shakespeare and Shaw, for example, and in our own time John Osborne, Christopher Fry, David Hare and Tom Stoppard) use words to do a great deal of explaining.

It is very tempting, especially with toes playwrights, to elucidate and make the most of everything, and this can lead to an over-emphatic and therefore monotonous delivery. So:

vary the emphasis. Use plus emphasis for some bits and minus emphasis for others; get rid of some of it.

For example, here's a short speech:

> I had a really bad time about eleven or twelve years ago. Or thirteen, I can't remember. It was soon after I'd left school, and I could not find any purpose in my life, so I just went to pieces. I was shattered. I was tired all the time, couldn't concentrate, couldn't enjoy anything; no friends. It was awful.

Here it is again, with suggested hesitations (/) and bits to throw away (a line over the words). By no means do I think this is the only or even the best way to arrange this speech; it is just one possibility:

> I had a / really / bad time about eleven or twelve years ago. / Or thirteen, I can't remember. It was just after I'd left school, and I could / not / find any / purpose / in my life, so / I just went to pieces. I was shattered. I was tired all the time, couldn't concentrate, couldn't enjoy anything; / no friends. / It was awful.

Sometimes, if you want to go faster, you can think of the next thing while saying the present one, and if you want to go slower, you can become preoccupied.

These little things help.

Feelings, Not Statements

To go one stage further: you could get rid of the whole of the following speech, feeling the heat the while, feeling listless and tired, not making any statements.

> Oh it's hot in here. Let's go out, shall we? Let's just sit outside and get cool. Oh, the thought of being cool! The thought of just a little air ... There's no air in here, you see. And perhaps we might have some tea or a drink or something. That'll refresh us. Yes. Let's go outside.

Make Paragraphs

'Let's make some paragraphs,' says the director one day. 'It's all a bit shapeless at the moment. It meanders. So let's start here, and everybody: close the gaps between speeches, and when we get to your line, Colin, stop. Colin's line stops you all. He's taken you by surprise. Then, Harriet, you start the next paragraph, and it can go pitter-patter pitter-patter for some time . . . until . . . Colin's next line, say. Then everybody stops again. Let's try it anyway. See if it works.'

If the director has chosen well, this rehearsal can be one of the most valuable of the lot. And then once you've got your paragraphs with the other players firmly established, you can free them up a bit, so they don't show.

No Emotion Is Static

If you laugh, if you cry, if you are cross, if you are happy: the laughter, the crying, the rage and the joy are ever-changing. It's good to think of this, it's good to remember it: it prevents that false switch-on of artificial, because generalised, emotions. So if you laugh, you can be laughing a little more or a little less than you were a moment ago. Or a lot more (with a sudden surge) or a lot less (with a sudden collection of yourself). The worst laughter always seems to accompany the stage-direction *exeunt* at the ends of scenes in Shakespeare's comedies, usually because it has not become organic, it has not grown; it has merely been switched on because somebody said so.

Ease Into The Play

Don't tell the audience too much about your character to start with: keep some surprises in store, keep some things back. Lead the audience gently into the world of the play. Be very true to start with, then you won't put the audience off.

Edith Evans said, 'When you're in a comedy, don't try for too many laughs in your first scene. The audience will tire of you, and be disappointed if you don't get funnier as the play goes on.'

Hints

Nevertheless, it's nice when constructing a character to give hints, however slight, of any big changes to come. Oswald in

Ghosts and Ophelia in *Hamlet* both go mad: the potential for madness must be there somewhere, lurking, right from the beginning; there should be a sign or two, here and there: a hint.

Positions And Think-Lines

Two actors are on stage, seated thus:

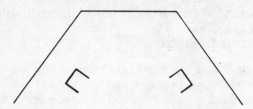

They sit comfortably in their chairs and talk. When they look at each other they incline their heads towards each other. When they don't look at each other, when they are thinking inside themselves, their heads return slightly towards the audience, square on their shoulders. That is their think-line. A gross simplification, this, but I've liked the idea of think-lines ever since I noticed how John Gielgud uses them a lot. Anthony Quayle did too, so I caught the habit while I was on the tour I've been talking about. He used them off-stage as well: he looked towards you and then away, to the same place.

Recently there was a play at the National Theatre when two characters were placed sitting at a table like this:

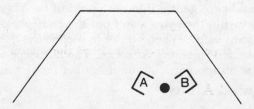

Those two chairs gave B a most unfair advantage over A: B's natural think-line gave her plenty of command over the audience:

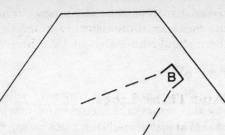

whereas poor A had a great deal of work to do to allow the audience sitting on the left-hand side of the auditorium to see anything of her face:

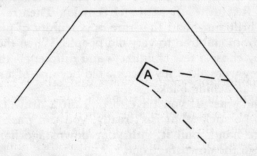

A much fairer placing would have been:

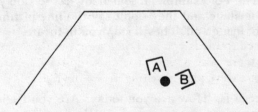

Being level with each other is not necessarily the fairest positioning: it depends where you are on the stage.

Look Around A Bit

When you have an intimate duologue, for example in a film or a television play, there is an area *around* the eyes of the other person which can attract your attention: the hair, the hairline, the brow, the mouth, the neck. Or even further away:

the space *around* the other character's head. There's no need to stare each other out all the time.

From Uta Hagen

When I was in New York in the winter of 1963, I went to a class given by this remarkable actress and teacher, and three things she said that afternoon have stuck in my memory.

The first was: 'When you have to be hot, or cold, or tired or whatever, don't try to be hot or cold or tired all over. Select a place, and concentrate on that. Your neck? A shoulder? The small of your back?' (Recently I saw a play called *The Dining Room* by A. R. Gurney Jr at the Greenwich Theatre. All six actors – all brilliant – had that rare opportunity of playing a lot of parts from children to very old people. When they were children they chose a few childlike – and different – things to do; when they were old, they became old because of a stiff leg, a slow walk, an aching back.)

The second was: 'If you have to pull on a drawer that is supposed to be sticky, but isn't really, you can push it with your upstage hand, pull it with your downstage hand, but believe only in the downstage one.'

The third was: 'Try not to *tell* your acting partners what to do: *make* them. For example, if somebody has to stop you from going off the stage and they don't say the line in time, don't ask them to, just go off. They'll stop you in future.'

Egg

If your speech is: 'How are you today? Are you feeling well? You look very tired,' and the reply is 'I'm fine,' you will leave egg on your partner's face if you pause between your sentences. Yet it often seems to happen.

Actions Which Speak . . .

In the original production of *The Deep Blue Sea*, Peggy Ashcroft dropped a handkerchief. The first time I saw it I thought it was an accident. Subsequently I realised it wasn't. She stooped to pick it up, and rose wearily on I can't remember now what line, and that heavy rise was an encapsulation of the weariness inside her.

Additional Words

I am often tempted – and fall to the temptation – to add 'Well,' or 'Oh,' or 'And,' or something to the beginning of an author's line. Sometimes the author has asked me not to, but I think a little licence is legitimate. However, sometimes (notably on television) the additions become incredibly complex, time-wasting and very boring to listen to. They can grow like this:

'Look . . .'
'Look, Nigel . . .'
'Yes, well . . .'
'Well, yes, but I mean . . .'
'Yes, well, but Nigel, look . . .'
'Oh, well, no, but Nigel, look . . .'
'Oh, well, yes, I mean, but Nigel, look . . .'
'Well yes, but you know, Nigel, I mean to say, look . . .'

Off-Form

You can be off-form for a performance, for a string of performances, for a whole play, or indeed, for a whole period. Everybody has their off-form times . . . you've only got to look at the very famous sports people.

I remember watching, on Italian television, a men's singles tennis championship. Although I couldn't understand a word of the commentary, it was easy to tell which player was winning and which was losing. The winning player, quietly confident, showed little emotion, and between rallies he stared at his opponent, or at his racket, which he twirled gently around. The losing player, who couldn't concentrate any more, gasped with indignation at his every mistake, and between shots looked around at the crowd and the cameras, and then tried to pull himself together.

One was relaxed, the other was tense. Oh, we've all seen it; and we've all felt it too.

Take The Hurdles As They Come

Yes, a loser anticipates disaster, working himself into a lather of uncertainty before each shot, and sure as eggs, disaster occurs. He who hesitates . . .

I was beginning to froth a bit before the transmission of a 'live' television play, going over bits and pieces which had always worried me. It was a two-hander, and my partner was Charles Gray, who said to me, very quietly, a few minutes before we went on the air, 'Don't worry it . . . don't fuss it . . . take the hurdles as they come.' I felt immensely calmed by that, and often think of it now.

PS 1991.   Things I Learned From Simon Gray

The first thing I noticed in Simon Gray's *Hidden Laughter* was how the dialogue was full of 'ums' and 'ers' and incomplete sentences and repeated words: full of the mess of everyday conversation. My first speech, for example, was:

'Um, hello – I do hope you don't mind – I was passing and heard voices – I'm, um, Ronald Chambers, the . . . the local – I'm so sorry. I'm intruding.'

I decided that as he had taken the trouble to put in all these things – which are usually the sort of things which actors supply – I'd better take the trouble to learn them accurately. I was relieved to notice when rehearsals started that the whole cast was similarly accurate, and became, after a bit of practice, adept at performing them really naturally.

So the first thing I learned from Simon Gray was from his writing. What surprised me as the rehearsals became a tour and the tour became a London production was the number of things I learned from his directing, especially since, on his own admission, he can't act for toffee.

The first note I remember him giving was after the first read-through, which was at the Groucho Club (of which he is an avid member), over sandwiches and wine, about a fortnight before rehearsals started. (A good idea, this preliminary meeting: it breaks the ice and reduces the tension at the more formal read-through at the beginning of rehearsals). He said, 'I want to say only one thing: that people behave differently in gardens from the way they do in rooms.' And he encouraged us all, in the interim, to observe what those differences were: a sort of aimlessness, looking at the garden while talking, sprawling on the grass, sitting on it, sunbathing on it, playing on it. And these things influenced greatly the placing and moves when we came to rehearse.

The second note he gave was after the formal read-through, with Michael Codron there and all. He said, 'I want to say only one thing: I noticed rather a lot of emotion was creeping in. Watch it! Trust the text! Do not ornament it! Do not add to it! It's enough merely to report that such and such a thing happened. There's no need, often, to *feel* it.'

He seemed to start by paring us down. He wanted us to be simple, and to be economical with gesture. On the first day, after we had blocked the first scene very roughly, he had some interesting comments on the text. 'When you're explaining God,' he said to me, 'don't make it sound like a sermon to Ben. Think it out. You've said it all many times in your life, but you always have to think out the words.' And: 'Sometimes when you don't finish a sentence it's for no reason at all. Sometimes it's because you can't think of a word. It's also a habit.'

On the third day of rehearsals, in the pub afterwards, Simon said to me, 'Let's talk about your relationship with this vicar, this Ronnie. I think you've got him. I know you understand him. But you are, so far, the raw Ronnie. Too much shows. You have a very expressive face, and too much shows. You see, he's had all his agonies for a long time and he can cope with them. He's had to. What you need now are a few layers of skin. To hide the rawness.'

Deftly, he pointed out to all of us, always privately, always quietly, so we didn't hear the notes to other people, the bits of our roles which were easy to say – 'That can come out more quickly, less gloomily' – and the bits which were difficult – 'Oh, she's really thrown you by saying, "You think I'm wicked don't you?" and you can take forever before you say, "No, I . . ."'

He had major notes about my relationship with the audience. 'Don't do so much out front. You're speaking to the other character, not to the audience.' And: 'Don't put your face upstage when you listen to someone who is upstage of you. I want to *see* your face. A conversation is between two people and I want to see both your faces. I know you do it out of generosity but you should eliminate it from your performance.'

We rehearsed every weekday, for four weeks, from 1 till 6. For me, those hours are ideal. The morning is free for getting on with things and for homework on the part. There is no lunch-break, which is always such a waste of time and energy. But what I did learn in this production is the value of the pub afterwards. Simon, Kevin McNally and I went every day, and the others joined us from time to time. The pattern of our talk was always the same: the first hour was spent in chewing over what had occurred at that day's rehearsal, what our worries were, what seemed to be getting better and what seemed to be getting worse, and the second hour, as the drink began to settle, went on ribaldry and gossip. And it was Kevin who said that because we knew there was ample time for gossip in the pub we didn't bother with it in the rehearsal room. We got down to work straight away. They were the most concentrated rehearsals I have ever known.

We opened securely in Brighton and then went to Guildford. While we were there Simon and I had lunch one day, over which he said, 'You need more pain now. Especially when you are describing the appalling holiday in Southsea with your wife. You remember I said you needed a layer or two of skin? You can take a layer off now.'

'More pain?' I said.

'More pain,' he said.

The result was that an already funny speech got louder laughs than ever. And this confirmed something I had thought for some time but had never really put into practice: that the only thing you are allowed to exaggerate in comedy is emotion, so that worry becomes frenzied anxiety, smugness becomes unbearable complacency and distaste becomes anguished indignation. Tony Hancock was past-master of this sort of comedy (the states he used to get into!), as are John Cleese, Richard Briers and Warren Mitchell.

Samuel West said to me one day at rehearsal, when we were talking about this, 'Actually it's just overcoming a larger obstacle, isn't it? Like if you're John Cleese in *Fawlty Towers* and you want a huge panic your intention will be to have the menu typed in fifteen seconds instead of thirty, and the typewriter sticks. It's still real, you see.'

I never heard Simon say, 'Do it this way and you'll get a louder laugh.' His notes were always couched in seriousness. In fact he said to me one day, 'Don't try to be funny when you're explaining the Church of England's views on abortion to little Natalie. Be more pastoral, more loving.' Louder laughs again.

I suppose the most influencing note he gave me was, 'When you have to, take your time.' I had always thought you should get on with it and not hang about. Felicity Kendal thought the same. But we both agreed it was a treat to be given permission to go slowly at times.

Maxims

As you get older you remain exactly the same, only more so.
The good things get better, the bad things get worse.
There is no substitute for repetition.
Don't expect praise.
Don't ask for opinions.
You can't make anybody love you.
It's easier to act with people you like.
Confidence and concentration go hand in hand.
Every part is a character part, but should look a straight one.
A good performance is one in which the actor seems to be
    conceiving the words and not merely remembering them.
Put a bit of mess in.
Everything is habit-forming.
Do remember to forget
    Anger, worry and regret.
Play your character from the character's point of view.
It isn't the time spent learning that matters, it's the time
    spent having learnt.
Say yes only if you want to.
Say no only when you have to.
You employ your agent.
Try to bring to every part something you've never thought of
    before.
Never stop looking – at people and things.
How you start in a play is more important than how you
    finish, because it is then that an audience makes up its
    mind about you.
Don't use more energy for an action than the action requires.
In every company find a chum.
If two people are whispering and looking at you, don't assume
    they are talking about you; and, if they are, don't assume
    that what they are saying is bad.
Don't try to impress people.
Don't plunge in at the deep end if you don't know the pool.

Hard work never killed anybody.

Be absurdly generous.

You can't please everyone.

You can't worry and think.

The first duty of an actor is to be heard.

Vowels travel easily, consonants don't.

Acting is giving; reticence has no part in it.

Mechanical acting just won't do.

(*And, from a letter written by Edward Fitzgerald*):

At all cost, a thing must live: better a live sparrow than a
   stuffed eagle.

Index